LIBRARY *of* GREAT AUTHORS

LIBRARY *of* GREAT AUTHORS

Albert Camus
Lewis Carroll
Fyodor Dostoevsky
Barbara Kingsolver
Gabriel García Márquez
Toni Morrison
Vladimir Nabokov
J.K. Rowling
J.R.R. Tolkien
Virginia Woolf

SPARK NOTES

LIBRARY *of* GREAT AUTHORS

J.R.R. Tolkien

His Life and Works

Stanley P. Baldwin

EDITORIAL DIRECTOR Justin Kestler
EXECUTIVE EDITOR Ben Florman
SERIES EDITOR Emma Chastain

INTERIOR DESIGN Dan Williams

Produced by The Wonderland Press and published by SparkNotes

Spark Publishing
A Division of SparkNotes LLC
120 5th Avenue
New York, NY 10011

10 9 8 7 6 5 4 3 2 1

Please submit comments or questions, or report errors to www.sparknotes.com/errors

Printed and bound in the United States of America

ISBN 1-58663-843-2

Cover photograph Copyright © 2003 by Corbis, Inc.

Library of Congress Cataloging-in-Publication Data available on request

Contents

Contents

III.

{ The Fellowship of the Ring }
55

Contents

$$\left\{ \begin{array}{c} \text{IV.} \\ \text{The Two Towers} \\ \text{103} \end{array} \right\}$$

Contents

Contents

{ # Topics In Depth }

**SPARK
NOTES**

The
LIBRARY *of*
GREAT AUTHORS
series explores the
intimate connection between
writing and experience, shedding light
on the work of literature's most esteemed
authors by examining their lives. The
complete LIBRARY *of* GREAT AUTHORS brings
an excitingly diverse crowd to your bookshelf,
from Fyodor Dostoevsky to J.K. Rowling.

Each book in the LIBRARY *of* GREAT AUTHORS
features full-length analysis of the writer's
most famous works, including such novels as
*Crime and Punishment, Lolita, The Lord of
the Rings,* and *Mrs. Dalloway.* Whether you
are a reader craving deeper knowledge of
your favorite author, a student studying the
classics, or a new convert to a celebrated
novel, turn to the LIBRARY *of* GREAT AUTHORS
for thorough, fascinating, and insightful
coverage of literature's best writers.

LIBRARY *of* GREAT AUTHORS

J.R.R. Tolkien

I

THE LIFE OF
J.R.R. TOLKIEN

1

One evening in 1930, a thirty-eight-year-old professor of Anglo-Saxon at Oxford paused while grading exams and reached for a blank sheet of paper. On it, he wrote, "In a hole in the ground there lived a hobbit." Sixty-seven years later, in January 1997, the *London Sunday Times* announced that its readers had voted *The Lord of the Rings* the greatest book of the twentieth century in a readers' poll conducted by Waterstone's bookstore chain. Two years later, in 1999, a poll of Amazon.com customers chose *The Lord of the Rings* as the greatest book not merely of the century but of the millennium. What began as a scribbled sentence became the now classic epic *The Lord of the Rings*.

John Ronald Reuel Tolkien (1892–1973) was born in Bloemfontein, South Africa, on January 3, 1892. The melodrama of his childhood recalls the suffering of boy heroes from **Charles Dickens** (1812–1870) novels. When Tolkien was an infant, a poisonous spider bit him. He would have died if a servant had not immediately sucked the poison from the wound. Tolkien was a sickly child, suffering various African illnesses. In the spring of 1895, his mother, **Mabel** (1870–1904), decided to take Ronald (as family and friends called Tolkien) and his younger brother, **Hilary** (1894–1976), back to England. She hoped the move would improve Tolkien's health. Tolkien's father, **Arthur** (1857–1896), remained behind in South Africa, where he worked as a bank manager.

On arriving in England, Mabel and her sons stayed with Mabel's family in suburban Birmingham. Initally, Tolkien's health did not improve.

Arthur Tolkien, still in South Africa, fell ill of rheumatic fever. By then, young Tolkien had rallied and was well enough to write his father a get-well letter, along with news of the family. Arthur Tolkien suffered a hemorrhage and died, never having received the letter. After recovering from her initial shock and grief, Mabel moved out of her parents' home and rented a small house at Sarehole, near Birmingham. The boys, unused to the local dialect, found it difficult to make friends. Money was tight, and to economize, Mabel home-schooled the boys.

Before long, Tolkien qualified for a scholarship at King Edward's School, where he reveled in his classes: medieval history and literature, and Greek. He took particular pride in reading *The Canterbury Tales* (1390s, unfinished), by **Geoffrey Chaucer** (c.1342–1400), in the original Middle English, an earlier version of the English language as we know it today. For the first time in his life,

J.R.R. Tolkien

Tolkien felt blessed. However, Mabel Tolkien soon fell ill with diabetes. She made arrangements with her Catholic parish, asking the church to oversee her sons' housing and schooling in the event of her death. She died in November 1904.

> "**T**allness is a quality of which he makes much in his books, so it is a little surprising to see that he himself is slightly less than average height — not much, but just enough to be noticeable."
>
> **HUMPHREY CARPENTER**, *J.R.R. TOLKIEN: A BIOGRAPHY*

After Mabel's death, the boys went to in a private home that sheltered orphans. Orphaned and poor, Tolkien read no daily newspapers. His boarding house had no radio. No horse and carriage waited for him to board. Happily, however, at age sixteen Tolkien fell in love with another orphan living in the home, nineteen-year-old **Edith Bratt** (1889–1971). Other than Edith and his classes, Tolkien found little that brought him joy or delight. After only a few dates with Edith, Tolkien wanted to marry her, but the church insisted that Tolkien wait until he turned twenty-one. In the five-year interval, Edith became engaged to someone else. When Tolkien turned twenty-one, he raced to propose to her. She broke off her engagement and agreed to marry Tolkien.

Tolkien entered Oxford in the autumn of 1911. There he won a prestigious academic prize worth five pounds, which he used to buy books. Still fascinated with the Middle Ages, he began studying Old Norse and Old German, and writing stories set in that era. When World War I (1914–1918) began, many students left and joined the English forces in France. Tolkien continued his studies at Oxford. In 1915, Tolkien was awarded a First Class Honours degree in English Language and Literature from Oxford. He soon received a commission as officer in the Lancashire Fusiliers. On March 22, 1916, while on military leave, Tolkien married Edith, now a Catholic. The marriage produced four children: **John** (b. 1917), **Michael** (1920–1984), **Christopher** (b. 1924), and **Priscilla** (b. 1929).

Tolkien returned to the military and served on the front line, where he saw a number of close friends die. In November 1916, the army sent Tolkien home. He had post-traumatic shock syndrome, compounded by a threatening case of trench fever. As Tolkien recovered, he buried himself ever deeper in ancient languages, reading Old Norse and Old German. He also took comfort in Nordic lore and began creating worlds, mythologies, and even languages of his own. Two years later, Tolkien had fully recovered and was hard at work on philological research. (Philology involves the study of oral and spoken literature, and the importance of the spoken language to cultural history.) In 1920, he began teaching at the University of Leeds, where he remained for five years.

In 1925, Tolkien moved back to Oxford, where he was named Professor of Anglo-Saxon. That same year, he published a new translation of the classic medieval poem *Sir Gawain and the Green Knight* (c. 1375). In 1931, Tolkien and several of his friends, including **C.S. Lewis** (1898–1963), author of *The Screwtape Letters* (1942) and *The Chronicles of Narnia* (1950–1956), began meeting twice a week at Oxford's Eagle and Child pub. The colleagues, who called themselves the Inklings, read their short stories and essays to one another and welcomed each other's criticism. In addition to literature, the friends discussed religion. Tolkien was a staunch Catholic, and his best friend Lewis was a high-church Anglican, a religion close to Catholicism in doctrine.

Several members of the Inklings published essays and works of fiction that explored issues of faith. The group was partly responsible for initiating a renewed interest in Christianity following the deep pessimism and agnosticism that enveloped the country after World War I, a war in which Englishmen accounted for one third of the young men who died in France and Germany.

Tolkien's children loved stories, so he began entertaining them with tales of a little creature that he called a hobbit. In 1937, Tolkien transformed his bedtime tales into a novel, which he published as *The Hobbit*. The novel received uniformly enthusiastic reviews. The *Times* of London predicted that *The Hobbit* would be "read and re-read by adults." The novel's first printing sold out within a few months, and

> **J**ust why Tolkien has established himself so strongly among the eager young is not yet clear, and his popularity there is probably much more significant than his gradual acceptance into those academic realms that are loyal to the likes of C.S. Lewis and [G.K.] Chesterton."
>
> **ROGER SALE**, "TOLKIEN AND FRODO BAGGINS," *TOLKIEN AND THE CRITICS*

the American edition met with as much success as the British. Tolkien received the *New York Herald Tribune* prize for the best children's book of the year. *The Hobbit*'s success helped Tolkien recover from financial difficulties. With the first royalty check, Edith paid doctor bills.

Tolkien continued to publish articles on mythology and literature, and in 1945, he was appointed Merton Professor of English Language and Literature at Oxford, a position he held until his retirement fourteen years later. In 1948, he finished the first draft of his three-volume epic *The Lord of the Rings*, but could not find a willing publisher for the massive manuscript, which was deemed too enormous an undertaking to be profitable. The first two parts of the novel, *The Fellowship of the Ring* and *The Two Towers*, were not published until 1954. The concluding volume, *The Return of the King*, was published a year later. Once again, Tolkien garnered positive reviews. The *Sunday Telegraph* of London hailed the novel as one of "the greatest works of imaginative fiction of the twentieth century." The initial print run of the first volume (3,500 copies) sold out in less than two months.

> "Here was a professor who looked like a professor. Tolkien wore cords and a sports jacket, smoked a reassuring pipe, laughed a lot, sometimes mumbled when his thoughts outstripped his words. . . . There was a sense of civilization, winsome sanity and sophistication about him."
>
> **DESMOND ALBROW**, *CATHOLIC HERALD*

Almost overnight, Tolkien became a celebrity, drawing the disapproval of some of his academic colleagues. It struck them as unsettling that a noted critic and professor of literature could achieve such widespread popularity and inspire a pop-culture following. At times, Tolkien found his celebrity status an annoyance. Photographers followed him, and reporters nagged him about mundane details such as the brand of tobacco he smoked. However, annoyance was balanced out by financial security. After the enormous success of *The Lord of the Rings*, Tolkien and Edith never again had to worry about money, which previously had been a constant concern.

As a writer, Tolkien became a legend during his own lifetime. Still, he remained a man of simple pleasures, enjoying a daily breakfast of bacon and eggs, a chocolate bar in the afternoon, and a mug of hot chocolate before bedtime. He also enjoyed drinking ale and smoking his pipe. The public pursued him, but the kind of life he continued to enjoy most was quiet, snug, and secure.

In 1957, Tolkien planned a trip to the United States to receive honorary degrees from Marquette University and Harvard, and to deliver a series of lectures. However, Edith fell ill, and Tolkien cancelled the trip. Tolkien retired from teaching in 1959 to begin collecting his short stories, essays, and sketches for publication. Edith died in November 1971, apparently from an inflamed gallbladder. Two years later, in the early hours of September 2, 1973, Tolkien died from a bleeding gastric ulcer infection. Four days after Tolkien's death, Oxford held a requiem mass in his honor. Today thousands of Tolkien's fans make the pilgrimage to his gravesite at Wolvercote, just outside Oxford, where thick ivy grows over one end of a double stone on which admirers often hang amulets and charms.

People, Events, & Trends

That Influenced Tolkien's Work

Modern Life: Throughout most of his life, Tolkien sought a quiet, safe haven away from the modern world. His difficult early life did not endear modernity to him. He struggled with his health in South Africa, almost dying there, and when his mother resettled the family in Birmingham, England, he lived near factories that emitted smoke and soot from their long-necked chimneys. Tolkien was happiest when exploring the gentle English countryside, with its deserted barns and vast fields of grain. As a teenager, he yearned for a home of his own, far away from the crowded, unfriendly world of manufacturing and commerce.

Halley's Comet and *Mona Lisa*: Tolkien's diaries and journals rarely mention world events. They do not note the appearance of Halley's Comet (1910), the Chinese Revolution (1911–1912), the theft of the *Mona Lisa* (1911), the sinking of the *Titanic* (1912), or the murder of Russian **Czar Nicholas II** (1868–1918).

J.R.R. Tolkien

World War I: Upon seeing the atrocities of World War I (1914–1918), Tolkien felt a responsibility to play his part in fighting the German aggressors. No one realized how brutal the war would be. Modern technology had transformed the way men killed one another. Poisonous gas, machine guns, bayonets, and primitive bombs decimated landscapes and soldiers alike. Tolkien came home with a serious illness. He had lost all but one of his friends in battle.

> "**B**ilbo found a scrap of black twist and tied it around his arm. The little hobbit wept bitterly. Somewhere in the world of fantasy that Prof. J.R.R. Tolkien created, this is happening at the news of his death. . . . Even at the ripe age of 81, it is sad to lose one who brought so much fresh air and poetry into our literature. The kingdoms that he created will not pass away."
>
> **TOLKIEN'S OBITUARY,** *DAILY TELEGRAPH*

World War II: In the early 1930s, as Tolkien began writing and assembling *The Hobbit*, Germany was marching its armies into neighboring countries and annexing them. **Adolf Hitler** (1889–1945), Nazi dictator of Germany from 1933 to 1945, used newsreels and radio to rally Germany's economically devastated citizens to war. Tolkien loathed Hitler and dreaded the prospect of another world war, especially one brought on by a megalomaniacal dictator who was perverting the nation that had produced some of humankind's greatest myths and epics. Tolkien's hatred of Hitler, the short, irredeemably wicked Austrian who hoped to conquer the Western world, shaped his ideas about evil.

Perhaps Hitler's greed for land and power influenced Tolkien's fictional creation Smaug the dragon, who lusts for gold in *The Hobbit*. As Tolkien wrote his masterpiece, *The Lord of the Rings*, World War II (1939–1945) raged. England, France, Canada, and the United States, along with their allies, fought to defeat the Germans. The founding of the United Nations in 1945, after the end of the war, seems to have strengthened Tolkien's belief in the importance of harmony and cooperation among nations.

Environmentalism: Tolkien's great popularity made his old age less peaceful than he might have wished, especially when environmentalists began embracing him as an icon. People scrawled "Frodo Lives!" on buildings, T-shirts, and posters throughout the English-speaking world, a tag that irritated Tolkien. An advocate of the importance of ecology long before the attitude became popular, Tolkien agreed with the philosophy of organizations like Greenpeace, founded in 1971 to oppose nuclear testing in Alaska and to promote environmental awareness. Tolkien cherished trees and wrote about his love for them long before anyone began hugging them for photographers. He did not, however, cherish the role of figurehead for environmental causes.

Tolkien's Literary Context

His Influences and Impact

J.R.R. Tolkien was an accomplished scholar of English literature. Even in his youth he demonstrated skill at reading Middle English. His ability to grasp Chaucer's *Canterbury Tales* while still a young boy indicated his strong interest in Anglo-Saxon literature, and his translation of *Sir Gawain and the Green Knight* proved that he had much to contribute to his field. Tolkien's eventual tenure as Oxford professor bore out his initial promise.

J.R.R. Tolkien

As a master of Old English works, Tolkien often reviewed and critiqued the work of his colleagues, who did the same for him. Undoubtedly, these friend-critics also influenced his work, and his work influenced them. One of Tolkien's best-known friends, **C.S. Lewis**, wrote his own multi-novel fantasy series called *The Chronicles of Narnia*. The popular novel *The Lion, the Witch, and the Wardrobe* is part of this series.

> " **I** can only speak very personally, from having taught Shakespeare and Tolkien: I don't see any difference."
>
> **JANE CHANCE**, *LORD OF THE RINGS: THE MYTHOLOGY OF POWER*

Tolkien's most popular works of fiction originated as bedtime stories for Tolkien's four curious children, a functional origin that puts them in the same category as *Alice's Adventures in Wonderland* (1865) and *Through the Looking-Glass* (1871), the fantastic stories that **Lewis Carroll** composed to entertain his child companions. Carroll compiled and refined the stories he originally shared with his young companions, among them the story's namesake, **Alice Liddell**. Eventually, he published what had begun as a tale told aloud. Similarly, Tolkien wrote down the stories he told his children about hobbits, Dwarves, and Elves, and published them to great acclaim from the general public.

Tolkien's work has inspired innumerable fantasy stories and series geared toward children, young adults, and even the general reading public. The best-selling *Harry Potter* series by **J.K. Rowling** (b. 1965) is indebted to themes and tropes from Tolkien's work. Recently, the first two installments of the film adaptation of Tolkien's trilogy have met with great success.

II

THE HOBBIT

The Hobbit

An Overview

Key Facts

Genre: Mythic fantasy novel

Date of First Publication: 1937

Setting: The Third Age in mythological Middle-earth

Narrator: Anonymous, omniscient (all-knowing) third-person

Plot Overview: Gandalf, a wizard, convinces Bilbo Baggins, a contented, home-loving hobbit, to accompany him and thirteen Dwarves on a long journey to confront the fearsome dragon Smaug. They want to kill the dragon and reclaim the Dwarves' treasure, which the dragon seized long ago.

Style, Technique, and Language

Style—Creating Mythology: Tolkien read myths all his life, mostly Nordic, Anglo-Saxon, and Old Germanic myths. Eventually, he realized that England had no independent mythology beyond the Arthurian tales. In his writing, Tolkien meant to forge his own version of an English mythology. Before Tolkien created hobbits, they did not exist, even in fantasy literature. After the publication of *The Hobbit*, these new creatures had a place in English lore. Readers knew what hobbits looked like, how they dressed, where they lived, what their houses were like, what they liked to eat, what made them happy, and what made them cranky. Tolkien fashioned three-dimensional lives for his hobbits. To his mythology of England Tolkien added not just hobbits, but goblins, Wargs, a Gollum, Dwarves, Elves, humans, and an arrogant, vain dragon. These standard ingredients for fantasy entered the common parlance because they were not sketched in, but fully realized. Like gods in centuries-old myths, Tolkien's creations seemed real and became so familiar that people could believe they had once actually existed.

Technique—Private Amusement: Shortly after the third volume of *The Lord of the Rings* appeared, the *New York Times* sent a reporter to Oxford to interview Tolkien. The interviewer asked how *The Hobbit*, a children's book, had developed into the serious novel *The Lord of the Rings*. Tolkien explained that *The Hobbit* did not evolve into a serious work, b ut stood on its own as a serious if amusing and often whimsical work. "I am a philologist," he explained, "and all of my work is philological. I avoid hobbies because I am a very serious person and cannot distinguish between private amusement and duty. I am affable, but unsociable. I only work for private amusement, since I find my duties privately amusing." Tolkien attributed his enduring popularity to his refusal to patronize readers, even young readers. Because of Tolkien's respectful attitude, critics have often compared him to Lewis Carroll, who addressed his audience in similarly serious fashion.

> "*The Hobbit* will be funniest to its youngest readers, and only years later, at a tenth or a twentieth reading, will they begin to realize what deft scholarship and profound reflection have gone to make everything in it so ripe, so friendly, and in its own way so true."
>
> **C.S. LEWIS**, AUTHOR AND MEMBER OF THE INKLINGS

Language—A Wealth of Detail: By imbuing his stories with detail, Tolkien enables us to visualize Middle-earth and its inhabitants with perfect clarity. He makes the Dwarves individuals, distinguishing them by their agility, obsessiveness, whininess, and coloring. As Bilbo and the Dwarves ride on their ponies, willows along the riverbank "bend and sigh," and a "wandering moon" appears in the sky. As they approach the Trolls' campfire, they grumble and drat, rustling and crackling. Tolkien particularly likes verbs that imitate the sounds they represent—for example, as Bilbo and the Dwarves descend toward Rivendell, their ponies slither and slip on the steep zigzag path. This kind of writing begs to be read aloud.

Characters in *The Hobbit*

Belladonna Took Baggins: The mother of Bilbo Baggins. From Belladonna, Bilbo inherits daring and adventurous "Took blood," which lies dormant until Gandalf and the Dwarves spark Bilbo's curiosity and desire for adventure.

Balin: A Dwarf who remembers the way Smaug killed Thorin's ancestors and devastated the countryside around Lonely Mountain. Balin lived in the village of Dale and witnessed its decimation, as did Bard. He hopes to restore the castle-fortress in Lonely Mountain.

Bard: A grim-voiced, pessimistic, but courageous warrior who lives among the Lake Men in Esgaroth. He and Balin witnessed the dragon Smaug's destruction of the townspeople of Dale.

Beorn: Gandalf describes Beorn as a "skin-changer." Sometimes Beorn appears as a huge man with a thick black beard, great bare arms, and legs with knotted muscles. At other times, he changes into a massive bear. Beorn offers his home as a haven for Bilbo and the Dwarves after they escape the wrath of the goblins.

Bilbo Baggins: A little hobbit. Bilbo, the central character in the Dwarves' quest for treasure, is the hobbit of the novel's title. As the novel begins, Bilbo is content to do nothing more than eat two breakfasts, share generous meals and tobacco with friends, and enjoy long, pleasant days in Hobbiton. Nevertheless, the Dwarves coax him out into the vast world of the unknown, where Bilbo proves to himself and to the Dwarves that he has untapped resources of cleverness, imagination, and heroism.

Bofur, Bifur, Nori, and Ori: Dwarves who play minor roles in the story. They accompany Thorin on the adventure and share Bilbo's longing for regular meals.

Bombur: The fattest of the Dwarves. He encounters an unusual number of obstacles during the Dwarves' quest for the dragon's treasure.

Lord Dain: A distant cousin of Thorin Oakenshield, Lord Dain lives in the Iron Hills, far to the east of Lonely Mountain. At a crucial moment, Thorin sends Roäc the raven as an emissary to Dain to ask for reinforcements.

Dori: Dori helps the short-legged Bilbo keep up with the Dwarves as they flee from goblins inside the Misty Mountains. Later, he saves Bilbo from the wild Wargs.

J.R.R. Tolkien

Dwalin: The first Dwarf to arrive at Bilbo Baggins's house for the unexpected party. It is Dwalin who realizes that Thorin is missing after Bilbo has rescued the Dwarves from the spiders.

Dwarves: The thirteen Dwarves who take Bilbo on an adventure. They are Thorin, Bifur, Bofur, Bombur, Dori, Nori, Ori, Oin, Glóin, Fili, Kili, Dwalin, and Balin. Dwarves, who are usually superior goldsmiths and silversmiths, are taller and more muscular than hobbits. All Dwarves have fiercely grizzled beards. Most are easily annoyed. Dwarves trust few non-Dwarf creatures, so Bilbo, a mere hobbit, must demonstrate extraordinary courage and daring before he can win their respect. Most of the Dwarves in *The Hobbit* descend from the Dwarves who used to reside in the castle-fortress inside Lonely Mountain.

The Elvenking: The king of the Wood Elves in Mirkwood Forest. He behaves petulantly when the Dwarves interrupt him and his Elves as they feast in Mirkwood. Greedy for the dragon's treasure, the Elvenking joins forces with the Men of Esgaroth and prepares to battle Thorin and the Dwarves for a share of the treasure. The Elvenking is the father of Legolas, an important character in *The Lord of the Rings*.

Elrond: A kind, hospitable Elf. He lives in Rivendell and welcomes Bilbo, Gandalf, and the Dwarves to his home, the Last Homely House, on their way to the Misty Mountains. (Tolkien uses "homely" to suggest something cozy, snug, and secure.)

Eru: The creator of Middle-earth. Eru sent Gandalf and four other wizards to help good folk resist evil.

Fili and Kili: The two youngest Dwarves. They search for a dry, safe cave in which the company can take shelter from a ferocious thunderstorm. They die in the Battle of Five Armies.

Galion: The Elvenking's butler. He persuades the chief of the guards to accompany him to the cellar to taste some potent new wine.

Gandalf: A good, wise wizard. He approaches Bilbo and asks him to accompany the Dwarves on their mission to reclaim the treasure. Although not invincible, Gandalf can produce magical effects like bolts of lightning and multi-colored, fiery pine cones. However, Gandalf cannot save the residents of Middle-earth, who must learn to fight for themselves.

Glóin and Oin: Two Dwarves. At the beginning, they think Bilbo looks more like a grocer than a burglar. They later accept him and fetch lighted torches for him when he explores the lair of the dragon.

Gollum: A lonely, slimy creature. He lives deep in the Misty Mountains and paddles around his dark pond in a small boat, using his large feet as oars. When Bilbo finds Gollum's ring of invincibility, it makes Gollum furious.

The Great Goblin: The ruler of the savage goblin forces. Gandalf kills him in a cave in the Misty Mountains, a murder the goblins never forgive.

Lord of the Eagles: Lofty and majestic, the Lord of the Eagles helps Bilbo and the Dwarves survive and succeed.

The Master of Esgaroth: A human who at first generously offers food and shelter to the Dwarves. Later, he reacts with cowardice when Smaug threatens the town of Esgaroth.

The Men of the Lake: The Men of Esgaroth, also called the Men of the Lake, join forces with the Elvenking in order to confront Thorin and his Dwarves and gain a share of the dragon's treasure.

Necromancer: An evil being, he uses black magic to communicate with the spirits of the dead and reveal the future. Gandalf wants to drive Necromancer out of the south of Mirkwood.

Roäc: A wise old raven. He tells Bilbo of Smaug's death.

Sackville-Baggins Family: Bilbo's greedy relatives. When Bilbo returns from his adventure, he finds them auctioning off his furniture and belongings and planning to move into his hobbit-hole.

Smaug the Dragon: An enormous, fire-breathing dragon. Calculating and arrogant, he has teeth like swords and breath like a breeze of death. Long ago, he destroyed the Dwarf kingdom in Lonely Mountain and then laid waste to the town of Dale, amassing a mighty treasure for himself.

Spiders: Fearsome creatures that live in Mirkwood Forest and almost succeed in eating the Dwarves.

Thorin Oakenshield: The tallest of the Dwarves and a direct descendant of the lords of Lonely Mountain. Thorin longs to avenge himself on Smaug.

Trolls—Bert, Tom, and William: Ugly, heavy, dangerous creatures. They complain about eating mutton, for what they really crave is "manflesh."

Wargs: Wild wolves with a keen sense of smell. Gandalf can understand the Wargs' language, and even he feels fearful as he listens to them discuss how to deal with the Dwarves.

Wood Elves: Elves that live in Mirkwood Forest, they are not as civilized as the Elves in Rivendell. Suspicious and selfish, the Wood Elves plan to hold the Dwarves captive until they explain why they have trespassed on Mirkwood.

Reading
The Hobbit

An Unexpected Party

The narrator introduces us to **Bilbo Baggins**, a hobbit. Like other hobbits, Bilbo is half the height of a human and has very large, hairy, leathery feet.

He lives in a large meadow on a hilly countryside, near lots of other hobbits, all of whom live in separate hobbit-holes that tunnel into hillsides. Hobbits furnish their spacious rooms comfortably with closets of colorful clothes and pantries filled with tobacco and food. Hobbits enjoy eating, as their plump stomachs reveal. Preferring the quiet life, hobbits do not travel, indulge in excitement, or look for adventure.

This morning, as Bilbo stands outside his hobbit house, smoking his long pipe and thinking about his happy life, he sees a tall wizard, **Gandalf**, walking down the road. Gandalf carries a staff and wears a pointed blue hat, a silver scarf draped around his neck, and a long gray cloak. His white beard hangs below his waist.

Bilbo asks the wizard to pause and have a smoke with him. Gandalf says he is looking for someone to share an adventure. Bilbo tells Gandalf he has come to the wrong place, for no one in Hobbiton goes adventuring. Staying home is more appealing than going on adventures, which wear you out, make you uncomfortable, and put you in danger. Gandalf reveals that he knows Bilbo's name, saying it surprises him that the son of **Belladonna Took Baggins** has no zest for adventure, since the Took family has always loved adventurers. Bilbo begins to recognize Gandalf. Long ago, when Bilbo was very young, Gandalf created wonderful fireworks and told marvelous stories of goblins and giants. Bilbo also remembers that Gandalf lured hobbits into adventures.

Gandalf says that Bilbo will enjoy this particular adventure, which will be amusing, good for him, and likely profitable. No adventures for him, says Bilbo, but then he does something he cannot explain: he invites Gandalf for tea the next day. Immediately after making the invitation, he scurries inside and closes his bright green door.

The next day, Bilbo's doorbell rings, and Bilbo remembers that he has invited Gandalf to tea. Flustered, he opens the door and sees not Gandalf, but a Dwarf with a blue beard who marches in and hangs up his cloak. Reaching for a seed-cake, the Dwarf identifies himself as **Dwalin**. The door bell rings again, and another Dwarf, a very old-looking one, dashes inside, hungry for tea and cakes. He introduces himself as **Balin** and hangs up his cloak. Within minutes, two other Dwarves arrive, then more Dwarves, until thirteen of them, including Dwarves named **Bofur**, **Bifur**, **Nori**, and **Ori**, are sitting around Bilbo's table. Gandalf joins them. The Dwarves ask for a bit more red wine, more seed-cakes, some raspberry jam, an apple-tart, mince-pies, cheese, eggs, cold pickles, and chicken. Bilbo tries to be the best host possible, bringing out plentiful food, coffee, beer, and wine. In the end, he invites them all to stay for supper.

After eating their fill, the Dwarves scurry around the table, singing a fierce song about breaking crockery and pouring milk on the pantry floor. Eventually, they relax and begin to smoke. Before long, they bring out clarinets, flutes, and a drum and sing more songs. **Thorin**, who is taller than the other Dwarves, brings his harp in from the porch, and they sing a long song about the Misty Mountains and treasures of gold stolen from the Dwarves.

Bilbo listens to the music, and his mother's "Took blood," her spirit of adventure, surges through him. He would like to see the great mountains and hear the wind in the pine trees, and he would enjoy exploring caves and drinking from waterfalls. He would even like to carry a sword instead of a walking stick, but he feels too insignificant to do these things.

Thorin says they are in the house of their friend and "fellow conspirator," Bilbo, a statement that makes Bilbo nervous. Thorin says they must set out before daybreak on this long journey from which they may never return. The Dwarves look at Bilbo, who quivers like a leaf. Most of them frown, doubtful that he has the necessary stamina, but Gandalf vouches for Bilbo. Despite Gandalf's word, **Glóin** and **Oin** think Bilbo looks more like a grocer than a burglar.

Gandalf shows everyone a map and a key. Thorin's grandfather drew the map, Gandalf says. The key, which Gandalf gives to Thorin, will unlock a secret door that leads to the underground fortress of **Smaug the Dragon**. In that fortress, Smaug keeps a vast horde of gold that he stole long ago from the Dwarves after plundering Thorin's kingdom and killing almost everyone in it.

"To look for a lost collar button is not a true quest. To go in quest means to look for something of which one has, as yet, no experience; one can imagine what it will be like but whether one's picture is true or false will be known only when one has found it."

W.H. AUDEN, "THE QUEST HERO," *TOLKIEN AND THE CRITICS*

To get back the gold, the Dwarves must gain entrance to the fortress by means of the secret door, which runes describe as five feet tall and wide enough for three people to walk through at once. (*Runes* are the characters of a special alphabet that Scandinavians and other Germanic people used around 300 A.D. Here, *runes* refers to any mythical or obscure symbols or writings that carry secret meaning.)

According to the Dwarves' ill-conceived plan, Bilbo will slip inside the fortress, and then they will decide what to do next. The Dwarves hope Smaug will be asleep when they arrive. Bilbo suggests that if they want to leave at dawn, they should go to bed and discuss their plans at length tomorrow. Thorin makes a point of asking Bilbo why he uses the word "they" instead of "we." After all, he asks, isn't Bilbo going too? Bilbo realizes that he has committed himself and confirms that he will act as their burglar. Relieved, Thorin tells him that for breakfast he would like ham and six fried eggs.

Bilbo takes more breakfast orders, then fixes beds on chairs and sofas and in spare rooms. Later, when he finally crawls into his own bed, he feels tired and afraid. He wonders what he has done. The Took blood that earlier raced through his veins begins to wane. He decides that he cannot possibly go on the adventure and falls asleep.

J.R.R. Tolkien

Chapter 1

Inventing the Hobbits: Tolkien opens his novel by describing hobbits and their homes, creating a careful portrait of these imaginary creatures living in an imagined world. He succeeds in making his landscape and characters believable, convincing us that Hobbiton and the fantastical creatures in it actually exist by writing in a confident tone and including familiar references alongside unfamiliar inventions. Tolkien uses a cinematic technique, first showing us a panoramic view of Hobbiton, a vast, hilly countryside where hobbits burrow tunnels into hills, and then zooming in for close-ups of hobbit holes. A multitude of details about the hobbits make them immediately appealing and colorful. We learn about their appearance, their temperament, and their fondness for eating, drinking, and smoking. Tolkien makes it easy for us to visualize hobbits by imbuing them with a combination of familiar human characteristics and unfamiliar, imagined details. Hobbits, about three feet high, resemble human children in height. In fact, they look much like humans, aside from their enormous, leathery feet. Tolkien implies at the beginning of Chapter 1 that his fantasy world, which he later dubbed Middle-earth, was once connected to our own world. He writes that hobbits "have become rare and shy of the Big People," which is why we no longer see them around.

> "I am a hobbit in every way, except height."
>
> J.R.R. TOLKIEN

The Unlikeliest Hero: Bilbo Baggins, small and lacking in courage, does not fit the conventional role of hero. Even the slightest surprise causes him to shiver and quake. Right from the first chapter, however, we feel sure that Gandalf has chosen Bilbo for a specific reason. When Bilbo feels his Took blood stirring within him, it seems to promise great things. Although his courage wanes at the end of the chapter, already he has begun to poke his head out of the safety of his hobbit-hole.

Bilbo's Odyssey: Besides incorporating elements of Norse and Old English tales, Tolkien draws on familiar themes from classical Greek literature. For instance, Bilbo and the Dwarves go on an *odyssey*, a long quest to obtain or find something.

The Greek poet Homer's *Odyssey* (written between 750 B.C. and 675 B.C.) is the Western model for literary odysseys. The main character, Odysseus, is a thinking man. At times dangerous and aggressive, Odysseus survives and inspires his men through cleverness and cunning. In the same way, Bilbo, not naturally aggressive or even athletic, will embark on a quest that tests his intellect and character. Tolkien also borrows the importance of hospitality from Greek literature and ancient Greek culture. Greek myths teach that any traveler who arrives at the door should be greeted with gracious hospitality, for the unknown visitor might be a god in disguise. In *The Hobbit*, Bilbo shows hospitality not only to Gandalf but also to the Dwarves, who demand almost endless food from his pantry.

Tolkien as Bilbo: In the preface to *The Lord of the Rings*, Tolkien conveys his distaste for allegory, a symbolic system in which characters and places stand for things outside the text. In the decades after writing *The Hobbit*, however, Tolkien openly acknowledged the link between hobbits and the English people of his own time. Furthermore, many similarities exist between Bilbo and Tolkien himself. Like Bilbo, Tolkien enjoyed middle-class comforts such as simple food, a pipe, and a quiet life. Like Bilbo, Tolkien had "adventurous blood"—his mother came from a family known for its extensive adventures. In a more general sense, Bilbo can be read as a gentle caricature of the English, a reserved, quiet people who can be roused to action when necessary, a trait Tolkien witnessed firsthand during his service in World War I.

CHAPTERS 2 & 3
Roast Mutton

When Bilbo wakes up late the next morning, he finds himself alone in his house. A fearful mess of dishes and pots greets him. Bilbo, assuming the Dwarves left without him, feels relieved. It seems nonsensical to imagine leaving his happy home and going forth to confront a dragon. Just as Bilbo finishes cleaning up his kitchen and enjoying a quiet breakfast, however, Gandalf comes in, complaining that Bilbo is late. The Dwarves are waiting for him at the nearby Green Dragon Inn. They want to offer him one-fourteenth of the treasure, should they recapture it. Bilbo is informed that he has only ten minutes to get ready.

Outside the Green Dragon Inn, the ponies stand ready, saddled with parcels, packages, and other paraphernalia. Bilbo complains that he has no hat, so Dwalin lends him a dark-green hood and cloak, and off they go. Before long, Gandalf joins them on a splendid white horse. The party of thirteen Dwarves, a hobbit, and a wizard is now complete. The adventure has begun.

After leaving hobbit country, the group passes through the Lone-lands. The weather suddenly becomes dismal. Cold, driving rain drenches them, and the wind whips them mercilessly as they descend into a deep valley. They decide to find a dry place for the night and bed down early. Shortly after they begin setting up camp, one of the ponies bolts and stumbles into the river. Although **Fili** and **Kili** manage to save the pony, they cannot save their food.

For unexplained reasons, Gandalf departs suddenly. The group sits glumly. Then Bilbo sees a light, and they decide to venture forward. Looking through the trees, they see firelight but cannot make out who is seated around the fire. The Dwarves urge Bilbo to investigate and agree that he should hoot like an owl if he gets into trouble. Inching forward, Bilbo sees three immense Trolls, **Bert**, **Tom**, and **William**. Bored and drunk, the Trolls complain about eating mutton every night when what they really desire is fresh manflesh. Bilbo decides that since he is now a burglar, he should slip forward and see what he can find. He gets caught stealing a key and a change purse from William.

The Trolls quarrel about whether to let Bilbo go. Soon, they spot the group of Dwarves. Trolls hate Dwarves, especially uncooked ones. They quickly bag them, momentarily forgetting about Bilbo, who escapes and climbs a thorn tree. The Trolls begin arguing again, this time debating whether to roast, mince, or boil their catch. At the break of dawn, Gandalf appears suddenly. He imitates the Trolls' voices, causing them to argue among themselves and lose track of time. The dawn vanquishes the Trolls, since Trolls turn to stone whenever daylight touches them.

Bilbo and Gandalf release the Dwarves from their sacks. They find the Trolls' cave but cannot budge the heavy stone door. Bilbo suggests trying William's key, and the key fits the lock perfectly. From the cave they take bread, cheese, bacon, and swords. They also take pots of gold, which they bury carefully.

A Short Rest

Back on the trail to Rivendell, no one speaks. Bilbo mistakes the Misty Mountain range for Lonely Mountain, their ultimate destination, but they have only just begun their journey. Gandalf leads the way, cautioning the travelers that if they lose track of the road, they will likely perish. They want to reach the home of **Elrond** in Rivendell. Elrond expects them and will have food and a warm hearth waiting. The landscape has become perilous. Bilbo and the Dwarves notice cracks in the earth, one of which cuts deeply into a valley with steep sides and dark ravines.

Bilbo notices that teatime has passed with no sign of tea or seed-cakes. Eventually, they stumble upon the secret valley of Rivendell that they have been seeking. The air grows warmer and smells of pine trees. Bilbo hears Elves singing about the Dwarves' beards and Bilbo, warning the other Elves of his appetite for seed-cakes. In song, the Elves invite the Dwarves to stay with them.

Bilbo likes Elves, although he has little experience with them. He knows that the gruff, bearded Dwarves do not particularly care for Elves, deeming them foolish and carefree. Finally,

SOWING THE SEED-CAKES ❧ Tolkien's background as a medieval scholar made him familiar with seed-cakes, a delicacy Geoffrey Chaucer mentions in *The Canterbury Tales*. The cakes, made in the shape of a medieval round shield called a "buckler," consist of yeast, flour, warm beer, salt, butter, sugar, and eggs. The batter, after being flavored with poppy seeds, anise seeds, or coriander, is poured into eight-inch greased pans and baked.

they reach Elrond's Last Homely House, where they stay for fourteen days, eating, resting, and talking. Elrond examines the swords that the Dwarves found in the Trolls' cave and explains that they are very old Elf swords. He suspects that the Trolls stole them and that the mountains contain many caves filled with such old and fantastic swords, as well as forgotten treasures of gold.

By moonlight, Elrond reads the runes on the Dwarves' map. The moon letters explain how to get into Smaug's fortress. The group must stand by a gray stone when the thrush knocks, and the sun that sets with the last light of Durin's Day will shine upon the keyhole. Durin's Day is the first day of the Dwarves' New Year, and on that autumn evening, the moon and sun appear in the sky simultaneously. The Dwarves leave on "midsummer's morning," a good omen. The ponies are rested, and the Dwarves are eager to continue their adventure. They ride away singing songs of farewell and good luck, their hearts filled with hope.

UNDERSTANDING AND INTERPRETING
Chapters 2 & 3

Comic Trolls and Dark Beginnings: Tolkien alternates comic scenes with dark, ominous ones. He often reverses our expectations for which will come when. For example, he turns the dangerous brush with the Trolls into a slapstick comedy. The Trolls endanger the lives of the band of adventurers, but their names—Bert, Tom, and William—sound not evil, but classically English and unthreatening.

MIDSUMMER'S EVE

Midsummer's Eve, which falls on the Saturday between June 20 and June 26, is celebrated in Scandinavian countries as well as in England.

Midsummer's Eve is one of the happiest holidays, because it marks the true beginning of summer and the release from the dreary darkness that engulfs these countries during the winter. On Midsummer's Eve, people traditionally light bonfires in order to symbolically cleanse and banish evil spirits. They also decorate their homes with greenery and flowers. Sometimes Midsummer's Eve traditions include a tall maypole, a symbol of fertility around which girls dance. In recent times, people have used Midsummer's Eve as an excuse to flock to lakeside cabins and forests in order to commune with nature.

Like cranky old men, they complain in cockney English about the quality of their food, wailing that mutton wearies them. When Bilbo musters sufficient courage to investigate the fireside, he plans to hoot if he finds himself in trouble. Precisely at his moment of need, however, he remembers that he does not know how to hoot. Tolkien also reverses our expectations by making the departure for Rivendell gloomy. This contradicts the usual trope of cheerful embarkations. As the group strikes out for Rivendell, the air is

GOR' BLIMEY Cockney English, a dialect spoken in London's East End, is stigmatized as a lower-class working accent. Tolkien uses it for broad humor by putting it in the mouths of fearsome-looking Trolls. Characteristics of clichéd cockney English include dropped h's (*'ere* instead of *here*), glottal stops (*p'raps* for *perhaps*), and generous use of the phrase *gor' blimey* (a contraction of "God blind me!").

"dark and drear," and the land opens up into gullies, dark ravines, and dangerous bogs. Tiny white stones dot the path they must follow. Bilbo's pony stumbles, and Gandalf's horse nearly falls. The reversal of our expectations in these two scenes suggests that facing the unknown is far more perilous and scary than facing a live, three-dimensional foe you can look at and assess. Danger lies in the unknown, where saboteurs might be lurking and ravines might be waiting to swallow up the careless traveler.

Not Yet a Hero: Bilbo still seems an unlikely choice for a hero. He commits to the adventure reluctantly and at the last second. Gandalf must rush him out of his hobbit-hole and send him scurrying to the Green Dragon Inn. Bilbo sounds distinctly unheroic when complaining that he has no hat, no pocket-handkerchiefs, and no tobacco. In appearance, rotund and beardless Bilbo cuts a comic figure in comparison to the grizzled Dwarves. The Dwarves seem ready to accept him, however, glad that they have a burglar along for the journey.

Comfort-Loving but Cunning: Bilbo's love of comfort does not preclude cunning. At first, we see only Bilbo's desire for luxury. On the way to Lonely Mountain, he often longs for his warm, snug hobbit-hole. Most of all, he longs for regular meals and teatime. He panics when one of the ponies flounders and most of the food supplies wash down the river. Eventually, however, Bilbo proves that he is not entirely soft and spoiled. When he sees the Trolls, he reasons that his small hobbit hand will make it easy for him to pick their pockets unnoticed. Even when caught, he manages to elude the Trolls. This small act of bravery makes us see Bilbo in a different light.

ALLUVIAL FAN ❧ The vast slope that Bilbo and the others tumble down is called an *alluvial fan*—a long, fanlike formation along the bottom of a mountain range, made of rocks and sediment that have been washed and wind-blown off the mountain tops for centuries. The material is often loose and is dangerous to traverse. These long "aprons," or fans, at the base of mountains can be extensive, angling downward for as many as five miles.

Noble Swords: The swords that the company steals from the Trolls' cave are a link to the tradition of heroic epic on which much of *The Hobbit* is based. Many heroic epics feature swords with mythic lineages and heroic names, the most famous example being King Arthur's legendary sword, Excalibur. The possession of a named sword symbolizes heroism and prowess in battle, so it is significant that Bilbo's short sword does not yet have a name. We know that these swords, although found in the Trolls' possession, originate with good men, because they were made for the Elves. The swords' noble origin makes them lucky weapons.

CHAPTERS 4–6
Over Hill and Under Hill

Long days have passed since the adventurers left the Last Homely House. From their position on the Misty Mountains, they can look back and see the countryside they have traveled. One day, with two thunderstorms raging, the Dwarves find a cave that seems dry and large enough to shelter them. In the cave, they dry their clothes and feed the ponies. Before long, they all fall fast asleep.

Bilbo wakes to see goblins jumping out of a crack in the ground, grabbing the Dwarves and carrying them down through the cracks. Bilbo cries out as goblins surround him, and Gandalf creates a lightning crash that strikes several of the goblins dead. The Dwarves and Bilbo find themselves chained together and driven forward to the **Great Goblin**. Thorin carries Orcrist (*Goblin-cleaver*), a sword from the Trolls' cave. The goblins call this sword "Biter." On seeing it, the Great Goblin becomes so enraged that he rushes at Thorin with his sharp-toothed mouth open. At that moment, the lights in the cavern go out, and Gandalf attacks. A sword sears through the air and plunges into the Great Goblin, killing him instantly.

Gandalf and the Dwarves flee, trailed by a battalion of armed goblins. Bilbo cannot keep up, so **Dori** lifts him onto his back. Gandalf and Thorin hang back, armed with their swords, *Goblin-cleaver* and *Foe-hammer*. Something grabs Dori from behind, causing Bilbo to bounce off and hit his head on a rock.

Riddles in the Dark

When Bilbo opens his eyes, he cannot see or hear anything. He begins to crawl forward in the dark. He feels a ring on the floor and absentmindedly pockets it. He imagines the safety of home. Suddenly, he splashes into an ice-cold pool of water. There he finds a slimy creature, **Gollum**. Gollum paddles around in his little boat, using his large feet as oars. He asks Bilbo who he is and why he is here, and Bilbo responds honestly, explaining that he is utterly lost. Toying with his victim, Gollum suggests a game of riddles. If Bilbo wins, Gollum will show him the way out: if Gollum wins, he will eat Bilbo.

Bilbo manages to solve each of Gollum's riddles. Then he must propose a riddle, so he asks Gollum to guess the contents of his pocket. Gollum cannot guess, and Bilbo wins. Gollum asks for time to go back to his island to retrieve something. He cannot find what he seeks, and Bilbo realizes that Gollum's missing object is probably the Ring.

Gollum, furious, realizes that Bilbo must have the Ring in his pocket. He sneaks toward Bilbo, intent on killing him, hissing, "What's it got in its pocketses?" Bilbo puts his hand in his pocket, and the Ring, with an apparent will of its own, slides onto his finger in the nick of time and makes Bilbo invisible. Gollum sits in front of the exit to his dark hole, moaning. Bilbo summons the courage to sneak past him. Invisible, he gets past goblin guards and makes it to a grove of trees.

Out of the Frying-Pan into the Fire

Bilbo sees that he has lost his hood, cloak, food, pony, and friends. He looks back, sees the Misty Mountains, and realizes that somehow he succeeded in emerging on the other side of the range and now stands on the edge of the Land Beyond. Hearing voices, Bilbo creeps forward and peers between two large boulders. He sees Balin dressed in his red hood. Bilbo slips off his magic ring and cries out, "Here's the burglar!" The Dwarves cheer. Bilbo entertains them with tales of his adventures but decides not to tell them about his magic ring.

Gandalf announces that they must make haste, because the goblins can smell their footsteps. They slip down a slope and crash into a forest. Amazingly, no one is injured. The group hears a howl in the distance and then a howl in answer. They realize they are hearing wolves. Gandalf tells his friends to climb as high in the trees as they can. Soon, everyone is safe except Bilbo, whose short legs prevent him from jumping up and grabbing a tree branch. Dori, the lowest down, lifts Bilbo out of the way just in time to rescue him from the enormous pack of wolves that snaps at Bilbo's toes.

The wolves are wild **Wargs**, and this clearing belongs to them. They speak a language that Gandalf can understand, and he does not like what he hears. The Wargs have assembled tonight to meet with some goblins and plan a raid on human settlers who have invaded their land. The humans have guns and have killed many Wargs, so the Wargs hope to kill as many humans as possible and share the freshly slaughtered corpses with the goblins. Gandalf grabs several pinecones and magically lights them with colored fire, tossing them into the midst of the circle of wolves. His plan works immediately. The wolves catch fire and begin to flee.

The **Lord of the Eagles** flies over and sees goblins taunting Bilbo, Gandalf, and the Dwarves. The Lord of the Eagles swoops down with other eagles to rescue Bilbo and his friends. Bilbo, who has never liked heights, lands in an eagle's nest. Gandalf and the Lord of the Eagles are old friends. The Lord feeds them roast game for supper, and then they go to sleep.

UNDERSTANDING AND INTERPRETING
Chapters 4–6

Entering Evil: In these chapters, the narrative moves from the relatively safe beginning of the journey to a more perilous leg. As this chapter begins and the group advances up the mountainside, the narrator gives us a panoramic view of the land below and far away. He wants readers to see, through the eyes of Bilbo, where the company has been. The narrator contrasts the safe and comfortable life that Bilbo used to know with the dangerous existence that he now faces. Down below, in the land that Bilbo has left behind, hobbits and Elves harvest hay and have picnics. This peaceful life now seems lost to Bilbo. The massive, frightening thunderstorm foreshadows the dangers that lie ahead. Gandalf prepares the travelers by revealing to them that they are headed into the Wild, where, after dragons drove Men from the land, evil flourished.

One Race, One Temperament: In Tolkien's fantasy world, beings of one race often share identical moral tendencies. Goblins, for example, are infamous for their ability to make cruel weapons and instruments of torture, and they are all evil. All Elves, in contrast, are good. The races of Middle-earth also share the same quirks. All hobbits love food, for instance, and all Dwarves love gold. The mythic theology of Middle-earth accounts for these race-wide characteristics. According to Middle-earth myth, the gods create creatures for specific purposes. Each race of creatures also has a specific relationship with nature. Of the various characters Tolkien depicts, Bilbo is the only one capable of making complex moral choices that test the boundaries of his racial characteristics.

Goblin Grudges: The Great Goblin hates Elves even more than he hates Dwarves. It is an old, festering hatred, born of centuries of war and killing. Thus, when he and his goblin soldiers see the two legendary elf-forged swords—Orcrist (*Goblin-cleaver*) and Glamdring (*Foe-hammer*)—they go berserk, screaming orders that the Dwarves be slashed and destroyed. Tolkien shows that old hatreds are often the fiercest.

Fear of the Unknown Gollum: Although Gollum is a slimy, lamp-eyed foe, he does not present the same kind of danger as a goblin. In fact, he is most terrifying when he is unknown. Before Bilbo sees him and speaks to him, Gollum terrifies the hobbit because for all Bilbo knows, he is more monstrous and unnatural than any enemy Bilbo has faced. When Bilbo sees Gollum and speaks to him, however, he can easily manage him. Gollum becomes almost comical, hissing, talking to himself, and referring to himself as "we," as if he were royalty.

Mind Games: Gollum's riddle game is likely inspired by epic literature. Riddles and riddle games often feature in Anglo-Saxon and Scandinavian epics, in which heroes are defined almost as much by their prowess with words as they are by their prowess with swords. In fact, many of the riddles exchanged by Bilbo and Gollum come directly from ancient Scandinavian or Anglo-Saxon poems. Bilbo's victory in the riddle game marks an important step in his development, but the eccentric manner in which he wins is closer to a modern comedy than to an ancient epic. Bilbo baffles Gollum with the question, "What have I got in my pocket?"

 EYRIE *Eyrie* (sometimes spelled *aerie*) is the name for an eagle's nest, which can be quite large. The nest of a bald eagle, for example, can measure up to five feet across. Eagles often use the same nest year after year, increasing the nest's depth and width as time passes. Over the years, some nests become huge, measuring as much as nine feet in diameter and weighing more than two tons. The eagles in *The Hobbit*, ancient ancestors of today's eagles, are twice the size of their modern-day counterparts.

which is not a true riddle at all. A true riddle must contain the clues necessary to solve it. Gollum, less quick than his foe, cannot even challenge Bilbo's question, let alone answer it.

Changing the Course of History: What seems a small moment in Chapter 5 is actually by far the most important event in all of *The Hobbit*. When Bilbo discovers the Ring, he changes the course of Middle-earth's history. Though neither Bilbo nor Gollum knows it, the Ring is an object of awesome power. Created by the Dark Lord Sauron, who appears in *The Hobbit* as the Necromancer of Mirkwood, it is his means to conquer and corrupt the world. The ring is pivotal to the plot of *The Lord of the Rings*. In *The Hobbit*, Tolkien hints at its importance only by commenting cryptically that Bilbo's discovery marks a turning point in his career.

CHAPTERS 7–9
Queer Lodgings

The next morning, eagles fly the company to safe ground. Bilbo enjoys the thrill for a moment before his fear of heights returns. Back on the ground, Gandalf announces that he will accompany them to the house of his old friend, **Beorn**, the skin-changer, and then he will leave them. Beorn sometimes takes the form of a strong, black-haired man with a massive beard and arms like oak trees. Sometimes he takes the form of a mammoth bear.

THE NECTAR OF THE GODS ❧ Mead is a honey wine often mentioned in Greek, Norse, Germanic, and Anglo-Saxon literature. Until humans began to cultivate grapes and produce wine from them, mead was the most popular alcoholic drink in the Western world. Writers often referred to it as "the nectar of the gods." Mead is relatively easy to make, since honey is highly fermentable. Mead consists of honey and yeast fermented for thirty days, strained, and dosed with sparkling water.

Beorn loathes goblins, and he sympathizes with the group when he hears that goblins caused them to lose their ponies, food, and luggage. The Dwarves enter Beorn's house a few at a time, to avoid startling him. Beorn does not particularly care for crabby, taciturn Dwarves, but he prefers them to goblins. Beorn invites everyone to eat and offers the company wooden drinking bowls full of mead. After ingesting their fill of food and mead, the company sleeps. Bilbo hears animals outside, snuffling and scuffling, and wonders if Beorn has become a bear. The next day, Beorn tells Bilbo that a large assembly of bears convened the night before to dance and tell stories. Beorn learned that goblin patrols are hunting for the company, intent on avenging the death of the Great Goblin and the burning of the chief wolf's nose. Beorn decides to give the Wargs and the goblins a little scare by killing one of each. He shows Bilbo a goblin's head stuck outside the gate and the skin of a Warg nailed to a tree.

Beorn warns the company about the dangers of Mirkwood Forest, through which they must travel. They must never drink water from its streams, and they must ration their food carefully, because they should not eat anything they find in Mirkwood. As the company travels and the days pass, the grass and flowers become scarce. Occasionally, Bilbo sees antlers among the trees and notices the shadowy form of a large bear prowling parallel to them. He mentions what he sees to Gandalf, but Gandalf tells him to hush and take no notice of it. Finally, the black and frowning wall of Mirkwood Forest appears before them. Gandalf says that he will ride on, leaving them at the edge of Mirkwood. He must attend to pressing business in the south. Gandalf advises them to take courage and keep their wits about them.

Flies and Spiders

Entering the dark and dangerous forest of Mirkwood, the company walks in a single file. Strange, unfamiliar creatures grunt and scuffle in the darkness. Above them, dark, dense cobwebs stretch from tree to tree. The air is rank and still. During the nights, Bilbo sees yellow, green, or red eyes gleaming from above, shining from a distance, and popping open next to him. Even more frightening are the thousands of large, hand-sized black moths that flap and flutter alongside flocks of monstrous bats. Food runs low, and the path the company is following peters out at a washed-out bridge.

As the company attempts to cross the water, **Bombur**, the fattest of the Dwarves, falls into the enchanted stream and nearly drowns. Almost immediately after the others pull him from the water, he falls asleep. Four days later, the Dwarves struggle through the forest still carrying his heavy, unconscious body with them. Balin sees a twinkle of light in the forest. When the company creeps forward, they discover Elven folk seated in a circle on felled trees, eating, drinking, and laughing merrily. Suddenly, the lights go out. The Elves disappear, leaving Bilbo and the Dwarves alone in the darkness.

Soon they see a distant blaze of light and hear singing and harps. They come upon a **woodland king** with a crown of leaves on his golden hair. This time, Thorin steps forward, but again the lights go out. Bilbo runs around calling to the Dwarves, but no one answers. He is alone in the silence and darkness. Bilbo falls asleep and dreams of bacon, eggs, toast, and butter. He awakens to find that an enormous spider has begun wrapping him in strong, sticky string. Bilbo frees himself by using his small sword. Thrusting his blade into the spider's eyes, he watches it die. Then Bilbo collapses.

When he wakes again, Bilbo decides to call his sword *Sting*. All alone, he slips on his golden ring of invisibility and begins searching for the Dwarves. He discovers huge, horrible **spiders**, creaking and hissing at one another about what fine eating the Dwarves will make. Looking up, Bilbo sees a dozen bundles, all wound in sticky spider thread, hanging in a dark row from a high branch. The spiders have captured the Dwarves and wrapped them up to season them for consumption.

Still invisible, Bilbo picks up several smooth, egg-shaped stones and hits several spiders with them, killing some and knocking others senseless. In the confusion, Bilbo manages to free the Dwarves. During the rescue, Bilbo must reveal to the Dwarves that the Ring can make him disappear. Alive but wobbly, the Dwarves regard Bilbo with great respect. Proud to have such a clever, beringed friend, they realize gratefully that they would have perished had it not been for him.

Suddenly, Dwalin realizes that Thorin Oakenshield is not among them. **Wood Elves** have carried Thorin away to their castle-cave and handed him over to their king, who questions him closely. When Thorin refuses to reveal the Dwarves' business in Mirkwood or their destination, the **Elvenking** throws him in a cell and vows to keep him there for a hundred years, or until he agrees to answer the questions.

> "I don't want to defend Tolkien or to attack him, but to describe how the strange power of his books casts a spell over readers, a spell some of them grow out of and others don't. Except that 'spell' is far too neat and unembarrassing a metaphor, really, for a process so alarming as the locking-on of the hungry imagination. It is possible for readers to live their whole lives through Tolkien's universe, for weeks and months and even longer."
>
> **JENNY TURNER**, *LONDON REVIEW OF BOOKS*

Barrels Out of Bond

The day after the battle with the spiders, as Bilbo and the Dwarves trudge forward in the green darkness, they find themselves suddenly surrounded by Wood Elves who leap out from all sides with bows and spears drawn. The Elves order the Dwarves to halt. Bilbo quickly slips on his golden ring of invisibility. The Wood Elves blindfold the Dwarves and march them to the castle of the Elvenking. Bilbo follows.

The Elvenking sentences all of the Dwarves to prison until they are willing to explain their mission. Each Dwarf must live in a solitary cell, far from the others. The king does grant them food and drink. For a long time, Bilbo scurries from place to place, hiding in the castle, hardly daring to sleep, unsure of what to do. He soon finds his days dreary and dull. One day Bilbo chances to discover that food and wine are brought upstream in barrels, which are then unloaded and sent back downstream, empty. He reasons that if he can somehow free the Dwarves and pack them in the barrels, they will be sent downstream.

Galion, the Elvenking's butler, asks the chief of the guards to come below with him and sample the first of the newly arrived wine. They drink large flagons of the beverage and eventually pass out drunk. Bilbo silently grabs the guard's keys and hurries off to free the Dwarves, who then escape in the barrels. Bilbo forgets to put himself in a barrel. As the last barrel rolls toward the hatch doors, Bilbo catches hold of it and splashes into the water, scrambling to hold on to the barrel as it floats downstream.

UNDERSTANDING AND INTERPRETING
Chapters 7–9

Darkening Tone: The novel's tone grows darker and more ominous the farther the company travels. The solace they find in Beorn's lair after escaping the goblins seems grim and violent compared to the solace they found in Rivendell after escaping the Trolls. Even after the company escapes the goblins, the coming perilous journey into Mirkwood makes the road ahead seem more frightening than the road behind. This gradually darkening tone builds tension. It also transforms the novel's dynamic from a lighthearted children's story into a more serious epic. The gradual change corresponds to the reader's immersion in the tale and to Bilbo's transformation into a true hero. As Bilbo travels farther from the safe and familiar comforts of Hobbiton, the dangers he faces increase, and he begins to evolve from a quiet, comfortable hobbit into a noble protagonist.

Pure Nature: Like the eagles, Beorn helps the company out of hatred for goblins, rather than love for Dwarves. Neither Beorn nor the eagles have any interest in the Dwarves' gold, but as representatives of pure nature, they are the sworn enemies of corrupted nature, represented by the goblins and Wargs. Beorn can be downright cruel to those unnatural beings that displease him. When he finds a goblin and a Warg prowling about in the woods, for instance, he puts the goblin's head on a stake and the Warg's pelt on a tree outside his house as a warning. Beorn, although he helps the company, is a dangerous man. He embodies the brute force of nature.

> "What an unforgettable experience it was for me as an undergraduate, hearing you [Tolkien] recite *Beowulf*. The voice was the voice of Gandalf."
>
> **W.H. AUDEN**, WHO ATTENDED TOLKIEN'S LECTURES AT OXFORD

Beorn and *Beowulf*: One of Tolkien's academic specialties was the Anglo-Saxon epic poem *Beowulf* (written between A.D. 680 and 800 by an unknown author). In fact, a year before *The Hobbit* was published, Tolkien published a classic, groundbreaking essay on *Beowulf*, which he entitled "*Beowulf*: The Monsters and the Critics." *Beowulf* influences *The Hobbit* in several places. Here, for example, Tolkien fashions Beorn's spacious, timbered home after *Beowulf*'s Heorot, the mighty mead hall of Hrothgar, King of the Danes. Both structures have wide, high gables and mammoth wooden pillars. In Heorot, Hrothgar freely shares his treasures with worthy men. Here, Beorn shares his own treasures—honey, cream, and mead—with the Dwarves. Along with playing host, he plays storyteller, a revered position in *Beowulf*. As torch lights and red beeswax candles flicker, Beorn tells of the wild lands on this side of the mountain. Also like *Beowulf*, *The Hobbit* features a dragon that must ultimately be defeated.

Learning Their Own Lessons: Until this point in the tale, Gandalf has guided the Dwarves and Bilbo. Now, for the first time, he leaves them to their own devices. Eru, the Creator, put Gandalf on Middle-earth to assist in the fight against evil, but Gandalf cannot do everything for the Dwarves and Bilbo. They must struggle by themselves sometimes. Gandalf and Beorn prepare the company for its adventure with words both encouraging and ominous. Gandalf tells the Dwarves that Bilbo possesses the courage and resourcefulness necessary for the rest of the journey, but he also reminds them that no shortcut to the Lonely

Mountain exists. Beorn warns them not to eat anything they find in Mirkwood and not to drink or bathe in the water. He wishes them "all speed" and reminds them that his house is open to them "if ever [they] come back this way again"—a kind invitation, but also a worrisome reminder that they may never return from their mission.

A Sword Named Sting: A turning point in Bilbo's development is his slaying of a savage spider. After killing the spider, Bilbo feels like "a different person." For the first time, Bilbo has defeated an enemy in combat, a victory that is a rite of passage. Bilbo marks this rite by naming his sword. In ancient epic literature, named swords are important symbols of courage and heroism, so by giving his sword a name, Bilbo signifies his new capacity to lead. The sword's name, *Sting*, is short and strikingly effective, like Bilbo himself. From this point on, Bilbo begins to take action and make plans on his own. His successful plan to free the Dwarves from the Wood Elves is the first instance of his newfound resolve. Bilbo cleverly draws the spiders away from the Dwarves by throwing stones, confusing and distracting the spiders. Bilbo's cunning succeeds again in the castle of the Elvenking, when he waits for a propitious moment and then frees the Dwarves from jail.

CHAPTER 10
A Warm Welcome

As Bilbo bobs along in the river, he sees Smaug's Lonely Mountain looming before him. Before he can feel too afraid, the river suddenly rushes into Long Lake. River men catch the barrels, planning to wash them later. When the river men leave to eat and rest, the Dwarves scramble out of the barrels. Thorin says they should all give thanks to Bilbo. Bilbo suggests they head toward the center of the lake town of Esgaroth, also called Lake Town. When they come to a guard encampment, Thorin reveals his name and identity to the guards. He is Thorin, son of Thrain, grandson of Thror, who was king under the Mountain. Excitement erupts immediately. For the people of Esgaroth, Thorin is a legendary figure. Thorin explains that the Dwarves with him are descendants of his father's people and that they have returned, as old songs prophesied, to reclaim what belongs to them. He asks the guards to take them to the **Master of Esgaroth**.

The Master hesitates to believe Thorin's story, in part because he does not want to make an enemy of the king of the Wood Elves, who is wary of Dwarves. Townspeople strike their harps and draw their bows across fiddles, and songs ring out. After resting for a week, the company feels ready to battle Smaug, the dragon of Lonely Mountain. As Thorin and the rest of the Dwarves prepare to depart, the Master offers them munitions and thanks them in advance for attempting to kill the dragon and regain Thorin's kingdom.

UNDERSTANDING AND INTERPRETING
Chapter 10

Egos and Esgaroth: Although Thorin Oakenshield is grateful when Bilbo rescues him from the Elvenking's imprisonment, he is convinced that he, Thorin, remains in charge of this adventure. He is a Dwarf, descended from the mighty Thrain and Thror, while Bilbo is only a hobbit. Therefore, after Bilbo and the Dwarves arrive at Esgaroth and extract themselves from their barrels, it is Thorin—not Thorin and Bilbo—who strides into town, albeit wet and bedraggled, and requests an interview with the Master of the town. The people of Esgaroth are impressed with this living legend with ties to the past, an era when Dwarves honored goldsmiths and silversmiths and ruled from Lonely Mountain. Thorin does come from noble ancestors, but his pride could cause problems.

The Power of Names: The way in which Thorin Oakenshield's name and the name of his grandfather command immediate respect in Lake Town despite Thorin's tattered appearance highlights the importance of ancestry in Middle-earth. We have already seen the importance of lineage in defining a person's character and prospects, through Bilbo's oscillation between his Took side and his Baggins side and through Thorin's obsession with his birthright, the treasure under the Mountain. When the party arrives at Lake Town, we see that lineage also influences social interactions. Since strangers often bring trouble, a well-known name is powerful. A mark of social and familial stability, a name like Oakenshield represents a time when peace and prosperity prevailed. For the people of Lake Town, the return of the grandson of the king under the Mountain recalls the time before Smaug, when gold came from the Lonely Mountain.

Lake Town Humans: The introduction of the people of Lake Town places humans in Tolkien's hierarchy of good and evil races. The human denizens of Lake Town are cautious when it comes to confronting the dragon. When the company sets off for the mountain, the humans refuse to go near it, leaving Bilbo and the Dwarves to fend for themselves. Though they are concerned most about themselves, the people of Lake Town cannot be blamed for fearing Smaug—they are convinced he is invincible. Though Tolkien here emphasizes human fallibility and fear, he portrays humans as generally good creatures.

CHAPTER 11
On the Doorstep

After two days of traveling on Long Lake, the company sees Lonely Mountain towering grim and tall before them. On the third day, they disembark. The land about them grows ever more bleak and barren. Thorin tells them that long ago the land was green and fair, but it changed after the dragon seized control of it. The travelers pin their hopes on the westernmost spur of the mountain. There they hope to find the hidden door that leads to the core of the mountain, where Smaug lives atop his treasure hoard. Bilbo scouts and finds a great stone door.

The company goes to the flat wall but finds no sign of a bar, bolt, or keyhole. The Dwarves beat on it and push at it, study the map, and speak fragments of old spells, but nothing budges the door. They complain about Bilbo's usefulness. They look down at the ruins of Dale, the town where Balin lived when Smaug destroyed the countryside. As evening approaches, Bilbo watches a nearly coal-black thrush, its yellow breast freckled with dark spots, cracking snails against a stone. A faint ray of light from the setting sun escapes through the clouds and falls on the smooth rock face of the mountain. The thrush gives a sudden trill, a crack forms in the stone slab, and a flake of rock falls away from the wall. Slowly, a keyhole appears about three feet from the ground.

Bilbo calls for the key. Thorin steps forward and inserts it. The key fits and turns. The sun sinks, and evening springs into the sky as the Dwarves all push together. Part of the rock wall gives way, and a door five feet high swings inward. A yawning mouth leads down into the mountain.

UNDERSTANDING AND INTERPRETING
Chapter 11

A Secret Key to a Secret Door: With the riddle of the secret door, Tolkien draws his readers into the story by presenting a confusing puzzle that we solve before the characters do. Tolkien employs this device often. He used it, for example, in the riddle game between Bilbo and Gollum. At the mountain, we have an advantage over the characters. The company has passed through many dangers since their last night in Rivendell, where Elrond interpreted the moon runes on the map for them, explaining that the door could open only on Durin's Day, one of the last days of autumn. The Dwarves have forgotten the line about "when the thrush knocks . . . ." We are more likely to have the message fresh in mind, since the narrator notes several times in Chapter 11 that "[a]utumn was now crawling towards winter." The difference between the reader's knowledge and the characters' ignorance, a situation of dramatic irony, adds to the suspense and urgency of their attempt to figure out the secret of the door. Tolkien builds tension by playing on our desire for the characters to figure out what we already know.

CHAPTER 12
Inside Information

For a long time, the Dwarves stand in the darkness in front of the door. At last, Thorin speaks, saying it is time for their burglar, Bilbo Baggins, to enter and earn his reward. Bilbo tells them he will explore whatever lies beyond the door. After all, he has already rescued them from two near-death calamities. As his father used to say, the "third time pays all." All alone, Bilbo creeps into the dark passageway , aware that ancestors of his Dwarf companions originally built it. Their superb craftsmanship made the passage straight as a ruler and gave it a gentle downward slope. Bilbo puts on his golden ring of invisibility and loosens his dagger in its sheath. Darkness surrounds him except for a red light at the far end of the tunnel. He hears a strange sound, like the purring of a huge tomcat. It is the dragon snoring .

When Bilbo reaches the dragon's vast horde, he finds the mighty "worm" still sleeping. On all sides of the monster lie countless piles of precious gold objects, gems, and jewels. Bilbo seizes a two-handled cup and flees as fast as his furry feet will carry him. "I've done it!" he exults to himself. The Dwarves celebrate Bilbo's return, but their joy is short-lived. A loud roar comes from within the mountain: Smaug has discovered that a cup is missing. Fire spews from the mountain as Smaug shakes its roots and roars like thunder. Smaug comes out of the mountain through the main gate. Bilbo and the Dwarves quickly hide in the tunnel, and Smaug does not notice them. He assumes that Men from the valley below invaded his lair, and he vows to make them pay in time. He appears to resume his nap.

Bilbo again slips on his ring and descends to the dragon's lair. When he arrives at the threshold, he pauses. Smaug seems to be sleeping, but in fact he is only pretending. He sees nothing because of Bilbo's ring of invisibility, but he smells a stranger. With mock courtesy, he invites the stranger in and urges him to take what he wants, for there is plenty. Bilbo tells Smaug he did not come to take anything, but merely to see if the dragon is as glorious as he has always heard. This claim flatters Smaug, who asks Bilbo's identity. Bilbo tells Smaug that he is a clue-finder, a web-cutter, a stinging fly, who drowns his friends and draws them again from the water. He is a friend of bears and a guest of eagles. He is known as Ringwinner, Luckwearer, and Barrel-rider. The dragon says he has heard enough of this blather.

The dragon then reveals that he has feasted on several ponies that stank of Dwarves and knows there are fourteen in the company. When Bilbo says that they have come for revenge, the dragon roars with laughter. The king under the Mountain has died, and Smaug ate the people of Dale long ago. No one threatens him because he has teeth like swords, claws like spears, and a tail like a thunderbolt.

Bilbo comments on Smaug's waistcoat of diamonds, saying it does look sword proof. He asks for a better look, and when Smaug shows it off, Bilbo sees a large bare patch in the hollow of Smaug's left breast. He tells Smaug to get some rest and runs up the tunnel. Smaug roars that Bilbo is a fool for mocking a live dragon, spouting jets of fire and steam toward the sound of Bilbo's feet and scorching the backs of the hobbit's head and heels.

After returning to his friends, Bilbo worries that the **Men of the Lake** may bear the brunt of Smaug's wrath. Perhaps he taunted Smaug too much. Nonetheless, Balin praises Bilbo for his cleverness in finding Smaug's vulnerable patch. Now, somehow they must pierce that spot. As they talk, a thrush listens to them. Bilbo feels certain that Smaug will come out soon, and he urges the Dwarves to hide inside the tunnel with him and close the door. It shuts with a snap and a clang. No trace of a keyhole remains. They are locked tight inside the mountain. A moment later, the mountain booms, its walls crack, and stones fall on their heads . Outside, Smaug is breaking rocks to pieces, lashing against the mountain with his huge tail, and scorching the grass and walls. The Dwarves huddle together.

UNDERSTANDING AND INTERPRETING
Chapter 12

Red and Gold: Tolkien describes the fearsome dragon as "red-gold," binding together two traditionally opposing colors. Anglo-Saxon mythology associates hell with red, fiery flames, and heaven with golden, gleaming streets. Here, the dragon combines the threatening, fiery-red hell of his body with the heaven of gold that the Dwarves seek. The journey to obtain Smaug's treasure is both a curse and a blessing.

Ancient and Modern: Smaug's character fuses elements from ancient epic literature with modern traits. Smaug has all the characteristics of legendary dragons, including an armor-like scaled hide, a love of treasure, and the ability to breathe fire. However, he also possesses a dark, modern sense of humor and an almost magical gift of speech that allows him to glean more information from Bilbo than the clever hobbit intends to convey. His speech is so persuasive that it even makes Bilbo doubt whether the Dwarves really plan to give him his share of the profits.

DRAGON'S HEEL

The term **Achilles' heel** refers to a person's weak spot or point of vulnerability. The term originated in a Greek myth about the Trojan War hero Achilles. When Achilles was born, his mother hoped to make him immortal by dipping him in the underworld's river Styx. As she slipped him into the river, she held him by one heel and forgot to dip him a second time in order to make that part of his heel resistant to all weapons. Achilles, therefore, remained vulnerable. Smaug's vulnerable spot is a small hollow near his left breast. A psychololgical vulnerability can be more dangerous than a physical one: Smaug's vanity might also be interpreted as an Achilles' heel, since vanity prompts him to show Bilbo his physical weak spot.

Brave Bilbo: It takes all the courage that Bilbo can muster to leave the Dwarves behind and go forward on his own, down the long corridor to the dragon's lair. It takes even more courage for him to poke his tiny head inside and survey the massive dragon. The second time Bilbo approaches Smaug, now wearing the ring of invisibility, the witty banter reminds us of the dangerous but humorous exchange Bilbo had with Gollum. Bilbo engages the dragon in a game of wits, describing himself in riddle-like conundrums. He lavishes such an excess of mock humble praise and awe upon the dragon that Smaug vainly shows his diamond-studded waistcoat, inadvertently revealing the vulnerable spot on his left breast.

CHAPTER 13
Not at Home

The company waits. Thorin tries the door but cannot budge it. They realize they must go through the dragon's lair if they want to escape. Bilbo advances down the tunnel once more, urging the others to follow him. He stumbles and rolls headlong into the great hall, which stands empty. Nothing moves. Bilbo calls for a light, and Glóin and Oin fetch him a small pine torch.

Bilbo begins climbing the great mound of treasure. At the top, he looks down and sees the gleam of a beautiful gem, the Arkenstone, flickering many-colored reflections. With a deep breath, he pockets it. Now, he realizes, he is a true burglar. He makes his way down the other side of the treasure pile and comes to the enormous doors at the far side of the room. He peeps through and sees more passages, but no sign of Smaug. Bilbo cries out for the Dwarves, who light torches and follow him. At the sight of the enormous mound of treasure, they pause in awe and then grow bold and fierce.

Thorin remembers this place well. He leads the Dwarves up long stairs to the ruins of the great chamber of Thror, the feasting and council hall. They pick through skulls and bones, scattered flagons and bowls. They come to the Front Gate of the mountain and look down toward the ruins of Dale. Balin urges them to begin a five-hour march to the southwest corner of the mountain, warning them that the going will be rough. They set forth, fording a stream without difficulty. They arrive with no sign of Smaug. Looking around, they see nothing threatening and bed down for the night.

Chapter 13

"In His Pocketses": Bilbo is not greedy, but curious. In Chapter 5, he put Gollum's ring in his pocket absentmindedly, not greedily. He did not snatch it because he realized it could grant him invisibility. In the same way, when Bilbo sees the fabled Arkenstone, he takes it as a souvenir of his success as a burglar. The marvelous gem, a glowing shower of snow-white lights, does not stir money-lust in Bilbo's heart. He never imagines the gem will serve important functions, as Gollum's ring will.

Hapless Dwarves: As the Dwarves get closer to their long-lost treasure, they become more stubborn and make poorer decisions. They come to rely almost entirely on Bilbo for common sense and relief from their own blunders. The Dwarves' increasing haplessness gives Bilbo no choice but to develop his new-found qualities of initiative, courage, and heroism. It falls to Bilbo, for example, to plan the next step of the quest, and all he can do is get the greedy Dwarves away from the gold in Smaug's chambers so they can look for a safer place to rest. It is partially Bilbo's frustration with the Dwarves' stubborn recklessness that prompts him to take and conceal the Arkenstone, the gem that Thorin covets.

Money-Loving Dwarves: The narrator explains the Dwarves' eagerness to plunder by saying that all Dwarves love money. One cannot expect much more from them, whether they are good or bad. As the tale progresses and the Dwarves' greed leads them to increasingly arrogant and foolish behavior, we feel less sympathy for Dwarves and more sympathy for Bilbo. The treasure fills Thorin, in particular, with pride and stubbornness, but he does not match his lofty rhetoric with any practical plan for confronting the dragon. Like the other Dwarves, he leaves this problem entirely to Bilbo.

CHAPTER 14

Fire and Water

The narrator adopts the past tense and focuses on Smaug, explaining what happened shortly after Bilbo provoked the dragon. Several people from Esgaroth saw a faint glow in the sky. **Bard**, a grim-voiced man, growled that they were probably seeing fire from an angry dragon. When the glow grew into a bright light that flooded the northern end of the lake, Bard shouted for the townspeople to prepare themselves. They filled every vessel in the town with water, ready to douse fires. The dragon swept down on the town, ignoring the arrows that snapped against his scales.

Smaug, furious at the defiance of the people, breathed fire at thatched roofs and smashed the walls of the Great House with his tail. Citizens cowered. Smaug stopped in mid-air to consider how he would most enjoy slowly destroying the people. Then, an old thrush fluttered onto Bard's shoulder and told him to look for a hollow on Smaug's left breast. When he saw the vulnerable spot, the thrush said, Bard should aim his black arrow at it.

Bard shot an arrow straight into the hollow in Smaug's left breast, killing him. The citizens praised Bard and his mighty shot, hailing him as King Bard. The town's Master, who had behaved in a cowardly manner by running away when Smaug attacked, crept up beside Bard to claim some of the fame. Work began on building a new town farther north.

UNDERSTANDING AND INTERPRETING
Chapter 14

A Good Human: Bard, the only human hero in *The Hobbit*, is grim, serious, courageous, and honorable. His actions emphasize the importance of family lineage. Bard understands the words of the thrush because of his descent from the people of Dale. Brave Bard is the last man standing when Smaug invades the town, and his skill and courage help him kill Smaug. Bard is also kind and reasonable, presenting the demands of the Men and the Elves as politely as possible to Thorin and asking only for what is needed to rebuild Lake Town and help alleviate his people's suffering.

Dragon-Slaying: The account of the dragon's death at Bard's hand might come as a surprise, since it may have seemed that Bilbo could battle and slay the dragon himself. However, Tolkien keeps Bilbo's character consistent by letting it fall to another man to kill Smaug. Bilbo's strength is not physical, but mental. By cunningly bantering with Smaug, he tricked the dragon into revealing a weak spot. He played his role in the vanquishing of Smaug by doing this much. His wit ferreted out Smaug's vulnerability, but his wit was not enough to slay the dragon. Furthermore, Bard has a personal vendetta against Smaug, and Bilbo does not. Bard once lived in the village of Dale, which Smaug burned to cinders. Bard had witnessed the near annihilation of the townspeople of Dale, and by killing Smaug he avenges them.

CHAPTER 15

The Gathering of Clouds

Back in the Dwarves' camp, Thorin looks at the sky and sees flocks of starlings, finches, and even carrion. **Roäc**, an old, enormous raven, slowly flaps down and begins talking to Thorin. He explains that the birds are gathering because Smaug is dead. The news stuns Thorin, who realizes that the treasure now belongs to them. The old raven interrupts Thorin, saying that already many others are gathering to take a share of the treasure. The Men of the Lake say that part of the treasure should belong to them because Smaug destroyed their town, and armies of Elves are mobilizing to make a claim. The raven counsels Thorin to talk with Bard, who is grim but honest. Thorin tells the raven to fly to Thorin's cousin **Dain** in the Iron Hills and urge him to come help defend the Dwarves' treasure.

Four days pass. The ravens report that the Lake Men have joined forces with the Wood Elves and are hurrying toward the mountain. Soon they arrive, armed for war, and set up camp close to the mountain. The next morning, a company of spearmen advance, bearing the green banner of the Elvenking and the blue banner of the Men of the Lake. Their spokesman, Bard, tells Thorin they are not his enemies, and they rejoice that he and the Dwarves are alive. They have come to talk. Bard explains that the people of Dale have a legitimate claim to some of the treasure. Recently, Smaug destroyed the homes of the Men of Esgaroth, and they need recompense.

For long hours during the past few days, Thorin has brooded on the vast store of gold and hunted for the fabled Arkenstone, and now he tells Bard that no one has a claim to the treasure except the Dwarves. They will pay the Men of the Lake for the goods and assistance they gave the Dwarves but will give them nothing else. If Bard wishes to speak further with him, he should send the Elves back to the woods and order the Men of the Lake to disarm.

UNDERSTANDING AND INTERPRETING
Chapter 15

Gold Lust: After they find the treasure, the Dwarves' greed escalates so quickly that Thorin seems more like a villain than a hero. Bilbo, an ally of the Dwarves, is stuck on the wrong side of the conflict. When the Elf and human representatives propose sharing the treasure, they speak kindly and reasonably, and Thorin reacts with irrational greed. The narrator observes that Thorin's lust for gold has been building since he entered the dragon's lair. This lust has made Thorin and most of the other Dwarves unreasonable.

The Destructive Power of Greed: More than a criticism of the Dwarf race, Tolkien's depiction of the Dwarves' money lust also serves as a warning against the destructive power of greed, which has turned those who were once friends—the Dwarves under the Mountain and the Men of Dale—into enemies. Humans, Dwarves, and Elves, all good people, ought to fight on the same side against their common enemies, evil creatures such as the goblins. When Smaug was alive, he guarded his treasure, and good people were united. They did not have riches, but they lived in peace. With the treasure suddenly up for grabs, however, greed creates conflict.

Modern and Ancient: Both ancient and modern traits exist in Bilbo. He helps Bard slay the dragon by finding Smaug's weak spot, and dragon-slaying is among the primary themes of ancient epic literature. At the same time, he wants to give away his portion of the treasure and forge peace, an impulse that would be out of place in Anglo-Saxon literature. In ancient Anglo-Saxon and Scandinavian epics, characters treat gold and treasure with the same seriousness and reverence with which the Dwarves treat it. The situation is not precisely parallel, for in epic literature gold is valued as much for its ability to create social stability as for its purchasing power, but the strife that treasure creates is exactly the same in *The Hobbit* as it is in epics like *Beowulf.* Tolkien explores epic heroism in Bard's slaying of Smaug, but he is also interested in exploring a more modern notion of heroism that combines courage with sympathy and modesty.

CHAPTER 16
A Thief in the Night

The days go by slowly. Many of the Dwarves spend their time sorting through the treasure. Thorin speaks of the priceless Arkenstone, which he longs to find. Bilbo, who has kept the Arkenstone wrapped in a bundle of tattered rags that he uses as a pillow, has an idea. One night, he pockets the Arkenstone, climbs to the top of a wall, and shimmies down on a rope. Bilbo awakens the nearby Elves and asks to speak to Bard.

Two hours later, Bilbo sits beside a fire, warming up and talking to the Elvenking and Bard. Bilbo explains that he is tired of this adventure and wants to go back to his hobbit-hole in Hobbiton, where people are more reasonable. He draws forth the Arkenstone, which dazzles the Elvenking. Bilbo explains that Thorin values the Arkenstone above all else in the world, so it will prove useful in bargaining with him. Bilbo gives the stone to Bard as a bargaining chip.

Bard and the Elvenking beg Bilbo to stay with them, fearing for his safety if the Dwarves discover what he has done, but Bilbo refuses to abandon his friends. As he turns to leave, an old man wrapped in a dark cloak rises and comes toward them. It is Gandalf, who congratulates Bilbo for proving that he is truly an extraordinary little hobbit. He urges Bilbo to keep his courage up, for good news will come.

UNDERSTANDING AND INTERPRETING
Chapter 16

Heroic Defection: In this section, the idea Tolkien began developing in Chapter 15—that the Dwarves are in the wrong and that the truly heroic path is the one that ends in peace—comes to a climax when Bilbo chooses to help the Elves and humans. Bilbo defects to the enemy camp for at least three reasons. First, he longs for a peaceful resolution to the conflict. Second, despite his friendship with the Dwarves, Bilbo feels a more natural camaraderie with Elves and, to a lesser extent, with Men than with Dwarves. Third, he longs to bring his adventure to a close and return home, so he must find a way to end the standoff. Though personal desire partially motivates Bilbo, his defection is nevertheless one of the most courageous, righteous acts of his short career as a burglar-hero. He risks his life to bring about peace, for when he confesses his theft, Thorin's angry hands could easily kill him.

Abandoning Virtues: Bilbo's defection brings out the strain of modern heroism in the novel, and the strain of heroism based on epic literature recedes. Loyalty to one's lord and solidarity to one's group count among the highest virtues in epic literature, but Bilbo abandons these virtues to make an independent moral choice to bring about the quickest, most just, and most peaceful outcome rather than the outcome willed by his leader, Thorin. Tolkien criticizes unquestioning loyalty by emphasizing Thorin's pigheadedness and greedy behavior, and praising Bilbo's independent thinking.

CHAPTER 17
The Clouds Burst

The next morning, Bard, the Elvenking, and an old man holding a box of iron-bound wood come to the mountain. The old man opens the box and asks Thorin if he will bargain for the Arkenstone of Thrain. Thorin says he will not bargain for it. It belonged to his father, he says, so it already belongs to him. Bard tells Thorin that they are not thieves, and they will give back the stone in exchange for their fair share of the treasure.

Bilbo admits he gave the Arkenstone to the visitors. Thorin, furious, shakes Bilbo savagely and rages that Gandalf should be here to see what devilment the hobbit has caused. The old man throws back his hood and reveals himself as Gandalf. He orders Thorin to put Bilbo down and listen. Bilbo explains that he wants his share of the riches to go to the visitors. Thorin fumes but agrees to exchange a fourteenth of the treasure for the Arkenstone. Gandalf chides Thorin, telling him that so far he is not nearly the splendid king that his father was.

Three days later, Dain and his formidable band of Men arrive. Bard sends messengers to the mountain, but no gold or payment awaits them. Thorin means to do battle with Dain's help. Gandalf appears and warns them that goblins are on their way, riding on wolves, bringing an army of bats, and followed by battalions of Wargs. In the face of this threat, the Dwarves ally themselves with the Elves and humans.

The Battle of Five Armies ensues. As the bat-cloud and wolf-riding army approaches, the Elves charge first, unleashing their long hatred of goblins. They pierce the goblins with arrows of stinging fire. Dain's troops charge in along with the Lake Men. Many goblins fall under Thorin's mighty axe. The goblins gain ground, however, and Bilbo must retreat to the Elves' camp, which is nearly surrounded. Bilbo looks up toward the sky and spots the eagles, line after line of them. A stone falls from above, hitting Bilbo heavily on his helmet. He falls to the ground, unconscious.

UNDERSTANDING AND INTERPRETING
Chapter 17

Good and Evil: The arrival of the goblins and the Wargs sharpens the moral hierarchy of race that Tolkien develops in *The Hobbit*. The appearance of these truly evil races forces the essentially good creatures to band together, and the armies line up according to fundamental divisions between good and evil, not according to claims for money. Money is still at stake in the Battle of the Five Armies, but the more urgent conflict is the one between good and evil. The Dwarves, Elves, and Men are all "Good People," and we see here that the classification of Good People runs deeper than the family pride of Thorin or even the long-standing feud between Dwarves and Elves. The alliance of Dwarves, Men, and Elves recalls happier days when the three races lived peacefully as neighbors and worked together to create great cities.

Pure Eagles: The evil creatures' increasing power and their near victory in the battle signal the fading glory of Middle-earth. Fortunately for the armies of good, one great race, the eagles, has been preserved almost untouched from the beginning of time. Nature, as represented by the eagles, takes the side of good when good and evil clash. The pure eagles would not have intervened in a war over gold, but the involvement of the goblins cries out to their instinct to fight evil and brings them down from the mountaintops. Tolkien reiterates an essential rule of his fantasy world: evil, characterized by the perversion of nature, may become powerful, but the essential nature of the world is good.

CHAPTER 18
The Return Journey

When Bilbo regains consciousness, he is cold and shaking, and his head burns. He hails an approaching man, shouting that he is Bilbo Baggins. The man, who has been searching for Bilbo, carries the hobbit down to Dale. Even Gandalf sustained an injury in battle, and his arm is in a sling, but he is overjoyed to see Bilbo. Gandalf hurries Bilbo inside the tent, where Thorin lies wounded, his mighty notched axe on the floor beside him.

Dying, Thorin says he is pleased that he is leaving as Bilbo's friend. Bilbo kneels and says he has been honored to share in Thorin's adventure. Thorin says the world would be a better place if there were more hobbits in it. Too many people value gold above all else. Thorin bids Bilbo a final farewell. Bilbo wraps himself in his blanket and weeps. While Bilbo grieves, aching in his bones to go home, the narrator explains the story of the eagles. When they realized the goblins had attacked, they flew to the aid of the Dwarves and dislodged the goblins from the mountain slopes, casting them over precipices and driving them downward. But the goblins outnumbered the eagles and might have been victorious had not Beorn appeared in the guise of an immense bear. Beorn crushed the leader of the goblin troops, causing the goblins to flee in all directions.

That evening, Gandalf tells Bilbo that the eagles have returned to their eyries. Bilbo hesitantly asks Gandalf if he will be going home soon. Gandalf chuckles and says they can leave as soon as Bilbo pleases.

Thorin is buried deep beneath Lonely Mountain, the Arkenstone lying on his chest. On his tomb, the Elvenking lays Orcrist, the mighty sword of ancient days. Dain tells Bilbo that since so many Dwarves have claimed portions of the treasure, there is little left to share. Bilbo expresses relief, for he wonders how he would have traveled home carrying a large amount of wealth. He will take only two small chests, one filled with silver and another with gold, just enough for one pony to carry comfortably.

Balin and Bilbo bid each other fond goodbyes. Bilbo tells Balin that if he ever visits Hobbiton, he should come in to Bilbo's hole without bothering to knock. Tea is always at four. Gandalf and Beorn accompany Bilbo on his journey home. The Tookish part of Bilbo's blood is tiring, and the comfort-seeking Baggins blood becomes stronger every day. He yearns to sink into a large armchair.

UNDERSTANDING AND INTERPRETING
Chapter 18

Vanity and Values: Before Thorin dies, he realizes how extraordinary Bilbo is. Thorin has been proud and arrogant, but now, nearing death, he changes. He sets aside his vanity and praises Bilbo for saving the Dwarves from death and imprisonment and for clinging to his values. Sincerely and specifically, he explains why Bilbo is superior to him, saying, "If more of us valued food and cheer and song above hoarded gold, it would be a merrier world." Bilbo possessed these values as a simple hobbit living in Hobbiton before he set out on his adventures with the Dwarves. He has never lost them. Bilbo's adventures have not made him proud, cynical, or materialistic. He is still humble and simple— qualities, Tolkien suggests, that seemed undesirable in a hero at first but turned out to be compatible with cleverness, sacrifice, and courage.

The Unchanging Essence of Bilbo: If *The Hobbit* has an overarching message, it is that even a small, unassuming person such as Bilbo possesses the inner resources necessary to perform heroic deeds and that a person who transforms into a hero does not have to erase his essential nature to do so. Bilbo constantly struggles to subdue his love of comfort and to nurture his love of adventure, but despite this struggle, he never really changes at his core. As he rests in Beorn's house, we see the old, comfort-loving side of Bilbo, the side that existed all the time next to Bilbo's heroic side and now longs for ease and armchairs.

CHAPTER 19
The Last Stage

On the first day of May, Bilbo and Gandalf reach Rivendell, greeted by Elves singing in trees. Gandalf now explains that when he left Bilbo and the Dwarves, he attended a council of wizards that finally drove the evil Necromancer from the south of Mirkwood Forest. Soon, Gandalf says, the forest will grow more wholesome. After a week, Bilbo and Gandalf set out again. They dig up the Trolls' gold, which they had buried a year before, loading up the pony so heavily that Bilbo decides to walk. At last, far in the distance, Bilbo can see his own hill, and he begins singing a song of homecoming. Gandalf turns to Bilbo and reminds him that he is not the hobbit he used to be.

Nearing home, Bilbo cries out in surprise. His front door is open, and hobbits are going in and out without wiping their feet. A sign advertises an auction of the effects of "the late Bilbo Baggins, Esquire of Bag-End." Already, many of his things have been sold, and Bilbo's cousins, members of the **Sackville-Baggins family**, are measuring his rooms to see if their furniture will fit in his hobbit-hole.

The return of Bilbo Baggins creates quite a stir. He has acquired a reputation as an eccentric, which does not really bother Bilbo. He throws out his cousins and reclaims his home. Bilbo is content to listen for the song of the kettle on his hearth as he anticipates daily tea. He spends much of his gold and silver on presents for his many nephews and nieces, giving them some useful items and some extravagant ones. He writes poems and visits the Elves, despite his neighbors' disapproval.

One autumn evening some years later, Gandalf and Balin come to the door. They talk of their grand adventure in the lands of Lonely Mountain. Balin says Bard and the Dwarves have rebuilt the town of Dale, and flowers and birds now fill the valley. Bilbo marvels that long ago the Dwarves' songs prophesied that they would regain their lands and treasure. Gandalf tells him that prophecies do come true and that Bilbo played an important part in the fulfillment of this prophecy. Bilbo's heroics were real, but, Gandalf reminds him, he is only a little hobbit in a big wide world. Bilbo sighs, "Thank goodness!" and passes the tobacco jar to Gandalf.

UNDERSTANDING AND INTERPRETING
Chapter 19

A Safer World: The wide-ranging benefits of the company's quest mitigate the greed that motivated it. The Lake Men rebuild Esgaroth. Humans once again live in Dale. Dain rules as King under the Mountain. The conquering of the goblins has made much of the wilderness of the east safer for travelers. Moreover, Gandalf joined a great council of wizards in driving the Necromancer out of southern Mirkwood. Perhaps to emphasize the great success of Bilbo's adventure, Tolkien humorously likens him to Odysseus, who, upon returning from his voyages, had to rout a passel of freeloading suitors from his house. Similarly, Bilbo must banish his greedy relatives from his hobbit-hole.

"Quite a Little Fellow": Tolkien suggests that perhaps other, grander adventures are taking place as we read about Bilbo's doings—for example, the dark lord's banishment from Mirkwood has enormous ramifications in *The Lord of the Rings*, and the account of the wizards' conference hints at the importance of this event. Still, Bilbo plays a crucial role in the fate of Middle-earth. Without Bilbo's intervention, Smaug would never have been killed, the treasure would never have been recovered, and the goblins would still roam the Misty Mountains. Without question, Bilbo is a hero, although the title hardly suits his tastes. In the novel's last passage, Gandalf jokingly chides Bilbo about his insignificance, telling him he is "only quite a little fellow in a wide world after all!" In part, this is a humorous admission that the meek Bilbo makes an unlikely hero, and in part, it is Gandalf making fun of himself. Even he could hardly have foreseen how brilliantly Bilbo would fulfill his role.

Conclusions

Tolkien originally told his stories of Bilbo Baggins to his children, hoping to ignite their sense of fantasy by creating a new mythical landscape and populating it with magical creatures. In novel form, *The Hobbit* shows the mark of its origins. Hobbits are three feet tall, about the size of a young child. Intricate details of weather, trees, food, and songs appeal to inventive young minds. Tolkien wrote to amuse and captivate, but *The Hobbit* also supports multiple and complex interpretations. Tolkien, writing as the political situation darkened in Europe, seeks to show that individual citizens, no matter how small, can make a difference in the course of history.

Tolkien has said, "Hobbits have what you might call universal morals. They are certainly capable of extraordinary bravery and humaneness." He once told his good friend C.S. Lewis that "the real life of men is of a mystical and heroic quality." Thus, we do right to think about human events as we read *The Hobbit* and to wonder what Tolkien meant his characters to demonstrate about our own lives. C.S. Lewis explains that in fact we must read fantasy and understand its applications to reality if we want to understand the human condition: "Man as a whole, Man pitted against the Universe, have we seen him at all till we see that he is like a hero in a fairy tale?"

III

THE FELLOWSHIP OF THE RING

The Fellowship of the Ring

An Overview

Key Facts

Genre: English fantasy; quest novel; first volume of epic trilogy

Date of First Publication: 1954

Setting: The closing years of the Third Age of Middle-earth

Narrator: Anonymous, omniscient (all-knowing) third-person

Plot Overview: Frodo Baggins, a simple but virtuous hobbit, inherits a magical ring with a mysterious past. With the guidance of the wizard Gandalf and the help of various friends, Frodo sets out on a journey to return the Ring to its place of origin. His goal is to destroy the Ring by casting it into the Mountain of Fire in the evil land of Mordor.

Style, Technique, and Language

Style—Kennings and Litotes: Tolkien, a scholar of language and literature, employs literary devices found in *Beowulf* and other Anglo-Saxon works. He uses **kennings**, compound expressions that name a person or thing by stating its characteristics. For instance, in Anglo-Saxon, the word *hranrade* combined the words "whale" and "road" to mean "ocean" (since oceans are aptly described as whales' roads). Kennings occurred often in Anglo-Saxon because the language was new, and words were constantly being invented. Tolkien calls a dragon a "wicked-worm" and refers to war spoils that pay for a relative's death as "weregild" (man-payment or man-gold). Sometimes Tolkien uses **litotes**, phrases that use negatives to mean the opposite, such as "Not a few times did he yearn for home," which suggests that the character often yearned for home. Litotes occur frequently in Anglo-Saxon literature. Occasionally, Tolkien has fun with **alliteration**, the repetition of initial consonants ("swords sang sweetly"), and he frequently uses **aphorisms**, short, concise statements that express some basic truth. Pippin voices an aphorism when he observes, "Short cuts make long delays." In Anglo-Saxon literature, such neatly phrased points were considered new and wise. *The Fellowship of the Ring* also makes use of **songs**, which characters usually perform at night around the fireside, giving us a flavor of the history of the people and reminding us of Anglo-Saxon poets, who used songs for educational as well as entertainment purposes.

> "**C**hildren, before we go on with this tale, let me remind you that all of this took place in prehistoric times, before the Internet, before mega-malls, before the inexorable spread of the mammoth 'chain' bookstores across the land. . . . Dark times indeed."
>
> **ESTHER M. FRIESNER**, "IF YOU GIVE A GIRL A HOBBIT," *MEDITATIONS ON MIDDLE-EARTH,*

Technique—The Meaning of Places: Throughout this volume of the trilogy, locations carry symbolic meaning. The **Shire** represents the hobbit culture, and so it is a place of relative peace and contentment. Elrond built **Rivendell** as a sanctuary for Elves, but it has come to represent much more than that. It is a cultural and educational center in Middle-earth, a place where leaders meet to exchange ideas and seek wisdom. **Lothlórien** represents a more private, mysterious facet of Elvish culture. As the epic progresses, these and other locations serve to remind us of the cultural or political interests of their inhabitants.

Language—Rich Details: Tolkien's narrative description is famously rich in detail. Instead of telling us that a scene is mysterious or frightening, he shows us it is by writing about dark figures entering "like shades of night creeping across a ground" or "standing like shadows of stone beneath a nearly moonless, starless sky." He shows us beauty by writing of a green hillside "studded with small golden flowers shaped like stars" and blossoms that glimmer year-round. Tolkien employs some images that are standard in the epic tradition: fair maidens have hair as golden as sunshine or as dark as ravens, for example. Most of his description, however, is fresh and powerful. Characters reveal their personalities through lively dialogue. Commoners in the Shire speak with cockney accents suggestive of London's East End in Tolkien's time, while Elves speak in a more refined manner, as do the nobility. Farmer Maggot uses a rustic dialect that Tolkien might have heard in rural Yorkshire in the mid–1900s, saying things like, "I'd best be turning for home. Mrs. Maggot will be worriting with the night getting thick."

Characters in
The Fellowship of the Ring

THE FELLOWSHIP

Aragorn (also known as Strider): Known as Strider throughout most of *The Fellowship of the Ring*, Aragorn is the rightful human heir to the throne of Gondor. He carries a broken sword, **Narsil**, which prophecies say will help him regain his throne. After Elven-smiths re-forge the sword in Rivendell, he calls it **Andúril.**

Boromir: The son of the Steward of the land of Gondor. Although a brave and decent human, Boromir cannot see the evils of the Ring. Despite several warnings, he believes he can use the Ring to save Gondor.

Frodo Baggins: The central character of *The Fellowship of the Ring*. Frodo, not a typical epic hero, must undertake an extraordinary quest to save Middle-earth. During his quest, he goes by the name Mr. Underhill.

Gandalf the Grey (known to Elves as Mithrandir): One of five wizards who came to Middle-earth to assist in the fight against evil. Gandalf can encourage and aid Frodo, but only in limited ways. The residents of Middle-earth must also fight for themselves. Gandalf carries the sword **Glamdring**, and his horse is **Shadowfax.**

Gimli: A Dwarf who joins Frodo on his quest. Gimli is an expert with the broad-bladed axe.

Legolas: A courageous Elf who accompanies Frodo on his quest. Legolas is a superb archer. Although Elves usually do not get along with Dwarves, Legolas and Gimli become close friends.

Peregrin (Pippin) Took: Another of Frodo's closest friends in the Shire, Pippin voluntarily joins the quest.

Meriadoc (Merry) Brandybuck: One of Frodo's closest friends in the Shire. Merry insists on accompanying Frodo on his journey.

Samwise (Sam) Gamgee: Frodo's gardener. Sam, a fiercely loyal servant, proves one of Frodo's best friends. His packhorse is **Bill**.

ELVES

Arwen Evenstar: The daughter of Elrond and Celebrían. She is in love with Aragorn (Strider). As an Elf, she can live forever, but if she marries Aragorn, a human, she will become mortal.

Celeborn: The Lord of Lothlórien and the husband of Galadriel. Although less powerful than his wife, he is a highly respected Elf.

Elrond Halfelven: The half-human, half-Elven Master of Rivendell. Elrond built Rivendell as a sanctuary for Elves, and it has become a center of wisdom and learning. He encourages Frodo to destroy the Ring.

Galadriel: A powerful opponent of evil, Galadriel possesses one of the Three Rings of the Elves. She helps rule the forest refuge of Lothlórien and assists Frodo. Galadriel is Arwen's maternal grandmother.

Gildor Inglorion: A leading Elf and friend of Gandalf. Gildor invites Frodo and his friends to spend the night with him when they first need to hide from the Black Riders.

Glorfindel: One of Elrond's chief Elves. He finds Frodo's group and helps them cross the Loudwater River, then loans Frodo his speedy steed.

HOBBITS

Bilbo Baggins: The central character of *The Hobbit*. After celebrating his 111th birthday, Bilbo leaves the Shire immediately, giving most of his belongings, including a magic ring, to his adopted son, Frodo.

Déagol: A brother of Gollum. Déagol found the One Ring several hundred years ago, but kept it only a short time. Gollum murdered him in an attempt to steal the Ring.

Farmer Maggot: A connoisseur of mushrooms. Maggot helps Frodo avoid the Black Riders early in the novel.

OTHER ALLIES AND BENEVOLENT BEINGS

Balin: One of Bilbo's Dwarf comrades in *The Hobbit*. Balin dies attempting to reoccupy the caverns of Moria, and the fellowship discovers his tomb.

Barliman Butterbur: The human innkeeper of the Prancing Pony in Bree. Butterbur is Gandalf's friend and welcomes Frodo. He has a letter Gandalf wrote to Frodo but for three months neglects to deliver it.

Glóin: Gimli's father. Glóin, one of the Dwarves who accompanied Bilbo in *The Hobbit*, plays a minor role in *The Lord of the Rings*, warning against the dangers of Sauron.

Goldberry: Tom Bombadil's wife. Goldberry is a beautiful water nymph, the "river's daughter," who has magical powers and excellent abilities as a hostess.

Gwaihir, the Windlord: The swiftest of the great eagles. Gwaihir rescues Gandalf from imprisonment by Saruman.

Isildur: An ancient human ruler of Gondor, he cut the Ring from Sauron's hand at the end of the Second Age. Isildur lost the Ring in a river, and Orcs killed him near the beginning of the Third Age.

Tom Bombadil: One of the most enigmatic characters in the epic. Tom has powers that rival Gandalf's. He appears to be a *Nature Valar*—a representative of the Creator, Eru, in human form—serving as guardian angel of trees, hills, and rivers.

ENEMIES AND MALAVOLENT BEINGS

The Balrog: The ancient monster with whom Gandalf engages in a battle to the death.

Black Riders (the Nazgûl, Ringwraiths): Representatives of Sauron and the forces of evil. They long to possess the magic Ring.

Gollum (Sméagol): The cave-dwelling being from whom Bilbo takes the Ring in *The Hobbit*. Gollum now begins a quest to regain the Ring.

Orcs: Large, powerful, semihuman creatures controlled by the forces of evil in Middle-earth. Cannibalistic and cruel, they abhor daylight, which limits their use in battle. When properly used, however, they make effective warriors. Orcs, prolific breeders, exist in great numbers.

Saruman the White: Chief of the Wizards, Saruman's ambition and vanity allow Sauron to corrupt him. Saruman has set up a fortress in the apparently impregnable tower of Orthanc in Isengard.

Sauron (the Evil One): The most powerful evil individual in Middle-earth. Sauron believes that he can achieve absolute control if he can regain possession of the One Ring. The Land of Mordor is his seat of power.

Uruk-Hai: A new strain of dark warriors that the evil master Sauron bred by blending Orcs with humans. Uruk-hai are taller, stronger, and more intelligent than ordinary Orcs, and they function better in daylight.

Reading *The Fellowship of the Ring*

Prologue

The Prologue explains the history and customs of hobbits, an ancient, unobtrusive people who love peace, quiet, and order. Despite their skill with tools, they dislike machinery more complex than a water mill or handloom. Hobbits are short in stature, standing between two and four feet, and tend to be a little fat. Although competent workers and very tidy, they prefer not to exert themselves or rush if they can avoid it. They enjoy a merry social life. Parties, ale, and food are important to hobbits, and they enjoy smoking a special homegrown "leaf" they call "pipe-weed" (see page 126). Hobbits dress in bright colors, especially yellow and green, but rarely wear shoes. Their large, tough feet have a thick covering of curly hair. Most hobbits have faces less beautiful than jolly, with rosy cheeks and quick smiles. Generally, hobbits care little for academics. The Shire hobbits dislike heights and water sports, and most of them cannot swim. They do enjoy

THE HISTORY
OF MIDDLE-EARTH

In his appendices, posthumous papers, and
other works, Tolkien created a long and
detailed history for Middle-earth, which is
the world as mortals know it and the land in
which *The Fellowship of the Ring* takes
place. According to this history, in the First
Age, Eru (the One) created Middle-earth
with the help of the Valar, lieutenants similar to angels. Some of the Valar became
jealous and resentful, rebelling against Eru
and seeking power for themselves. Morgoth
led the rebels. In the Second Age, Sauron,
a servant of Morgoth, replaced Morgoth as
leader. Sauron forged the One Ring and
based his operations in Mordor. Forces for
good, an alliance of Elves and humans,
killed Sauron and took the Ring, but Sauron's evil spirit lived on in hiding. In the
Third Age, Sauron's spirit has come out of
hiding and now seeks to recover the Ring
and rule Middle-earth.

studying genealogical lore, and they like old stories, but hobbits prefer books that contain information they already know. Most hobbits converse in Common Speech, a common language throughout most of the lands of Middle-earth.

The narrator also briefly relates how Bilbo Baggins, the first hobbit to make a name for himself, found and won the Ring from Gollum, a story we read about in detail in *The Hobbit*. He says we know about the hobbits' history because their story has been passed down to us in the form of a travel narrative called the *Red Book of Westmarch*, written by Bilbo Baggins.

UNDERSTANDING AND INTERPRETING
Prologue

Red Book of Westmarch: We may be surprised to learn that *The Hobbit*, Tolkien's earlier novel, is actually one of the narrator's archival sources, supposedly part of a larger book called the *Red Book of Westmarch*. Tolkien asks us to believe that *The Hobbit* was discovered, not created. In presenting the hobbits' tale in this way, Tolkien follows in the tradition of many great works of West ern literature. In Miguel Cervantes's *Don Quixote*, for example, Cervantes pretends to have discovered the manuscript of the novel and published it. There is a long line of works that claim not to be authored by their authors. One result of this device is that the characters' world and the readers' world are brought closer together. If Bilbo's narrative found its way into our everyday lives, then perhaps we could find our way into Bilbo's world.

Historical Chronicle: Just as *The Hobbit* turns out to be penned by Bilbo, Tolkien now tells us that *The Lord of the Rings* is not a fictional novel, but a chronicle of history written from the perspectives of both Elves and Men, folklore and oral tradition, and the narrator's meticulous knowledge of the language and customs of the peoples he describes. By presenting his work as nonfiction, Tolkien allows us to believe more firmly in the fantastical worlds he creates.

BOOK I, CHAPTER 1
A Long-Expected Party

Everyone in the Shire enthusiastically anticipates September 22 in the year 3001 of the Third Age, for on that date **Bilbo Baggins** will celebrate his eleventy-first (111th) birthday with a party of special magnificence. Bilbo is a hobbit, as are most of the residents of the Shire. He is notoriously wealthy, and his neighbors have considered him a marvel since his unexpected disappearance and return sixty years earlier. Legends abound to explain Bilbo's wealth. His residence, Bag-End, supposedly includes a complex of tunnels loaded with gold, silver, and jewels. Best of all, Bilbo, like most hobbits, is a very generous fellow.

Frodo Baggins will turn thirty-three, the age of official adulthood, on September 22. Bilbo adopted Frodo, his favorite cousin, twelve years before and made him his heir. At the party, Bilbo plans to announce that he is permanently leaving the Shire and giving most of his property to Frodo. Bilbo's old wizard friend, **Gandalf**, creates grand fireworks for the party, including rockets that turn into a flight of birds and a lifelike red-golden dragon spouting fire from his eyes. At his birthday dinner, Bilbo announces his impending departure and mysteriously disappears in a blinding flash of light by putting on a magic Ring.

Shortly after dinner, Gandalf goes to Bag-End and insists that Bilbo leave the Ring with Frodo along with his other property. Bilbo initially refuses, but then he offers the Ring to Gandalf. Gandalf rejects it, saying the Ring might have evil powers. Gandalf sets off on a journey, intending to learn more about the magic Ring.

UNDERSTANDING AND INTERPRETING
Book I, Chapter 1

Life in the Shire: The novel opens in the hobbits' Shire, an area of about forty by fifty leagues (120 miles by 150 miles) in "the North-West of the Old World, east of the Sea." Early on, the hobbits divided their Shire into four districts, but they have almost no government. Extended families live close to each other and manage their own affairs. Every seven years at the Midsummer Free Fair, the hobbits elect a Mayor of the Shire, but he has few duties beyond presiding at banquets. The Mayor does appoint both the Postmaster and the "Shirriff," so he has some control over messenger services and what passes for law enforcement. The Shire's economy depends on agriculture, particularly corn. Most families grow large gardens for personal use. The earliest known hobbits lived in burrows, caves, or tunnels (called *smials*). At the time of the novel, only the very poor and the very rich continue to live in *smials*. Rich hobbits often build elaborate underground complexes. Most hobbits now own long, modestly comfortable homes that sit at ground level. Doors and windows are usually round. The Shire is rustic and peaceful; the last battle in the Shire took place several hundred years ago. With its cozy homes, small gardens and inns, and good-natured farmers, the Shire is an idealized version of the English countryside in which Tolkien grew up.

Strange Bilbo: The townspeople treat Bilbo with suspicion. Their provincialism partly accounts for this attitude, but their suspicion is somewhat valid. For instance, we find that despite his advanced age, Bilbo seems not to have aged at all. Tolkien wants us to question Bilbo as the townspeople do. He hints that the Ring might be largely to blame for Bilbo's change in character. Whenever the subject of the Ring comes up, Bilbo's behavior becomes strange, unpredictable, and defensive. Bilbo has kept the Ring secret all these years, and he sneakily attempts to keep it even after promising to hand it over to Gandalf. Bilbo makes the mysterious and surprising admission that, in a way, it will be a relief finally to be rid of the Ring. Bilbo's strange behavior and remarks raise a sense of foreboding about the Ring, making us curious about its powers.

BOOK I, CHAPTER 2
The Shadow of the Past

Over the next seventeen years, Frodo sees little of Gandalf. Frodo's best friends, **Pippin** and **Merry**, sometimes travel the Shire with him and annually celebrate his birthday, remembering the absent Bilbo each time. The friends live peacefully but hear rumors of trouble rising in the Land of Mordor, far to the southeast, where **Sauron**, the Evil One, rules and longs for total control over Middle-earth.

The April before Frodo's fiftieth birthday, Gandalf makes a visit to divulge what he has learned about the magic Ring, which is sometimes called the One Ring. Gandalf warns Frodo that the Ring is of dark origins and will eventually possess any mortal who keeps it. Frodo has already noticed that the Ring changes size and weight on its own. For safekeeping, he usually carries it on a chain around his neck.

Gandalf astonishes Frodo by hurling the gold Ring into the middle of a nearby fire. The Ring appears unchanged, and even after a few minutes, one can remove it from the fireplace with a bare hand. Gandalf points out an almost invisible alteration on the Ring, which is now marked with ancient runes in the Mordor language. Gandalf translates the words, which say, "One Ring to rule them all, One Ring to find them, One Ring to bring them all and in the darkness bind them."

Gandalf explains that this Ring originally belonged to Sauron the Great, and now Sauron needs to possess the Ring to dominate Middle-earth. Sauron has learned that a hobbit has the Ring, and soon he will send forces to recover the prize. Gandalf explains that the Ring can only be used for evil; no one can use it

THE WIZARDS
OF MIDDLE-EARTH

Elsewhere, Tolkien writes that around the
year 1050 in the Third Age, at least five wizards first appeared in Middle-earth. Eru the
Creator apparently sent them, and they
may be angels. These wizards assume
human form and attempt to guide the
inhabitants of Middle-earth toward ethical
and moral behavior. While it is not their
role to overcome evil themselves, they do
oppose evil and help the inhabitants of
Middle-earth fight Sauron. Wizards have
magical powers, but because they live in
human form, they can become hungry,
tired, thirsty, and even angry. They have
freedom of choice, as do mortals, and are
capable of both good and evil. Gandalf is
one of these wizards.

for good. For the Ring to be destroyed, it must be returned to its origins in Mordor and cast into the volcanic Cracks of Doom on the Mountain of Fire. Gandalf believes that it is Frodo's destiny to go on a quest to the Mountain of Fire and destroy the Ring.

Frodo tries to give the Ring to Gandalf, suggesting that he take care of it, but Gandalf vehemently rejects the offer. He refuses to accept the temptation of the Ring, which could allow him to rule Middle-earth, but only in the service of evil. Gandalf urges Frodo to leave soon and travel under the name of Mr. Underhill. Without warning, Gandalf leaps to the windowsill and, reaching out, grabs Frodo's faithful gardener, **Sam Gamgee**, who has been eavesdropping. Sam wants to accompany his master on the quest, especially if it could involve meeting Elves. Gandalf allows Sam to go with Frodo.

UNDERSTANDING AND INTERPRETING
Book I, Chapter 2

A Powerful Ring: The history of the One Ring helps explain its unique power. Around the year 1500 of the Second Age, Sauron convinced certain skilled Elf-smiths to forge the Rings of Power, which he claimed would fairly divide power among different creatures. Elves received three rings, Dwarves seven, and humans nine. No one knew that in secret, Sauron made for himself the One Ring, a ring endowed with many of his own powers, with the ability to control all the rest of the Rings and, he hoped, the power to make him ruler of Middle-earth. When an alliance of Elves and humans defeated Sauron, one of the human leaders, **Isildur**, a ruler of Gondor, cut the Ring from Sauron's corpse and kept it as a battle prize. Near the beginning of the Third Age, Isildur lost the Ring—perhaps it slipped off his finger of its own volition—while swimming across a river to escape Orcs. **Déagol** found the Ring more than 2,500 years later. His brother **Sméagol** (usually called **Gollum** because of the guttural sound he makes) killed Déagol and stole the Ring, hiding underground with it for centuries. In *The Hobbit*, Bilbo encounters Gollum, takes the Ring, and uses it to escape. However, Bilbo does not understand the Ring's powers. Even Gandalf does not understand the intricacies of the Ring initially, but his suspicion leads him on an investigation of the Ring's history. After investigating, Gandalf concludes that Frodo must attempt to destroy the dangerous and powerful Ring.

BOOK I, CHAPTER 3
Three Is Company

Gandalf tells Frodo that he should travel to Rivendell, a center for Elves located nearly five hundred miles to the east of Bag-End. In Rivendell, he can plan the rest of his quest. To keep his purpose secret, Frodo sells his home at Bag-End and purchases a small house at Crickhollow on the eastern edge of the Shire. Shortly after Frodo's fiftieth birthday, he sets out for his new house. At remote Crickhollow, few people know Frodo or care about his business. Pippin joins Frodo and Sam for what seems like an easy journey.

On their way to Crickhollow, the three become suspicious of a large, ominous-looking **Black Rider** on a huge black horse. Sam recalls that a similar fellow visited Bag-End and inquired about someone named Baggins. A cloak hid the rider's features, and he spoke with an odd voice. The travelers briefly hide to avoid the rider. Shortly after resuming their hike, they meet a group of Elves whose leader, **Gildor**, knows Gandalf. Hearing of the Black Rider, Gildor asks the three hobbits to spend the night in the woods under his protection. Sam can hardly contain his delight at meeting Elves.

UNDERSTANDING AND INTERPRETING
Book I, Chapter 3

Blissful Bag-End: One of the first significant symbols in *The Fellowship of the Ring* is Bilbo's home at Bag-End. Large and comfortable, the hobbit-hole includes a complex of tunnels that supposedly holds Bilbo's treasure. Bag-End represents Bilbo's tranquillity as much as it does his station in life. During the sixty years since his return from adventuring, Bilbo has lived as a rich country gentleman. When Bilbo leaves Bag-End, he leaves his comfortable life behind, and some hobbits wonder why he would choose to spend his last years anywhere else. Bag-End represents a similar kind of peace for Frodo. Although he is young, Frodo is content to devote most of his time to studying nature and enjoying the comforts of home. Given their relationship to Bag-End, neither Bilbo nor Frodo seems a likely candidate for adventure.

Nature versus Industry: Many critics have argued that Tolkien characterizes the battle of good and evil as a conflict between the natural world and industrialization. Sauron's power is tied up in his Ring, an object that does not occur naturally, but must be forged in fire. Elves, clearly a force of good, are intimately linked to the forest. The Elves and hobbits stop for the night in a bower, an enchanted and natural place. The great hall in the middle is made of living trees, as are the beds in which the hobbits sleep. Though Tolkien resisted overly allegorical readings of *The Lord of the Rings,* it is hard not to notice his repeated characterizations of the natural as good and the industrial or artificial as evil. Sauron, with his despoiling armies and dark forges, recalls the forces of industrialization that overtook the English countryside of Tolkien's childhood—a place for which Tolkien felt immense fondness, which comes out in his loving depiction of the Shire. The Elves, who take their power from that natural world, represent the sort of purity and mysticism Tolkien saw in the unspoiled English countryside.

BOOK I, CHAPTER 4
A Short Cut to Mushrooms

The next morning, the three hobbits breakfast on fruit and bread left by the Elves, who have already gone for the day. Rest, food, and a bright dawn lift the travelers' spirits. However, a Black Rider continues to menace the three. They try traveling off the road through thick bushes. They come to **Farmer Maggot**'s farm, where Frodo, as a young lad, once received a beating for stealing mushrooms. Farmer Maggot discovers the trespassers and recognizes Frodo. Farmer Maggot cheerfully welcomes the three to supper. He mentions that a Black Rider just visited the farm, looking for someone named Baggins.

For safety's sake, Farmer Maggot puts Frodo, Pippin, and Sam in a farm wagon and takes them to the ferry they must use to cross the Brandywine River. The trip seems ominous, but no harm comes, and the three hobbits find Merry waiting to join them at the ferry. He has heard of the journey to Crickhollow and wants to tag along.

UNDERSTANDING AND INTERPRETING
Book I, Chapter 4

Good, Evil, and the Ring: In these chapters, as in *The Lord of the Rings* as a whole, it is not difficult to figure out who is good and who is evil. The Black Riders have shrouded figures, hissing voices, and dread-inspiring demeanors. We quickly understand that they are evil. The Elves, with their light, clear voices, laughter, and wisdom, immediately appear fundamentally good. As we see later in the novel, the Elves, especially the High Elves, have great power, and they counterbalance the evil power of Sauron. On the whole, Tolkien makes good and evil polar opposites, with no blurring of the boundary between them. The one complicating factor, however, is the Ring. As we already know, the Ring has the power to corrupt the best intentions. In Chapter 2, even Gandalf refuses to take responsibility for the Ring, not feeling sure of his capability to resist the Ring's seductive power. The Black Riders have some connection to the Ring, which we know because Frodo feels an overwhelming desire to put the Ring on his finger when the Riders near. In a fictional universe of moral absolutes, the Ring is the one subversive element, the one thing that bridges the gap between good and evil.

BOOK I, CHAPTER 5
A Conspiracy Unmasked

With great relief, Frodo and his three hobbit friends cross the Brandywine River on a large, flat ferry boat and enter the tiny country of Buckland, where Frodo purchased his home in remote Crickhollow. On the far shore, a dark figure watches. At Crickhollow, the four bathe, eat, and rest, grateful to have survived the unexpected anxieties of the first leg of their journey. Frodo has decided on a change of plans. Instead of staying at Crickhollow indefinitely, he will leave for Rivendell at first light.

Merry, Pippin, and Sam have a surprise for Frodo. Sam eavesdropped on Gandalf and Frodo's entire conversation and told Merry and Pippin about what he heard. The three insist on accompanying Frodo on his journey. Merry has already prepared supplies and acquired six packhorses. Frodo decides to start out through the neighboring Old Forest in order to avoid the Black Riders. The stories about the Old Forest are nightmarish. Every traveler has trouble there. Some have gotten lost in the forest and never been seen again. At dawn the four set out.

UNDERSTANDING AND INTERPRETING
Book I, Chapter 5

Of Epic Proportions: While reading *The Lord of the Rings*, it is helpful to consider the ways in which the novel is an epic. Traditionally, epics are long narratives that celebrate the achievements of a significant hero. The victories of the hero have national, historical, or social significance. Critics speak of two types of epic: primary and secondary. A primary, or traditional, epic develops from the legends or oral tradition of a people, and eventually a poet or scribe writes down a version of the story for posterity. The medieval Anglo-Saxon *Beowulf* (created orally around the eighth century A.D., was passed down orally until written circa A.D. 1000) and the ancient Greek *Odyssey* (composed 750–675 B.C.) are examples of primary epics. Secondary epics are literary, the product of one writer who composes a story by creatively using aspects of traditional epics, including cosmic setting, spiritual relevance, heroic action, exciting battles, long, sometimes exotic journeys or quests, supernatural beings, the intervention of gods, and magic. Examples of secondary epics are *The Lord of the Rings* and the American novel *Moby Dick* (1851) by **Herman Melville** (1819–1891).

Frodo as Epic Hero: At the center of the traditional epic is an epic hero, an individual of impressive physical, spiritual, and mental stature who embodies the values of his people. National heroes are usually men, partly because men have usually written history and epics. (One complaint sometimes lodged against *The Lord of the Rings* is that it features almost no significant, interesting, or powerful women.) The epic hero may begin as a stumbling adolescent, but he soon demonstrates unusual prowess and an admirable character. He rises above those around him. Some attributes of the epic hero apply to Frodo, but most do not. Tolkien consciously undercuts traditions and presents an

> "**B**ecause of Tolkien, the universe will forever genuinely contain magic, even when all of it passes, and the covers of the book, for the last time, are shut."
>
> **DIANE DUANE**, "THE LAST SUNDAY," *MEDITATIONS ON MIDDLE-EARTH*

unconventional epic hero. Bilbo and Gandalf speak of Frodo as the most outstanding hobbit in the Shire, but he is the best of a pleasure-loving, quiet race not likely to produce heroes. However, his hobbit blood turns out to be exactly what makes him the ideal Ring-bearer. Frodo is courageous and honorable, but he is mostly an ordinary fellow, and it is this ordinariness that makes him immune to the temptations of the Ring. Unlike traditional heroes, he does not burn with passion, self-confidence, or ambition, qualities that would make him lust for the power of the Ring. Frodo is not meant to be a leader of men, and this is a blessing, for men with the qualities of leadership would never be able to resist the Ring.

BOOK I, CHAPTER 6
The Old Forest

The travelers sense that the trees of the Old Forest are watching them in a hostile way and whispering to each other. Pippin complains that individual trees move to bar the travelers' progress. He angrily shouts at them to let him pass, but Merry says yelling will do more harm than good. At the far side of a glade, the hobbits find a clear path to follow, but it soon leads them in the wrong direction. As noon approaches, the air becomes so hot and stuffy that the travelers can barely move. They soon become lost.

Near a dark brown river, they stumble upon a group of ancient willow trees. Exhaustion sets in, and the hobbits become unbearably sleepy. Merry gasps, "Must have nap." He collapses at the base of one of the willows. Yawning, Pippin joins him. Without warning, the giant tree comes alive, attacking with its huge branches and roots. A crack in the trunk suddenly gapes open and draws Pippin in completely. Frodo and Sam beat on the tree trunk, pleading for their friend's release. Merry falls into a crack in the willow and cannot escape. Sam threatens to burn the tree or chop it down, but the willow slowly begins to swallow Merry.

Not knowing what else to do, Frodo screams for help. To his surprise, a voice answers from deep in the forest. A figure emerges from the brush wearing a battered hat, a blue coat, and bright yellow boots. His blue eyes sparkle, and his long beard bounces with each step. The stranger is singing. This jolly visitor introduces himself as **Tom Bombadil**. Tom asks what seems to be the problem. Frodo frantically points out that the willow is swallowing two of his friends.

Tom responds that Old Man Willow is misbehaving again and needs a song. Tom puts his mouth near the tree trunk and begins singing in a low voice. As the tree loosens its grip on Merry, Tom briefly scolds Old Man Willow and tells him to behave himself. The willow releases Pippin, who springs from the trunk as if someone had kicked him. Tom insists that the travelers come home with him to eat supper and spend the night. He seems to have been expecting the guests. His wife, **Goldberry**, has food waiting on the table.

UNDERSTANDING AND INTERPRETING
Book I, Chapter 6

A Sensitive Forest: Although the term had not yet become fashionable in the mid-1950s, *The Lord of the Rings* passionately advocates environmentalism. In *The Fellowship of the Ring*, plants, especially trees, are conscious beings, and their feelings matter. As the hobbits enter the Old Forest, Merry says he knows from previous experience in the forest that "everything is very much more alive, more aware of what is going on" than in the Shire. These trees do not like strangers because their long experience tells them that strangers bring destruction. Tom, a model of environmental responsibility, respects all life in the forest.

Danger Looms: Buckland, although still within the Shire, is not as safe as the comfortable confines of Hobbiton and Bag-End. A motif that will recur emerges in this chapter: the presence of a road signifies the nearness of danger. The natural world around Buckland does not resemble the domesticated countryside that surrounds Bag-End. It is a more sinister place, with the Old Forest on one side and the Brandywine River—in which, we learn, Frodo's parents drowned—on the other. Buckland, unlike Hobbiton, has a protective hedge around it, with guards and gates. Tolkien clearly appreciates the beauty of the natural world, but implies that he prefers a more domesticated form of nature to untamed nature, which can be dangerous and unpredictable.

BOOK I, CHAPTER 7
In the House of Tom Bombadil

The guests join Tom and Goldberry for a refreshing supper that includes yellow cream and honeycomb. Goldberry fills drinking bowls with a clear liquid that warms the travelers' hearts and causes them to relax and join Tom in merry song. After supper, the hosts show the hobbits to their sleeping quarters. Sweet applewood burns in the hearth. Goldberry extinguishes the lamps and goes off to bed. Tom lingers to say goodnight and sing a last tune.

The next day is rainy, and the hobbits accept Tom's hospitality for another day. Tom entertains the guests with songs and tales of the forest. He makes it impossible for the hobbits to discern whether the fascinating stories last one day or many days. Before supper, Frodo asks Tom to explain who he is, and Tom says he is the "Eldest," older than everything on Middle-earth, even Sauron. Frodo feels that he is in a magical place and that Tom has mysterious powers. To Frodo's surprise, Tom asks if he may hold the Ring, which no one has mentioned. Tom places the Ring on his little finger and holds it up to the candlelight with a laugh. Tom does not disappear. He spins the Ring into the air and startles Frodo by making it disappear. Finally, Tom appears to snatch the Ring out of thin air and then returns it to Frodo.

The travelers intend to leave at dawn. Tom warns them to stay away from the Barrows, a series of hills containing caves whose occupants may be dangerous. He teaches them a rhyme to sing if they should run into trouble and need to call him.

UNDERSTANDING AND INTERPRETING
Book I, Chapter 7

The Mystery of Tom Bombadil: Tom is one of Tolkien's most enigmatic characters and the object of great debate among Tolkien scholars. Perhaps the only thing we know for certain about him is that he is joyously immune to the power of the Ring and therefore a uniquely neutral third party in the War of the Ring that is to come. Tom reminds us of a male personification of Mother Nature, the master of the land and its creatures, albeit only within his own territory. Perhaps he is a *Nature Valar*, a human representative of the Creator, Eru. He clearly has great powers, perhaps greater even than Gandalf's. Perhaps the Ring does not affect him because he lived before Sauron was born. It may seem strange that he does not destroy the Ring, but the same limits constrain him that constrain Gandalf. Eru mandates that powerful beings cannot quickly tidy up the problems of lesser beings, doing everything for them. Tom does not go with the hobbits to fight Sauron, and we get the feeling that perhaps his power has diminished somewhat in the later ages of Middle-earth. Tom's presence contributes to the elegiac tone of *The Lord of the Rings,* a sadness for the lost past.

Pastoral Ideal: The importance of Tom Bombadil gives clues about Tolkien's conception of nature. When the hobbits arrive at Tom's house, Goldberry tells them that now they need not worry about "untame things." This wording, combined with the perfectly manicured landscape around Tom's house, suggests that Tolkien does not necessarily equate nature with wildness or pristine wilderness. Nature, without the controlling hand of man, can be unruly and perhaps even unsafe. The most idyllic places in Tolkien's world—whether the comfortable confines of the Shire, the magical bower of the High Elves, or Tom's domain—are places where nature has been tamed but not trampled upon. The idealization of domesticated, softened nature is often cited in literature, music, and the visual arts as the pastoral.

BOOK I, CHAPTER 8

Fog on the Barrow-Downs

The next day begins briskly with a washed autumn sky of light blue. The hobbits have seen no Black Riders since they arrived at Crickhollow, and they set out in good spirits. By noon, they have traveled farther than they expected, and they stop for lunch and a nap in the warm sun. The hobbits wake in a dense fog. They try to continue traveling north toward Rivendell, but the going is slow. Frodo turns to talk to his companions and discovers that he is alone. He calls for them in vain. A dark figure appears and coldly says, "I am waiting for you!" The figure seizes Frodo, and Frodo loses consciousness.

Frodo awakens inside a barrow in a cave. A *barrow-wight* has captured all four hobbits and taken them to its cave. Frodo sees his three friends lying on their backs, a long sword resting across their necks and jewelry adorning them. Frodo notices a hand on a long arm groping its way into the room, its fingers moving like legs of a spider. As the arm approaches the sword on the hobbits' necks, Frodo grabs a short sword from the floor and chops off the crawling hand, which shrieks but then begins to growl. Frodo remembers the rhyme that Tom taught them and begins to recite it, calling for help.

After a long, slow moment, Tom's voice answers in song. He bursts into the cave, chases off the barrow-wight, rescues the hobbits, and helps himself to the barrow-wight's treasure. Tom leads the travelers to the main road and suggests they spend the night in the village of Bree, which lies only a few miles ahead. There they should stop at the Prancing Pony Inn and ask for **Barliman Butterbur**, a worthy innkeeper and a friend.

UNDERSTANDING AND INTERPRETING
Book I, Chapter 8

Evil Fingers Grasping: The encounter with the barrow-wight reveals Tolkien's vision of evil. Sauron emerges as the major figure of wickedness, the being whose nefarious intentions shape the plot of the novel. But Sauron does not have a monopoly on immorality or selfishness, and the presence of the barrow-wight—or mound demon, as we might call him in more modern English—reminds us that nastiness in Tolkien's work comes in many shapes and sizes. Nothing indicates that the barrow-wight has any connections to Sauron or acts to further Sauron's aims. The demon works as a free agent of evil. Even so, we can discern similarities between the barrow-wight and the Dark Lord. Like Sauron, the barrow-wight goes in search of jewelry and will kill to get it. Moreover, the independently moving arm of the barrow-wight, which walks spookily on its fingers, reminds us of the severed finger of Sauron, chopped off when Isildur took the Ring from him. Neither the barrow-wight nor Sauron has a personality in *The Lord of the Rings*; they are incarnations of wickedness rather than fully formed characters. They reach and grab with no soul or personality, as if they have desirous hands but no hearts or minds.

Tempted by the Ring: The power of the Ring appears as a temptation here, one that must be resisted. Sauron's power is not only an external threat, but an internal one. It afflicts the mind and the heart, working its insidious effects from the inside out, curdling a good being's heart and turning it to evil. During Frodo's confrontation with the barrow-wight, his first instinct tells him to put on the Ring, become invisible, and save himself by running away. This would solve the immediate problem, but it would indirectly cause the death of Frodo's friends, left behind in the mound. In this episode, Frodo struggles not just with a wicked demon, but with himself. One part of him wants to save his own skin at any cost, and another part cares about those dear to him.

BOOK I, CHAPTER 9
At the Sign of the Prancing Pony

The hobbits follow Tom's advice and proceed without incident to the village of Bree. They take rooms at the Prancing Pony. In a private parlor, Frodo and friends enjoy a supper of hot soup, cold meats, bread, beer, and a blackberry tart. The guests enjoy the wholesome Shire food. Frodo, Pippin, and Sam decide to join a mixed group of humans, Dwarves, and hobbits in the tavern for relaxing conversation and song before bedtime. Merry prefers to go out for a stroll.

In the tavern, Frodo notices a strange, weather-beaten man sitting alone in the shadows, a hood hiding his features. Butterbur says the man is known as **Strider**, one of a wandering group called the Rangers. Strider waves over Frodo and tells him to keep his friends from talking too much. Pippin has been especially gregarious as he enjoys his beer, and Frodo realizes that Pippin might inadvertently reveal the nature of their journey.

To attract attention away from Pippin, Frodo jumps onto a table and begins to dance and sing a song about the Man in the Moon's visit to a pub. During one verse, Frodo leaps into the air, slips, and crashes to the floor. One of his fingers jams into the Ring in his pocket, and Frodo abruptly disappears. He crawls across the floor to Strider, removing the Ring and hoping Strider will not notice anything odd. Strider already knows about the Ring and asks if he may have a quiet word with Frodo. As Frodo leaves the tavern, Butterbur also asks to speak to him privately. Frodo begins to suspect dark designs.

UNDERSTANDING AND INTERPRETING
Book I, Chapter 9

The Mysterious Stranger: Strider dominates this chapter, though his modest entrance belies his great importance to the novel. At first, his dark, shrouded appearance and knowledge of Frodo's business inspire suspicion rather than confidence. We soon see that Strider's downtrodden appearance is due to years of hard travel, and we learn that his knowledge comes from Gandalf, his own keen ears, and his many years spent fighting the Enemy. Moreover, the grandness of the poem that Gandalf quotes in reference to Strider, or Aragorn, hints at the Ranger's greater destiny. With Strider, as with the hobbits, a humble outward appearance hides inner greatness. As we continue to see throughout *The Lord of the Rings*, Tolkien prefers his heroes this way. Even Gandalf, Strider hints, is much greater than the mere clever old wizard the hobbits take him to be.

Two Humble Heroes: At this point, the hobbits have at least two surprisingly powerful figures aiding them. This fact is not only comforting, it also suggests that Tolkien conceives of a hero or great man as one who has an old-fashioned, chivalric concern for those less powerful than himself. The fate of the Ring concerns all of Middle-earth, but Gandalf and Strider were protecting the Shire long before the significance of Bilbo's ring was known for certain. For all their involvement in great deeds, neither Strider nor Gandalf becomes arrogant or loses sight of the fact that he is fighting the evil power of Sauron to protect seemingly inconsequential people such as hobbits.

BOOK I, CHAPTER 10
Strider

Frodo, Pippin, and Sam meet with Strider in the parlor. Strider reveals that he knows about Frodo's quest and has a deep interest in the Ring. He says he can be of help to the hobbits, and he wants a reward: to join them on their journey. Two Black Riders have been to Bree, and Strider feels certain they soon will return with reinforcements. Without his help, Strider says, the hobbits will never make it to Rivendell.

Butterbur enters the room and tells Frodo he has a letter for him from Gandalf. Butterbur was to send it to the Shire by messenger three months before, but he failed to see to its delivery. In the letter, dated the end of June, Gandalf warns Frodo to get out of the Shire as soon as possible. He says he has received alarming news and advises Frodo to pass through Bree, where he might meet a friend, Strider, who will take Frodo to Rivendell, where Gandalf will meet him. Strider's true name is **Aragorn**. Gandalf encloses a poem that refers to a broken sword and includes the cryptic lines, "All that is gold does not glitter, / Nor all those who wander are lost; / . . . The crownless again shall be king."

Strider is Gandalf's friend, and he carries an ancient, broken sword. Although Strider welcomes Gandalf's endorsement, he knew nothing about the letter. Strider swears to defend Frodo to the death. Merry rushes into the parlor, slamming the door after him. He saw at least two Black Riders on the streets of Bree. Strider urges the hobbits not to sleep in their assigned rooms. The next morning, they will all travel together toward Rivendell.

UNDERSTANDING AND INTERPRETING
Book I, Chapter 10

A Late Letter: The late letter from Gandalf to Frodo serves several purposes. First, it summons up an atmosphere of mystery, mentioning a distressing development without explaining it. It also increases our conviction that great danger stalks the hobbits. We learn that Gandalf wanted Frodo to leave the Shire no later than the end of July, and it is already the end of September. The letter also introduces Strider, whom Gandalf calls a friend. Frodo trusts Gandalf's commendation implicitly, and he knows that the man in front of him is actually the Strider of whom Gandalf writes because Gandalf describes Strider's physical characteristics, his real name, and his broken sword. The eight-line poem serves as a riddle, only part of which Frodo can understand, but he realizes that it, too, refers to Strider.

BOOK I, CHAPTER 11
A Knife in the Dark

As the hobbits sleep, three Black Riders approach Frodo's house in Crickhollow. They break into the house, realize Frodo is gone, and ride off furiously toward Bree. At dawn, Strider awakens the hobbits, who slept in the parlor. When they investigate their rooms, they find that someone broke in, slashed the beds, and ransacked the place. Butterbur has more alarming news. Every horse and beast in the stable has vanished. There is only one available horse in town, a bony, dispirited animal for which they pay the exorbitant price of 12 silver pennies. Sam will become especially fond of the horse, calling him **Bill**. The journey resumes. They take a wandering course through brushes and marsh, hoping to elude the Black Riders.

On October 6, they approach Weathertop, a hill near the main road that serves as a prominent landmark. A stone atop the summit is marked with a rune that might be a "G," Gandalf's sign, followed by three strokes. Strider thinks that this is a message left by Gandalf, possibly saying he was on the hill October 3 but had to leave in a hurry. The hobbits take heart, but worry that Black Riders might have forced Gandalf's departure.

As night approaches, Frodo and Merry notice several Black Riders assembling on the road below the hill. Strider warns them that the Black Riders will be even more dangerous in the dark, because they can sense shapes without the aid of light. He helps the hobbits set up the best defense they can around a bright fire. During the night, black shapes suddenly appear over the crest of the hill. Frodo feels an overwhelming urge to put on the Ring, and he obeys it. Though all else remains dark, the shapes, which were dim a moment before, become terribly clear. He observes five tall figures, three advancing rapidly. Frodo can even make out merciless eyes burning keenly in white faces. He draws his sword.

One of the Black Riders, taller than the others and wearing a crown, springs forward and bears down on Frodo, stabbing him in the left shoulder. Frodo lunges with his sword and cries out the names Elbereth and Gilthoniel. Just before losing consciousness, Frodo slips the Ring from his finger and closes his right hand tightly around it.

UNDERSTANDING AND INTERPRETING
Book I, Chapter 11

Foreboding Runes: As he does in *The Hobbit*, in *The Lord of the Rings* Tolkien sometimes uses runes to convey secret messages. Runes are cryptic alphabetical letters that Anglo Saxons and other Germanic people used during the historical period (circa A.D. 300–1300) that parallels Middle-earth's Third Age. On Weathertop, Gandalf apparently left a message in runes in order to tell Strider he had been there on October 3. The use of runes in this chapter adds to the dark mood of unknown danger.

THE STAR QUEEN ❦ Frodo probably postpones disaster by invoking the aid of Elbereth, whose name means "star-queen" in Elvish. Elbereth is Queen of the Valar, the special spirits who assisted Eru (the One) in the creation of Middle-earth. Elbereth gave Eru essential help when he kindled the stars. She acts as a guardian angel to Elves, humans, and hobbits. Elves sing her praises during Frodo's visit with them in Chapter 3, and Frodo would also know of her from ancient legends told by Bilbo. The servants of Sauron dread her name.

The Power of Language: Despite Frodo's physical weakness and inexperience, he does have the weapon of words at his disposal, and he wields this weapon effectively on a number of occasions. After the confrontation at Weathertop, Strider tells Frodo that it was not his sword thrust that hurt the king of the Riders, but rather the Elvish words Frodo cried out as he lunged: "O Elbereth! Gilthoniel!" Though it may seem strange that a mere name would cause the Black Riders to flee, we see time and again that language is always potent in Tolkien's world. A passionate student of philology— the study of language—Tolkien built his entire history of Middle-earth around languages he himself invented. Whenever we see these brief glimpses of foreign words in *The Lord of the Rings*, we must keep in mind that they are not nonsense, but part of a comprehensive, structured linguistic system. Tolkien's Elvish language, along with the Dwarvish language and the language of Mordor, among other languages, has a system of characters, grammar, and vocabulary. It is fitting, then, for Tolkien to give great power to language in Middle-earth. Frodo is not immune to this power either. Though Frodo's Elvish incantation serves as protection, Strider warns the hobbits against even mentioning the name of Mordor while out in the open and unprotected, as it could bring them great harm.

The Dubious Power of the Ring: The Ring displays its powers again here, but also its limitations. When Frodo dons the Ring to escape the notice of the Black Riders, he can suddenly see through the Riders' cloaks to their pallid faces and horrifying eyes. Yet, despite the insight the Ring affords Frodo, Tolkien invites us to doubt the practicality of this enhanced vision. Endowed with the power of the Ring, Frodo does not act like a superhero. The others in the Fellowship are active throughout their quest, while Frodo's role is observational and detached rather than participatory or aggressive. At this moment, Frodo poses no threat to the Riders, while Aragorn wildly brandishes two burning logs as he lunges. The Ring, for all its power, is not an effective tool in a quest such as Frodo's.

BOOK I, CHAPTER 12
Flight to the Ford

Frodo regains consciousness. Strider says that the puncture itself is not serious, but the King of Black Riders stabbed Frodo with a poisoned or cursed knife. Although he tries to treat the wound with herbs, Strider can only hope that Frodo survives until they reach Rivendell, where he can receive expert treatment. The group leaves as soon as possible. Frodo rides on the horse, and everyone else carries the supplies. Frodo, in nearly unbearable pain, lapses in and out of consciousness. He runs a high fever, and his left arm is lifeless. Ten days later, provisions are running perilously low. Rivendell is only a few days away, just beyond the Loudwater River Ford. On the twelfth day, the travelers come upon three large Trolls that frighten them until they realize someone turned the Trolls to stone.

That evening, as they approach the Loudwater River Ford, a shallow place where horses or people might wade across, an Elf on a magnificent white steed approaches. He is **Glorfindel,** one of many Elven-folk whom **Elrond** has sent from Rivendell in search of the party. Glorfindel reports that there are five Black Riders farther back on the road and probably four more lying in wait. He insists that Frodo ride the white steed and leave the others behind. This strategy will keep Frodo and the others safer. Frodo will have a better chance of outrunning the Black Riders, who will not harass the others if Frodo is not with them.

The next day, Glorfindel hears the Black Riders and calls to Frodo to make for the Ford. As Frodo nears the river, he finds four more Black Riders lying in ambush. With great speed, the white stallion crosses the river just ahead of the Black Riders. The nearest Black Rider is about to reach shore when "a plumed cavalry of waves" sweeps down the river, washing away the Black Riders in torrid foam. Frodo watches the Black Riders disappear. Exhausted, he loses consciousness.

UNDERSTANDING AND INTERPRETING
Book I, Chapter 12

Behind the Black Riders: Various clues suggest that the nine Black Riders represent Sauron and possess extraordinary powers. Although Strider does not explain who the Black Riders are, it is clear that he understands these riders' history. They are the **Nazgûl**, or **Ringwraiths**, nine former human kings who originally received the Nine Rings designated for humans in the Second Age. Because the nine humans lusted for power, Sauron easily corrupted them. They became subservient to Sauron and lost their humanity, turning into "wraiths," or ghosts. Like vampires, they can live indefinitely, but could die under certain circumstances, such as the destruction of the One Ring. With Sauron's defeat at the end of the Second Age, the Ringwraiths went into hiding. They appeared again when Sauron began to seek complete control of Middle-earth in the Third Age. They fear fire and prefer to avoid the light of day, which is why they travel under elaborate black capes and hoods. Ringwraiths themselves are almost invisible unless the viewer is wearing the Ring or has special powers. We do not know the names of the individual Ringwraiths.

Learning on their Feet: This chapter brings to a close the first book of *The Lord of the Rings* and the first half of *The Fellowship of the Ring*. Throughout Book I, the hobbits prove themselves in constant need of rescue, whether by Farmer Maggot, Tom Bombadil, Strider, or the raging waters of the Bruinen River. Despite their bumbling ways, however, the hobbits also demonstrate a bit of pluck and ability, as we see in Frodo's stands against the barrow-wight and the Black Riders, and in Sam's resistance to the wiles of Old Man Willow. The hobbits are adept at learning on their feet.

BOOK II, CHAPTER 1
Many Meetings

When Frodo awakens, he finds himself in a strange bed and wonders aloud where he is and what time it is. To his surprise, Gandalf answers, telling Frodo he is in Rivendell, at the House of Elrond, and it is ten o'clock on the morning of October 24. Frodo has been unconscious for four nights and three days. Frodo asks after his companions, all of whom are fine. The Black Riders targeted Frodo and paid little attention to the others. The rushing river saved Frodo thanks to Elrond, who commanded the river to wash away the Black Riders. Gandalf expects more trouble from the Black Riders, but Rivendell provides sanctuary for now.

Gandalf tells Frodo that he just barely escaped a fate worse than death. Elrond, an expert in occult medicine, discovered that a tiny sliver from the knife had remained inside Frodo and was working its way toward his heart. Had it reached its destination, it would have made Frodo like the Ringwraiths, only weaker and under their control. Sam can hardly contain his joy at his master's recovery or the thrill of being around so many Elves.

As darkness falls on Rivendell, Frodo awakes again and finds that he does not need any more rest. He is hungry and thirsty, and yearns for companionship. Elrond has planned a feast, which is just what Frodo desires. Elves crowd into the main hall, along with Dwarves, humans, hobbits, and one wizard. One fair lady captivates Frodo's gaze. She is **Arwen**, also known as **Evenstar**, daughter of Elrond. Her mother, **Celebrían**, passed "over Sea" to an Elvish afterlife, following a violent attack by Orcs.

Frodo speaks at length with **Glóin**, one of Bilbo's old companions. Following the feast, Elrond and Arwen lead the party into the Hall of Fire, a large room where guests share songs and stories. On most days, the Elves use the Hall of Fire as a center for meditation. To Frodo's delight, dear old Bilbo is sitting at the end of the Hall, having skipped the feast to sit, think, and compose songs. Bilbo has been largely at Rivendell since he left the Shire seventeen years ago.

Almost immediately, Bilbo inquires after the Ring. Frodo begins to hand it to his adopted father but draws back when he sees Bilbo turning into "a little wrinkled creature with a hungry face and bony groping hands." Bilbo realizes the Ring is not for him and tells Frodo to put it away. Bilbo performs a long historical song in the chanting manner of a *scop*. The music and story mesmerize Frodo, sweeping him away to another place and time. Bilbo takes a walk in the garden, and Frodo goes off to bed.

UNDERSTANDING AND INTERPRETING
Book II, Chapter 1

Internal Wound: Frodo's wound is symbolically important. More than a mere injury to the flesh, Frodo's wound strikes his inner self. Indeed, the physical wound barely affects Frodo's outer self at all. Tolkien does not focus on blood, scar tissue, or any external damage done by the knife. Rather, he focuses on the internal activity of the knife blade, which breaks off inside Frodo and moves toward his heart. The blade of the Nazgûl lives inside Frodo like a cancer. We learn that if the knife had reached Frodo's heart, it would have been the end of him—but not the death of him. Frodo would have become an undead wraith like the Ringwraiths. Personality and selfhood are crucial in *The Lord of the Rings*, in some cases even more important than life and death.

Center of Civilization: Elrond established Rivendell in the 1690s of the Second Age as a refuge from Sauron. If Sauron regains the One Ring, he will likely overcome Rivendell, but for the time being, it remains a safe haven. Despite its initial purpose, Rivendell has become not simply a fortress, but primarily a center of learning, meditation, and the arts. The overwhelmingly beautiful grounds sit

THE CHARACTER OF ELVES

Tolkien's Elves were the first "speaking-peoples" on Middle-earth, existing when beasts and ancient trees dominated the countryside, long before the struggle between good and evil began. They are the "Firstborn," the "Elder Race," and the noblest of Eru's creations. They cannot die of old age, but they can die from violent attacks. Elves must accept human mortality if they marry a human, which becomes an issue for Arwen. These Elves are similar to humans. Elrond is taller than the wizard Gandalf. In the First Age, Elves were friends of the Valar, and thus they are very spiritual. Elves have a deep respect for nature and can communicate with certain trees. They have acute sight and hearing, frequently noticing the presence of enemies before hobbits or humans do.

beside clean running waters in pristine forests. Even during peaceful times, the chief elders of Middle-earth gather at Rivendell to confer with each other and seek Elrond's wisdom.

BOOK II, CHAPTER 2
The Council of Elrond

Because of growing concern over Sauron's increasing power, Elrond has scheduled a meeting of leaders of the great races of Middle-earth, a council that Tolkien conceived of as a United Nations of Middle-earth. The Dwarf Glóin speaks first, revealing that about a year ago, Sauron approached the Dwarves with an offer of friendship. In exchange, he wanted the Dwarves to help him find a certain Ring, which he claimed was a mere trifle of nostalgic value. The Dwarves refused. Now, they seek Elrond's advice on the best way to deal with Sauron.

Elrond openly discusses the Ring. He regrets that Isildur kept it as *weregild* ("man-gold" or "man-payment") rather than casting it into the Cracks of Doom on the Mountain of Fire. Elrond suspects that someone must destroy the Ring, but he wants to hear more. **Boromir**, a representative from the land of Gondor, reports that his people have already endured military attacks from Sauron. He says he had a dream about a broken sword, something called Isildur's Bane, and a Halfling. The meaning of the dream suddenly becomes clear as Strider stands and reveals himself to be Aragorn, the heir and direct descendant of Isildur, keeper of Elendil's broken sword. The Halfling, as hobbits are sometimes called, is Frodo, who stands and displays the Ring, which is known sometimes to humans and others as Isildur's Bane.

Gandalf assures everyone that the Ring in Frodo's possession is the One Ring, as proven by its inscription and known powers. The elf **Legolas** mentions that Gollum, past owner of the Ring, has escaped from his dungeon. Gandalf sought counsel from **Saruman**, the only wizard who outranks him, but Sauron had corrupted Saruman by appealing to his arrogance and lust for power. When Gandalf refused to join the dark side, Saruman imprisoned him in a high tower. Gandalf escaped when **Gwaihir the Windlord**, swiftest of the great eagles, came to his rescue. Unable to find Frodo in the wilderness upon his return, Gandalf left a runic message on Weathertop, just as Strider suspected.

After listening to the speakers, Elrond makes a decision. For the short term, the Ring could help the council fight Sauron. Inevitably, however, the Ring would corrupt them and serve evil. Thus, they must destroy the Ring. Bilbo bravely offers to carry the Ring, but Elrond decides that Frodo must take the Ring to the Mountain of Fire. Gandalf and Sam will go with him.

THE SONGS OF *SCOPS*

As a scholar of Anglo-Saxon literature and culture, Tolkien was an expert on *scops* (pronounced "shop" in Anglo-Saxon), performing poets who created songs, developing the works over a period of years and then presenting them to audiences at court or in villages. The scop usually chanted to the accompaniment of a harp rather than singing his songs. Audiences were usually familiar with the story told in the scop's song, as is the case in Tolkien's epic. The scop took pride in his ability to recite the history of his people in an entertaining, often beautiful way. Oral formulas helped the scop remember long passages. Several scops might collaborate, creating an epic over a period of decades or even centuries, as was probably the case with *Beowulf.*

UNDERSTANDING AND INTERPRETING
Book II, Chapter 2

The Right to the Ring: Tolkien borrows the term *weregild* directly from the Anglo-Saxon language, in which the word is usually spelled *wergild*. The word combines *were* and *gild* to mean "man-gold" or "man-payment," just as the word *werewolf* combines *were* and *wolf* to mean "man-wolf." The concept of *weregild* involves more than goods taken in battle. In Anglo-Saxon literature, if a lord or one of his top warriors dies in battle, the opponent owes money calculated by the deceased's political or social status. In a full-scale war, the relatives or comrades of the fallen warrior justify looting by saying it is their *weregild*, their due. During the assembly of the council, Elrond refers to Isildur's ancient claim to the Ring as *weregild* because Sauron's forces killed Isildur's brother and father. Isildur had a right to the Ring through *weregild*, but Middle-earth would have been better off if he had destroyed it.

Christian Heroism: In *The Lord of the Rings*, heroism demands selflessness, a willingness to give oneself to a larger cause. Sauron, a selfish being, understands only the desire for power. This single-mindedness is a weakness for Sauron's enemies to exploit in defeating him. Sauron would never expect that someone like Frodo would deny himself the power of the Ring and destroy it. We can see Tolkien's Christian sensibility in his idea that resisting evil means, in part, resisting desire. Christianity demands the subjugation of one's own desires, whether sensual, material, or intellectual—indeed, excessive thirst for knowledge is considered one of the most dangerous desires. In the book of Genesis, the irresistible promise of forbidden knowledge leads to Adam and Eve's expulsion from Eden.

BOOK II, CHAPTER 3
The Ring Goes South

Frodo and his friends stay at Rivendell for two months while Elrond sends scouts to look for the Ringwraiths and to assess the situation. There is no sign of the enemy in the vicinity. Elrond decides to allow eight individuals to accompany Frodo. The **Fellowship of Nine** will balance, at least numerically, the Nine Ringwraiths. Merry and Pippin insist on joining Frodo and Sam to represent the hobbits. Legolas, an expert archer, will be the lone elf. One Dwarf, **Gimli**, son of Glóin, will contribute his powerful skill with the broad-bladed axe. Aragorn and Boromir will join. They are humans and proven warriors. The wizard Gandalf will go with his magical staff and an Elven sword.

Bilbo calls Frodo aside and gives him a sword, **Sting**, as well as a beautiful, strong, but light shirt of armor. This mail breastplate is harder than steel. Bilbo regrets that his age prevents him from joining the quest. He intends to stay in Rivendell to write his memoirs. On a cold day near the end of December, the nine set out. After two weeks, they have traveled south forty-five leagues (about 135 miles). Gandalf expects they will encounter difficulties trying to cross the freezing heights of the Misty Mountains. As they begin to cross the mountain range, they run into a terrible snowstorm almost certainly whipped up by the enemy. In the distance, they hear shrieks and cackles, suggesting the Ring-wraiths. Eventually, they are forced to turn back. If they cannot cross the Misty Mountains, they must take a dangerous, dark, secret underground passage.

UNDERSTANDING AND INTERPRETING
Book II, Chapter 3

Setting Fantasy Precedents: Elrond chooses The Fellowship of Nine to represent all the Free Peoples of Middle-earth: hobbits, Elves, Dwarves, and Men. Such an assembly of races in cooperation became a staple element in the fantasy genre originating in large part with Tolkien's works. Although Tolkien never considered himself a fantasy writer—in fact, he spoke of the genre with disdain—an enormous amount of fantasy literature and gaming is derived from his writing. Tolkien thought of his work, with its concern for the origins of mankind and its universal scope, as far more than fantasy. He envisioned it as something between fiction and mythology. On a narrative level, this cooperation of races allows Tolkien to act out in miniature some of the historical conflicts of Middle-earth, such as the traditional rivalry between Elves and Dwarves, which we see in the early interactions of Legolas and Gimli. The diversity of the Fellowship also allows Tolkien to personify some of the traits he earlier describes only on a more general, archetypal level, such as the lightness and quickness of Legolas the Elf, the stolid determination of Gimli the Dwarf, and so on. Some readers may find this stereotyping a bit limiting, but Tolkien fleshes out his characters beyond the stock traits of their particular races.

Excellent Elrond: Elrond represents an ideal of leadership, combining great courage with wisdom, effective government, and an appreciation for intellect and art. Because of his skill, representatives from all the free beings of Middle-earth flock to him to lead their discussion of what to do with the Ring and how to defend against Sauron. Elrond holds one of the Three Rings originally granted to Elves. With it, he has done great good. He realizes that destroying the One Ring might weaken the Three Rings, but he bases his ultimate decision on how best to serve all of Middle-earth. His diplomacy and ability to make wise decisions come from brutal experience. Fierce in battles against Morgoth and, later, Sauron, Elrond earned the respect of all free creatures. During the Second Age, he established Rivendell in a hidden valley deep in the foothills of the Misty Mountains, making it a sanctuary from Sauron and the forces of evil.

Fair Arwen Evenstar: Although over 2,000 years old, Arwen looks like a beautiful young woman because she is an Elf. Arwen has flawless skin, an important attribute of beauty, especially in medieval literature. She has the light of the stars in her eyes and a slender, graceful body. Few mortals have had the privilege of looking at Arwen. Frodo has never observed or even imagined such loveliness.

Faithful Sam: Sam is remarkable for his tender heart and loyalty. As soon as Frodo volunteers to take the Ring to the Mountain of Fire, Sam begs Elrond to be allowed to accompany Frodo. Although Sam has no business at the council of leaders, Elrond concludes that it is hardly possible to separate Sam from Frodo, so Sam may go on the quest. Sam also demonstrates his great compassion by his love for Bill, the feeble packhorse. He often talks to Bill and implies that he understands what Bill wants to say.

Slippery Saruman: Saruman, Chief of the Wizards, came to earth to battle against the power of Sauron. Although initially determined and loyal, Saruman's pride eventually made him vulnerable to corruption. When Gandalf criticizes his defection to Sauron, Saruman justifies himself by claiming he is strong enough and wise enough to manipulate Sauron and turn evil into good. Gandalf sees through Saruman's denial, however, and realizes that Sauron now controls Saruman completely. No being on Middle-earth has the strength to turn the One Ring against Sauron, not even the most powerful wizard.

BOOK II, CHAPTER 4
A Journey in the Dark

Pippin wishes that the fellowship could simply return to Rivendell. Frodo and Gandalf convince him they have what is probably the only opportunity to destroy the Ring before Sauron can capture it. Gandalf leads a search for the Mines of Moria, through which the fellowship could travel under the Misty Mountains. First, they must find the entrance. Dwarves built the mines forty years ago, and Gimli, a Dwarf, now tries to help Gandalf.

THE FOUNDING OF THE UNITED NATIONS

During the period when *The Lord of the Rings* was taking shape in Tolkien's imagination, the world's leading states established the United Nations, whose charter calls for maintaining worldwide peace and security, developing friendly relations, and cooperating to solve economic, social, cultural, and humanitarian problems. Delegates from fifty countries gathered in San Francisco on April 25, 1945, and spent two months developing the charter for this new organization, which was meant to replace the ineffectual League of Nations (1920–1946). The charter, signed on June 26, became effective on October 24, 1945, after ratification by a majority of signatories. By 1952, the United Nations had established its permanent headquarters in New York City. Tolkien's Council of Elrond is fashioned after the United Nations. It includes representatives from all the "Free Peoples of the World," which involves every group outside of Sauron's forces.

When Gandalf and Gimli at last uncover the doors leading into the mines, they discover they need a password to open them. High on an arch over the doors is a riddle inscribed in interlacing letters that Gandalf identifies as "Elven-tongue of the West of Middle-earth in the Elder Days." Gandalf is fluent in the language and translates the message as, "Speak, friend, and enter." Gandalf immediately begins trying every password he can think of, in all the tongues of Middle-earth. The blank gray stones do not stir. Gandalf reverses orders, mixes languages, and shouts single words and long passages. Nothing happens. At last, he throws his staff on the ground and sits down in disgust.

After a few minutes, Gandalf springs to his feet, shouting, "I have it! Absurdly simple, like most riddles when you see the answer." Gandalf slightly mistranslated the inscription on the arch, which actually reads, "Say 'Friend' and enter." The password is the Elvish word for "Friend." Because the path inside the mines will be dark and sometimes narrow, Sam must bid farewell to his packhorse, Bill. Although he fears for Bill's safety in the wild, Sam releases the animal and bids him farewell.

Inside the mines, the travelers follow the dim glow from Gandalf's staff as they trudge along a seemingly endless complex of tunnels and caverns. After several days, they come upon a tomb that Gandalf identifies as the Dwarf **Balin's**. Gandalf concludes that they will soon reach the eastern exit.

UNDERSTANDING AND INTERPRETING
Book II, Chapter 4

A Comedy of Errors: Occasionally, Tolkien presents a lighthearted scene to relieve the tension of his characters' quest. In Chapter 4, for example, we and the Fellowship get a bit of comic relief when Gandalf tries to figure out the password that will open the doors of the Mines of Moria. Gandalf is a proud, sometimes pompous, wizard. When he sees that opening the doors calls for a password, Gandalf assures Boromir that he is quite capable of opening them. He once knew every spell in all the tongues of Elves and humans, and one door should not pose a problem. When Gandalf fails to open the door, his undermined attitude of superiority makes the failure humorous. He finally solves the puzzle only by admitting he made a mistake.

A Dwarf History: Tolkien uses this section to better acquaint us with the Dwarves, about whom we have heard little before this point. As a race, the Dwarves are not only the traditional rivals of the Elves, but their opposites in many ways. The Elves are tall, slender, and fair; the Dwarves short, stout, and dark. The Elves make their home in the light, among the trees; the Dwarves live largely in the dark, mining deep within the earth. Perhaps most importantly, the Elves live in harmony with the natural world, whereas the Dwarves mine the earth for its riches. Perhaps this mining led to the doom of the Dwarves of Moria .

They have great skill at building and forging, but they have also been greedy, and their greed has cost them. They were driven from Moria. Then, fifty years after Bilbo returned to the Shire, their Dwarf-king Balin returned to reclaim the Dwarves' glorious realm of old and met with an untimely end at the hand of Orcs. This history of the Dwarves, especially their great desire for mithril, which led them to dig too deep and wake something evil in the earth, exemplifies one of Tolkien's central ideas in the novel: even desires that are not in themselves evil can lead to evil ends.

> "I am fond of *The Hobbit*, which is rarely pretentious, but *The Lord of the Rings* seems to me inflated, over-written, tendentious, and moralistic in the extreme. . . . I am not able to understand how a skilled and mature reader can absorb nearly fifteen hundred pages of this quaint stuff."
>
> **HAROLD BLOOM**

BOOK II, CHAPTER 5
The Bridge of Khazad-dûm

As the Fellowship of Nine slowly moves along, they hear a great rolling, drumming noise from the depths of a cavern. Then, large, semihuman creatures called Orcs attack. After a brief skirmish, Gandalf manages to bar a door in the path of the Orcs. The Fellowship flees for a mile or more, at last arriving at a narrow stone bridge they must cross to reach the eastern gates. The company rushes for the bridge, Gandalf bringing up the rear.

When everyone but Gandalf has crossed the bridge, a huge monster, the **Balrog**, attacks. To keep the Balrog from crossing the bridge, Gandalf strikes the bridge with his staff, causing it to break and the Balrog to fall into the gulf below. At the last moment, the Balrog lashes Gandalf's legs with a whip, capturing the wizard and taking him down into the gulf. Gandalf yells to his friends to flee. The eight remaining members of the Fellowship run into the golden light of a bright midday. They collapse in grief.

UNDERSTANDING AND INTERPRETING
Book II, Chapter 5

Tolkien as Director: "The Bridge of Khazad-dûm" contains the longest stretch of continuous action in *The Fellowship of the Ring,* and Tolkien's skill at sustaining the dramatic action in the chapter is remarkable. The drums the Fellowship hears owe some of their frightfulness to the fact that Tolkien evokes their sound with the word "doom" (or sometimes "doom-boom") rather than the more typical "boom." The pulse of the Orc drums punctuates the action and hints at something that has been awakened from its dormancy deep beneath Moria. Tolkien's visual descriptions further the sense of drama. As the tension builds throughout Chapter 5, so do the noise and the visuals, until finally at the bridge itself there converge roaring Orcs, flying arrows, leaping flames, Trolls, a fearsome demon, a sword and a whip of fire, and the bridge itself, thin and arching over a gaping chasm of nothingness. After Gandalf and the Balrog fall, the flames die and the noise fades. Like a film director, Tolkien tailors sound and image to reinforce the emotions of the characters.

Prophecy and Fate: When Gandalf plunges into the chasm, arguably the climax of *The Fellowship of the Ring,* he fulfills one of the many prophecies foretold in *The Lord of the Rings.* In the chapter before Gandalf's battle with the Balrog, Aragorn makes a strange warning when reluctantly consenting to enter Moria. He tells Gandalf, "I will follow your lead now—if this last warning does not move you. It is not of the Ring, nor of us others that I am thinking now, but of you, Gandalf. And I say to you: if you pass the doors of Moria, beware!" It is unclear whether Aragorn is recalling some prophecy he once heard or whether he is having a prophetic insight of his own. Such prophecies tie *The Lord of the Rings* to the mythological tradition that precedes it. Greek myth is one of the most familiar arenas of prophecy. Every mortal and god in Greek myth is subject to the predictions of the oracles. By placing prophecies in the mythological world of Middle-earth, Tolkien

> "**T**he Lord of the Rings** is one of those things: if you like you do: if you don't, then you boo!"
>
> **J. R. R. TOLKIEN,** HUMPHREY CARPENTER'S
> *J. R. R. TOLKIEN: A BIOGRAPHY*

emphasizes the importance of fate. Though Tolkien does not explicitly refer to any gods or higher powers that actively govern the workings of Middle-earth, these prophecies imply an overarching consciousness or direction that controls events, including those events, like Gandalf's death, that seem illogical and unfair.

BOOK II, CHAPTER 6

Lothlórien

Despite their grief, the friends agree they must move on quickly. Aragorn becomes unofficial leader of the Fellowship. The company approaches Lothlórien, a magnificent forest kingdom of Elves east of the Misty Mountains. Legolas is eager to enter "the eaves of the Golden Wood," but Boromir argues against it, saying the Golden Wood has a wicked reputation in his homeland, Gondor. Legend has it that those who enter will perish or suffer miserably.

That night, the travelers sleep in trees for protection, a natural course for Legolas but an unnatural one for the hobbits, who dislike heights. As Legolas climbs a great gray trunk, he discovers Sylvan Folk (forest Elves) watching him. They are friendly and willing to aid the company. Something bothers Frodo, however. He has noticed a shadowy figure slipping around the rocks and trees. At night, he sees two pale lights that might be eyes. The figure runs bent over, almost on all fours.

The next day, Elves lead the company into the depths of the Golden Wood. Elves do not trust Dwarves, so Gimli, a Dwarf, must wear a blindfold so he cannot remember the path. Aragorn worries about unity and orders all the members of the Fellowship, including Legolas, to wear blindfolds. At the end of a long day's walk, the Elves remove the blindfolds. Frodo is lost in wonder as he sees the regal beauty of the forest. He feels as if he has stepped through a window into a vanished world. Standing beside Frodo, Sam says, "I feel as if I was *inside* a song, if you take my meaning."

UNDERSTANDING AND INTERPRETING
Book II, Chapter 6

Panic and Peace: After the tumult and tragedy of the journey through Moria, Tolkien leads us into the near-heavenly peace of the Elvish forest of Lothlórien. This pattern of hairbreadth escapes followed by intermissions of peace recurs throughout the novel. Usually, peace comes in the realm of the Elves. The Elves live in a world set apart and protected—a world of the past, as Frodo notes during the stay in Lothlórien. Tolkien's pattern of action followed by respite serves, in part, to propel the narrative without wearying us with uninterrupted frenzied battles and chases. This pacing also mirrors the embattled, tumultuous state of Middle-earth. As Elrond says, Middle-earth is increasingly a place in which a sea of darkness surrounds small pockets of goodness and safety. To move from one to another of the islands is to move from safety to danger and back again.

Blending Middle-earth with Earth: Tolkien's Middle-earth is entirely his own creation, but his intimate knowledge of the natural world allows him to ground it in real details. He blends the invented and the real in the forest of Lórien. Along with the mystical *athelas* and *mellyrn* trees, Lórien contains more familiar fir-trees, harts-tongue, and whortle-berry. In Middle-earth, Orcs and Trolls exist alongside wolves and ponies. This blending of the authentic and the fantastic allows Tolkien to sustain the conceit that Middle-earth, with its magic and great deeds and battles between good and evil, is nonetheless the universe as it was in the time before our own time. Some elements of this older world remain in our world, Tolkien suggests, but many have disappeared.

BOOK II, CHAPTER 7
The Mirror of Galadriel

As the sun sinks behind the Misty Mountains, the Elves lead the members of the company into Caras Galadhon, known as the City of Trees, where they meet **Lord Celeborn** and **Lady Galadriel**, highly respected Elves who govern the city and the forest. The lord and lady are tall, noble, and beautiful. It is impossible to guess their age from their appearances, but they both have lived through the Second and Third Ages, so they must be thousands of years old.

After expressing grief at the loss of Gandalf, Galadriel promises to support Frodo in his quest, as Gandalf intended. She has an uncanny ability to see into the souls of each of the travelers. Without words, she makes each believe that she could grant his greatest wish if he turns away from the quest. Boromir suspects that Galadriel is testing them and questions her motives, but Aragorn quickly puts a stop to that. He allows no one to speak ill of Galadriel. Aragorn has visited Lothlórien before and says that the only evil in this land comes from outsiders.

> "While the Elves of *The Hobbit* are silly, capricious, and given to singing nonsense rhymes, . . . the Elves of *The Lord of the Rings* are glorious, responsible, and poetic."
>
> **KATHARYN W. CRABBE,** *J. R. R. TOLKIEN: REVISED AND EXPANDED EDITION*

In the magical atmosphere of the Golden Wood, no one notices how much time passes. Everyone feels peaceful. Even Legolas and Gimli, Elf and Dwarf, become close friends. One cool evening, Galadriel approaches Frodo and Sam.

She shows them a "mirror," a wide, shallow basin of water in which the hobbits can see visions from the past, present, or future. Sam sees Frodo lying fast asleep under a dark cliff. He sees himself in a dim passage and on a winding stair. Finally, he sees disturbing images of destruction in the Shire. Frodo thinks he sees Gandalf on a winding road. After a brief glimpse of Bilbo in his room and assorted flashes of war, Frodo sees a single eye in a black abyss, filling the mirror. It seems to seek Frodo. The Ring on Frodo's neck grows heavy, dragging Frodo toward the water. Galadriel speaks, and the image disappears.

Galadriel tells Frodo that she is the keeper of one of the Three Rings granted to Elves. She can use it for good, especially to ward off Sauron, unless the Evil One regains the One Ring. Frodo impulsively offers to give Galadriel the One Ring, confident that she could defeat Sauron and save Middle-earth, but she refuses, saying it would make her as evil as Sauron. She suggests that Frodo and the company depart at dawn.

UNDERSTANDING AND INTERPRETING
Book II, Chapter 7

Melancholy Paradise: Lothlórien is, in Aragorn's words, "the heart of Elvendom on earth," and Tolkien spares no superlative in describing it. Everything in the forest is perfect. The Elves have magical gifts, and they bestow upon the Fellowship long-lasting food and enchanted, chameleonic cloaks. However, as much as Tolkien evokes a sense of perfection in Lórien, he also evokes an elegiac sense of loss. As Frodo notes, "[i]n Rivendell there was memory of ancient things; in Lórien the ancient things still lived on in the waking world." The loss and the fading that the Elves repeatedly describe is felt most acutely here in the heart of their realm. Lórien is the Eden of Middle-earth, the paradise that will inevitably be lost whether or not Frodo succeeds.

Seeing the Future: Galadriel's mirror is a powerful image of prophecy and also represents the limitations of prophecy. Her water-filled basin provides images of things to come, including images we will see before the end of the trilogy. But while Galadriel's mirror is undoubtedly powerful and accurate, it is of limited utility. Galadriel herself warns of the danger of attempting to decipher what one sees in the mirror, but concedes that without interpretation, evaluation and action are impossible. Like the Ring that allows Frodo to see the Riders but not to fight them, the mirror allows seers to glimpse the future but not to do anything about it. The mirror shows us again that magic implements may be wondrous, but ultimately courage and determination count for more.

BOOK II, CHAPTER 8
Farewell to Lórien

As Frodo and his friends prepare to leave the next day, Celeborn and Galadriel give them clothing, supplies, food, including *lembas*, and gifts. Celeborn provides them with three small boats with which to travel down the Anduin, the "Great River." Boromir begins to express reluctance to destroy the Ring. Aragorn receives a silver-and-gold sheath for his sword. Galadriel also gives him a precious brooch that once belonged to the love of Aragon's life, Arwen. Galadriel is sympathetic toward the lovers and implies that Arwen would want Aragorn to have the brooch. To Boromir, she presents a gold belt, to Merry and Pippin, clasps wrought like golden flowers, and to Legolas, a magnificent bow strung with Elf hair and a quiver of arrows. Galadriel gives Sam, who is a gardener, a small box of earth from her orchard. Gimli shyly asks for a strand of the fair lady's golden hair, which Galadriel gladly gives him. To Frodo, she gives a tiny crystal phial that can magically light the way in dark places. Galadriel sings a song as her guests sadly depart.

UNDERSTANDING AND INTERPRETING
Book II, Chapter 8

Reminders of Peace: The gifts Galadriel offers to the group are useful and urgently needed. The *lembas* cakes provide nourishment, and the cloaks, warmth. In addition, many of the gifts symbolize what is missing from the bleak landscape of the war-threatened Middle-earth. Galadriel gives Frodo her phial of light, reminding us of the "dark times" (as a character in the next volume of the novel describes them) that currently prevail in Middle-earth. Her gift of magic soil to Sam reminds us of how little regeneration and growth there has been in this time of warfare and destruction. Finally, Galadriel's gift of a strand of her hair to Gimli may be meant as a gesture of reconciliation between the Elves and Dwarves, but it also reminds us how few females there are in Tolkien's work. In Tolkien's universe, women and girls are associated with times of peace, prosperity, and happy home life—none of which can survive the darkness of Sauron. As such, Galadriel's gifts are more than just a fairy-tale addition to the adventure. They remind us of all the fruits of civilized and peaceful life for which the Fellowship fights.

J.R.R. Tolkien

BOOK II, CHAPTER 9

The Great River

As they travel down the Anduin River, the members of the company must ward off attacks by Orcs. Frodo escapes death when an arrow bounces off his *mithril* corselet. A log that seems to be stalking the boats is actually a creature. They agree that it might be Gollum, still hoping to retrieve the One Ring. After ten days, the company has traveled as far as it can on the Great River. It is time to decide whether to go west with the Ring, hoping that it will help defend Gondor, or to attempt to take it east through Mordor to the Mountain of Fire and destroy it as soon as possible.

UNDERSTANDING AND INTERPRETING
Book II, Chapter 9

Constant Dread: The Fellowship experiences almost constant anxiety on their journey, as typified by Gollum's eerie presence. The various skirmishes with barrow-wights and tentacled monsters are challenging and violent, but it could be argued that unceasing dread, not isolated bursts of action, is more characteristic of the travelers' everyday experience and more difficult to endure. An unknown and unseen enemy is far more terrifying than one clearly viewed and recognized. Gollum, like the dark shapes of the Ringwraiths, frightens more because of his obscurity and elusiveness than because of the actual harm he causes. He haunts and stalks rather than ambushing or attacking, so his threat is never-ending. Gollum's pale, staring eyes and the ever-present patter of his footsteps in the distance symbolize the constant paranoia with which the Fellowship lives.

BOOK II, CHAPTER 10

The Breaking of the Fellowship

Aragorn announces that the time has come for each member of the company to make a decision. Frodo must decide whether to take the Ring into Gondor to help Boromir's people fight Sauron or go directly to Mordor and hope to reach the Mountain of Fire. His friends may or may not accompany him. Frodo asks for some time alone.

As Frodo sits on a stone and considers his decision, Boromir approaches. Despite warnings from Gandalf and Galadriel, Boromir believes himself virtuous and strong enough to make the One Ring serve the forces of good. Frodo disagrees and insists that he must not delay. The Ring is absolutely evil and must be destroyed. He will go to Mordor. Boromir loses control and tries to overpower Frodo and steal the Ring. Frodo manages to place the Ring on his finger. He vanishes and escapes.

Two powerful forces tear at Frodo from within. One tells him to join Sauron, the other orders him to remove the Ring. After a long moment, Frodo manages to slip the Ring off his finger. Frodo decides to continue on his own. As he climbs into one of the boats to row across to the eastern shore, Sam suddenly joins him. He suspected that Frodo would try to leave alone. The two old friends set out together.

UNDERSTANDING AND INTERPRETING
Book II, Chapter 10

Worthy to Bear the Ring: Frodo's struggle with himself dramatically represents the role free will plays in the battle between reason and desire. Both duty and desire affect Frodo, but he does not identify totally with either. This state makes him like every human being. What makes Frodo unique, however, is his willingness to meditate on the forces that pull at him. As he sits on the rock, he considers himself, the action of a wise being. It is impossible to imagine an evil warlord like Sauron struggling with the conflict between duty and desire, as Frodo does. Frodo's wisdom also distinguishes him from characters like Boromir, for example, who suffer stormy fits of passion and desire. Though we are given indications throughout *The Lord of the Rings* that Frodo is fated to be the Ring-bearer, Tolkien uses episodes such as the one at Amon Hen to remind us that self-knowledge, and the wisdom that springs from it—and not just fate—make Frodo worthy of his destined role.

Conclusions

The Fellowship of the Ring considers the formation and dissolution of a team designed to save the world from the forces of evil. As the poet and critic **W.H. Auden** (1907–1973) writes in "The Quest Hero," a quest is a search involving unknown but important consequences. Ability and courage are important for the hero of a quest, but faith and determination, which Frodo possesses, are essential.

IV

THE TWO TOWERS

The Two Towers

An Overview

Key Facts

Genre: Fantasy novel; quest novel; second volume of epic trilogy

First Published: 1954

Setting: The closing years of the Third Age on Middle-earth

Narrator: Anonymous, omniscient (all-knowing) third-person

Plot Overview: After Frodo and Sam depart for Mordor, Orcs kill Boromir and capture Merry and Pippin. Aragorn, Legolas, and Gimli pursue the Orcs in hopes of rescuing their friends. Several surprises, including a visit from an old friend, greet the characters in Fangorn Forest. Frodo and Sam pursue their quest with the unlikely assistance of Gollum, who proves untrustworthy. The volume ends with Frodo imprisoned and Sauron's forces on the move toward Gondor.

Style, Technique, and Language

Style—The Power of Song: Many songs are sung in *The Two Towers,* and Tolkien nearly always provides the complete lyrics, set off in italics from the rest of the text. As a scholar of early cultures, Tolkien understood that before the advent of published books and the spread of literacy, culture and religion were kept alive largely through the singing of songs. Songs functioned not merely as entertainment but as a way of preserving the collective memory of a culture. We find songs fulfilling such a function in *The Two Towers,* as when Fangorn sings about his childhood at the dawn of the world, sharing his memories, which are far older than those of any other living creature. Songs also have an emotional impact that stirs characters to action, as when Aragorn sings about Gondor in Book III, Chapter 2, concluding with the appeal, "Let us go!" For Tolkien, songs represent everything noble and good about ancient cultural traditions.

> "**M**uch that in a realistic work would be done by 'character delineation' is here done simply by making the character an elf, a dwarf, or a hobbit. The imagined beings have their insides on the outside; they are visible souls."
>
> **C.S. LEWIS**, "THE DETHRONEMENT OF POWER," *TOLKIEN AND THE CRITICS*

Technique—Nature Reveals Mood: In a sense, it is unavoidable that a fantasy novel set in ancient times, following the progress of creatures wandering over meadows and mountains, focuses significant attention on the natural environment. *The Two Towers* is full of forests, fields, pools, mountains, gorges, and caves—a loving attention to natural scenery that made Tolkien a favorite writer of the back-to-nature activists of the 1960s. Yet nature in *The Lord of the Rings* is more than merely a scenic backdrop to the plot. The state of nature closely mirrors the state of the world, reflecting the time of crisis leading to the War of the Ring.

In his writing about nature, Tolkien borrows ideas from Romantic poetry, most notably the idea that the external world often reflects the minds of men. In *The Two Towers*, nature reflects the state of man's condition. In Saruman's corrupt realm of Isengard, for instance, the landscape itself has become corrupted. The realm is barren and desolate where once it blossomed with greenery. Similarly, the land of Mordor has become sterile in the presence of Sauron's evil.

Language—Epic Techniques: In *The Two Towers*, Tolkien adapts Anglo-Saxon epic language. For example, he uses kennings, creative descriptions used as nouns, calling a "vocabulary" a "word-hoard," for example.

Tolkien reverses sentence structure while making effective use of standard epic phrases such as "fair of face": "Very fair was her face, and her long hair was like a river of gold. Slender and tall she was in her white robe girt with silver." He writes of arrows that "fall thick as rain," and horses "white as snow."

Occasionally, Tolkien reverses a cliché. For example, he reverses gender depictions standard in epics, characterizing the female Éowyn as strong and "stern as steel," "fearless and high-hearted," a natural leader. Tolkien uses especially rich epic descriptions, as when we hear a detailed, exciting account of Gandalf's battle with the Balrog. Songs play an important part in this section of the epic, especially those sung by Aragorn and Legolas at Boromir's funeral. Characters sometimes rely on aphorisms, tidy little statements of some rule of life. Describing his own imprisonment, for example, Gandalf says, "The guest who has escaped from the roof, will think twice before he comes back in by the door."

Characters in *The Two Towers*

THE FELLOWSHIP

Aragorn (Strider): A human, he is the rightful heir to the throne of Gondor. When he was known as Strider, he carried a broken sword, **Narsil**, which prophecies say will help him regain his throne. He became the unofficial leader of the Fellowship after Gandalf's death.

Boromir: The son of the Steward of the Land of Gondor. Boromir, although a brave and decent human, does not see the evils of the Ring until after he has tried to steal it from Frodo. After Frodo departed with the Ring at the end of *The Fellowship of the Ring*, Orcs attacked and wounded Boromir.

Frodo Baggins: The novel's central character. Frodo and his friends must undertake an extraordinary quest to save Middle-earth. Frodo now attempts to reach the Mountain of Fire with Sam at his side and Gollum as a guide.

Gandalf (Mithrandir): One of five wizards who came to Middle-earth to assist in the fight against evil, Gandalf encourages and aids Frodo. Gandalf carries the sword **Glamdring** and rides a horse named **Shadowfax**.

Gimli: A fierce Dwarf hero, expert with a broad-bladed axe.

Legolas: An Elf, Legolas is a superb archer possessed of superhuman eyesight. Although Elves usually do not get along with Dwarves, Legolas and Gimli have become close friends and make a formidable duo in battle.

Meriadoc (Merry) Brandybuck: One of Frodo's closest friends in the Shire, Merry insisted on accompanying Frodo on his journey. Along with Pippin, he spends much of this volume trying to rejoin the Fellowship.

Peregrin (Pippin) Took: Another of Frodo's closest friends in the Shire, Pippin voluntarily joined the quest. With Merry, he tries to rejoin the Fellowship.

Samwise (Sam) Gamgee: Frodo's gardener. Sam, more practical and more emotional than Frodo, proves to be one of Frodo's best friends. He and Frodo travel together in this volume.

ELVES

Celeborn: Galadriel's husband. Celeborn, the Lord of Lothlórien, is not as powerful as his wife.

Galadriel: A powerful opponent of evil, Galadriel possesses one of the Three Rings of the Elves. She helps rule the Elven forest refuge of Lothlórien and assists the hobbits from a distance.

HUMANS

Denethor: The father of Boromir and Faramir. Denethor serves as the Steward of Gondor in the absence of a rightful heir to the crown.

Éomer: The nephew of King Théoden of Rohan. Éomer opposes court adviser Wormtongue. Gandalf helps Éomer win the king's trust despite Wormtongue's lies about his loyalty. Éomer's horse is **Firefoot**.

Éowyn: Éomer's sister. Éowyn, a strong leader, serves as Marshal of Rohan in the king's absence. She displays a romantic interest in Aragorn.

Faramir: Boromir's brother. An officer in the Gondor Army, Faramir leads Frodo and Sam to a secret hideout where they spend the night in safety.

Isildur: An ancient ruler of Gondor. Isildur cut the Ring from Sauron's hand at the end of the Second Age. Isildur lost the Ring in a river, and Orcs killed him near the beginning of the Third Age.

Théoden: King of Rohan. Gandalf helps Théoden resume his role as powerful leader. The king's horse is **Snowmane**.

OTHER ALLIES AND BENEVOLENT BEINGS

Ents: Woodland creatures as old as the trees. In ancient times, Ents were indistinguishable from trees. Elves woke them and taught them to speak. Ents usually move slowly and deliberately, but they grow incredibly strong and mobile when angry.

Gwaihir the Windlord: Swiftest of the great eagles, Gwaihir carries Gandalf to Lothlórien after Gandalf's fight with the Balrog.

Tom Bombadil: One of the most enigmatic characters in the epic, Tom has powers that rival Gandalf's. He may be a *Nature Valar*, a representative of the Creator, Eru, in human form, serving as guardian angel of trees, hills, and rivers. Although he does not appear in this volume, Tom deserves mention because he shares certain important characteristics with Treebeard.

Treebeard (Fangorn): The oldest surviving Ent. Fourteen-foot-high Treebeard is a shepherd of trees in Fangorn Forest. It is unclear whether he is named after the forest or the forest after him. He appears to be a gentle ecologist, but he can be a fierce warrior when roused.

ENEMIES AND MALEVOLENT BEINGS

The Balrog: An ancient monster that lives underneath the Mines of Moria. On a bridge exiting the Mines of Moria, Gandalf engaged in a battle with this beast.

Black Riders (the Nazgûl, Ringwraiths): Former human kings turned slaves to Sauron. They seek the Ring on his behalf.

Gollum (Sméagol): After losing the Ring to Bilbo in *The Hobbit*, Gollum begins his own evil quest to regain it.

Orcs: Large, powerful, semihuman creatures who work for the forces of evil. Cannibalistic and cruel, the Orcs abhor daylight and must attack at night.

Saruman the White: The Dark Lord of Mordor and the most powerful Wizard in Gandalf's order. Once a force for good, he becomes corrupted by power and defects to Sauron's side, breeding a new race of Orcs that do not fear sunlight.

Sauron: The Dark Lord of Mordor. Sauron, who created the One Ring, is driven only by his desire to retrieve it. He never appears in the novel; we see only his Great Eye and Dark Tower in Mordor.

Shelob: The giant spider of Cirith Ungol. Shelob nearly murders Frodo, but Sam gets the better of her with some distant help from Galadriel.

Uruk-hai: A new strain of dark warriors that the evil master Sauron breeds by blending Orcs with humans. Uruk-hai are taller, stronger, and more intelligent than ordinary Orcs, and they function better in daylight.

Wormtongue (Gríma): The top adviser of Théoden, the King of Rohan. Wormtongue has steadily wormed his way into King Théoden's trust and destroyed Théoden's self-confidence as well as his faith in his top officers. Gandalf proves that Wormtongue is a treacherous traitor actually in the service of Saruman.

Reading *The Two Towers*

BOOK III, CHAPTER 1
The Departure of Boromir

While looking for **Frodo** and **Sam** on a hill near the Anduin River, **Aragorn** hears the harsh cries of attacking Orcs in the woodlands below. **Boromir**'s horn sounds a call of alarm from the same area. Aragorn runs to help his comrade, but he is too late. Mortally wounded, Boromir sits with his back against a large tree. Numerous Orc arrows have pierced his body. Around Boromir, more than twenty Orcs lie dead.

Boromir confesses to Aragorn that he tried to steal the One Ring from Frodo. He says the Orcs took **Merry** and **Pippin**. He asks Aragorn to go to Minas Tirith, Gondor's capital city, and help defend Boromir's people. **Legolas** and **Gimli** find Aragorn kneeling by Boromir, clasping his hand and weeping. Because of symbols on the Orcs' shields and helmets, Aragorn concludes that the Orcs represent **Saruman**, the corrupt Chief Wizard, and **Sauron**, the most evil being on Middle-earth.

Aragorn follows Frodo and Sam's tracks and realizes they have rowed away toward Mordor. He thinks Frodo chose to leave the Fellowship because he did not want to endanger his friends. He also attributes Frodo's departure to his fear

> "The Lord of the Rings deals with questions fundamental and timeless, the nature of good and evil, of man, and of God. Because of that, over and above its sheer readability, it endures, and undoubtedly will endure, as the plays of Shakespeare, or *Alice in Wonderland*, or *The Adventures of Huckleberry Finn*, do and will."
>
> **PAUL ANDERSON**, "AWAKENING THE ELVES,"
> *MEDITATIONS ON MIDDLE-EARTH*

that members of the Fellowship might be tempted to steal the Ring. Aragorn decides to track the Orcs to rescue Merry and Pippin. Legolas and Gimli will accompany him.

Before leaving, the three arrange a funeral bier on one of the boats and cast it adrift in the Anduin River. They lay Boromir's body in one of the two remaining boats, folding his cloak beneath his head. Boromir wears the golden belt that **Galadriel** gave him at Lothlórien. Across his lap lies the warrior's broken sword. Weapons from his enemies lie at his feet. The three beings let the river's current sweep the boat away. In later days, storytellers will say the boat rode through crashing falls and foaming pools, eventually carrying Boromir past Gondor to the Great Sea.

UNDERSTANDING AND INTERPRETING
Book III, Chapter 1

A Dearth of Hobbits: The opening chapters of *The Two Towers* mark the first time the hobbits have been absent from the narrative of *The Lord of the Rings*. The absence of the hobbits continues throughout much of *The Two Towers*. The hobbits are at the center of everything that occurs, and the other characters discuss them constantly, yet they are kept offstage. Their absence pushes them to the center of the narrative, however, as we worry about them. Tolkien puts us in the position of Aragorn and his company, constantly hoping to see the hobbits. Through Aragorn's eyes, we study the tracks on the forest floor, hoping in vain for a glimpse of Merry and Pippin.

Treachery Is Evil: Tolkien often equates treachery with evil. The evil of the Orcs is evinced not just by their cruelty, but by their inability to fight in close union with each other. Unlike Gandalf's alliance of Elves, Dwarves, hobbits, and Men, who overcome long-standing animosities to fight with vows of unity and solidarity, the Orcs kill each other as well as their common enemy. Boromir exemplifies the conception of evil as treachery. Boromir, a noble and tragic figure, dominates the opening of the novel. Although he fell prey to the lure of the Ring, he redeems himself by realizing the scope of his error and humbly repenting. Boromir's death in battle, which comes right after his attempt to commandeer the Ring, can be interpreted as a fated punishment for his lapse into selfishness and ambition.

BOOK III, CHAPTER 2
The Riders of Rohan

As Aragorn, Gimli, and Legolas travel through Rohan, a country to the north of Gondor, they come upon the corpses of five dead Orcs. Aragorn, an expert tracker, examines the area and decides that the Orcs must have been killed by their own comrades. There is no sign of Merry or Pippin. A few days later, Aragorn finds a silver belt clasp exactly like those Galadriel gave to Merry and Pippin. From the size of nearby footprints, Aragorn concludes that Pippin was there and must have dropped the silver belt clasp to indicate he is alive and with the Orcs.

One day, Legolas, whose remarkable eyesight allows him to see for great distances, notices over one hundred horsemen approaching from the direction of the Orc trail. The riders are not Orcs, but Men. Gimli is cautious, but Aragorn asserts that the horsemen are probably the Riders of Rohan, a mighty force but a just one. They would not assault strangers without listening to them first.

The horsemen approach, and the leader introduces himself as **Éomer**, Third Marshal of Riddermark.

Éomer explains that Saruman has Orcs under his command and has attacked Rohan from the west. This has strained Rohan's capacities, for it also must fight Sauron to the east. Éomer agrees to loan Aragorn horses, but he informs Aragorn that they will discover no living Orcs. The Riders of Rohan fought and killed the Orcs that captured Merry and Pippin, but they found no hobbits. Éomer assures Aragorn that he checked all the slain. His Men despoiled the carcasses, stacked them, and burned the lot.

Éomer tells Aragorn to be careful about mentioning their mutual friend **Gandalf** if Aragorn visits Rohan to return the horses. King Théoden is still angry with Gandalf for "borrowing" the king's finest horse, **Shadowfax**, during a recent visit. When Shadowfax returned, he would serve no rider other than Gandalf. The three comrades again pick up the Orc trail and soon come upon an open glade filled with a great pile of weapons and ashes still hot and smoking. A large Orc head impaled on a stake rises from the pile of weapons. Gimli builds a small campfire, and the three prepare for a night's rest.

BURIAL AT SEA

Boromir's ceremony is an abbreviated version of a traditional Anglo-Saxon ship funeral. Tolkien read about such funerals in the epic *Beowulf* and learned more about them while studying discoveries at the 1939 Sutton Hoo archeological site in East Anglia, now Suffolk, in eastern England. In a traditional burial at sea, the deceased king or great warrior was placed on a vessel and surrounded with battle weapons and treasure, including swords or ornaments belonging to his defeated enemies. It was thought that the king or warrior could take these possessions to the afterlife. Sometimes a ship was set adrift in memory of a deceased king or warrior, as was the case in the Sutton Hoo dig. Archeologists found no evidence of a body at Sutton Hoo, and some scholars concluded that the boat at the site was a cenotaph, a monument honoring a king whose body was burned or buried elsewhere.

Gimli has a vision of a mysterious, bent old man appearing at the edge of the firelight. He says nothing and quickly disappears. Legolas soon notices that the horses they borrowed from Éomer have vanished. Gimli suspects that the old man was Saruman, who sometimes travels in disguise.

UNDERSTANDING AND INTERPRETING
Book III, Chapter 2

Visions of Saruman: Gimli's vision of Saruman indicates the power and danger of the corrupted wizard. While Gandalf and other attendees of the Council of Elrond discuss Saruman in *The Fellowship of the Ring*, Saruman himself does not appear in the first volume of the novel. Gimli's bizarre dream is our first direct contact with Saruman, and it is a strange and hallucinatory encounter. Gimli does not know whether he has really seen Saruman or whether Saruman used magic to appear in his mind. The Dwarf's vision, along with the warnings of Éomer and the mysterious disappearance of the horses, makes Saruman a figure of ominous fascination.

Two Old Men, One Good, One Evil: Saruman appears as an old man in a cloak, with a staff and a wide-brimmed hat, cutting a figure strikingly similar to Gandalf's. This similarity highlights the ambiguous nature of good and evil. When Gandalf reappears later in *The Two Towers*, the company initially thinks he is Saruman. Tolkien stresses the similarity between the good Gandalf and the corrupt Saruman to show that good and evil can be nearly indistinguishable. Saruman, in particular, blurs the line, for he is evil not by nature, but by choice. He was once good, but he betrayed his side to sate his own ambition. As Gandalf notes later in *The Two Towers*, Saruman could have remained a force of good, likely more powerful than Gandalf himself, but he decided to embrace wickedness. Through *The Lord of the Rings*, Tolkien explores the question of whether evil is a matter of choice or an uncontrollable outside force.

Halflings: Because they live in a sheltered corner of Middle-earth, hobbits are relatively unfamiliar to many of the other inhabitants of Tolkien's world. Although we as readers have been introduced to hobbit lore and culture in *The Hobbit* and the Prologue to *The Fellowship of the Ring*, many of the characters in *The Two Towers* do not know what a hobbit is. Gimli must explain to Éomer that hobbits are neither children nor Dwarves, but Halflings. This description of hobbits as hybrid beings makes us realize that even we, for all the background knowledge Tolkien has provided, do not really understand the true origin of the hobbit race.

BOOK III, CHAPTER 3

The Uruk-hai

The narrative shifts back in time. Pippin and Merry lie captive in the Orc camp, bound hand and foot. Pippin has a dark dream in which he calls out to Frodo but sees only Orcs around him. Pippin recalls Boromir's great battle, in which he caused fear among the Orcs but could not summon other warriors to help him. Pippin's last memory of the battle is of seeing Boromir trying to pull an arrow out of his own body. Pippin regrets that Gandalf ever asked him to come along, because he feels like little more than a burden.

Pippin hears the Orcs talking among themselves. One Orc asks why the hobbits cannot simply be killed. Another answers that orders have been given not to kill, search, or plunder the hobbits. They must be captured alive. Pippin realizes that the two Orcs use the Common Tongue to communicate, since they do not speak the same language. Some Orcs work for Sauron, some for Saruman.

The Orcs travel with great speed and usually carry the hobbits, who otherwise could not keep up. One day, a fight breaks out among the Orcs. A warrior dies and falls on top of Pippin. His unsheathed knife falls near Pippin's wrists, and Pippin cuts the cords that bind him and frees his hands. Pippin conceals this fact and bides his time, hoping for an opportunity to escape. Later, he manages to drop the silver clasp that Galadriel gave him.

> **"I** n Tolkien's professional life the intersection of language and the past came in the realm of philology. In the inward life of his imagination, it came in his creation of a new version of Middle-earth."
>
> **JARED LOBDELL,** *ENGLAND AND ALWAYS: TOLKIEN'S WORLD OF THE RINGS*

The Isengard Orcs snatch Merry and Pippin and escape with them, running from the other Orcs. After outdistancing the other Orcs, the Isengard Orcs search Merry and Pippin for the Ring. Suddenly, the Riders of Rohan happen upon the Orcs. Although the Orcs outnumber the Riders two to one, the Rohan warriors fight with great skill and courage and outmaneuver their enemies. Merry and Pippin find themselves lying at the edge of the battle. Pippin grabs a fallen Orc's sword and cuts his friend loose. Merry and Pippin do not wait for the outcome of the battle. Although they have heard warnings against entering nearby Fangorn Forest, the hobbits prefer its mystery to the dangers of remaining in the open. As the sun climbs in the sky, they scramble through the trees and flee.

Book III, Chapter 3

A Bond among Hobbits: Pippin's dream of calling out to Frodo reminds us of the strong bond the four hobbits share—the bond that Gandalf predicted would count for much when he argued for Pippin and Merry's inclusion in the Fellowship in the first volume of the novel. Pippin and Merry suffer when the Orcs keep them away from each other. The narrator describes the great sense of relief the hobbits feel when they are close enough to talk quietly for a while and can take comfort in camaraderie even when bound and in captivity.

Squabbling Orcs: In contrast to the hobbit's camaraderie, the Orcs exhibit an almost total absence of cooperation. The Orcs squabble constantly, at times even fatally. Their frequent lapses into native Orc dialects, incomprehensible to other Orcs of different tribes, shows how little the creatures care about communication and unity. The Isengard tribe betrays the other Orcs—the most obvious example of disunity—but even the Isengard tribe quarrels among itself, snarling and cursing each other with a bitterness usually reserved for enemies. While the two hobbits would do anything for one another, the Orcs' squabbling makes it almost impossible for them to carry out their kidnapping.

BOOK III, CHAPTER 4
Treebeard

Going as fast as they can, Merry and Pippin hike deeper into Fangorn Forest, moving through the stuffy, dim air. For nourishment, they have only a couple of cakes of *lembas*, and they have no blankets. Suddenly, something lifts Merry and Pippin off their feet. They come face to face with one of the most extraordinary beings they have ever seen, a "Man-like, almost Troll-like figure" standing at least fourteen feet tall. The creature, which is covered in greenish-gray bark, has a huge head, no neck, and large, knobby hands. The creature's beard looks like moss-encrusted twigs. It has deep eyes that look as if they hold deep wells of memory.

"I am an Ent," the giant says, introducing himself as **Treebeard**. Ents were the first speaking beings of Middle-earth. In the earliest days, Ents were indistinguishable from trees. After Treebeard places Merry and Pippin back on the ground, they identify themselves. Just from touching the hobbits, Treebeard can discern much of their past. He can see that something important is afoot that involves Gandalf and forces of evil. Treebeard asks after his old friend Gandalf, who is, he says, the only wizard who cares about trees. The hobbits explain that Gandalf is dead. Treebeard seems doubtful but does not argue.

Treebeard explains that Ents care for trees. The Ents once had wives, called Ent-wives, but the wives moved away. Since then, there have been no baby Ents. Treebeard invites Merry and Pippin to dine and spend the night at one of his homes, a wide opening in the side of a hill. The hobbits accept his offer. The next day, Treebeard calls an Entmoot, a council of Ents. An Ent named Quickbeam explains to the hobbits that the Orcs have behaved cruelly, cutting down trees for no reason. The council resolves to overthrow Saruman. Several dozen Ents march toward Saruman's fortress at Isengard. Pippin notices that groves of trees are marching with the Ents. Fangorn Forest is going to war.

UNDERSTANDING AND INTERPRETING
Book III, Chapter 4

Two Tree Lovers: Treebeard might remind readers of **Tom Bombadil**, the Nature Valar in the Old Forest in *The Fellowship of the Ring*. Both characters are ancient and have existed since the First Age, and both respect the environment and insist on treating nature, especially trees, with kindness. Saruman encourages wanton destruction of the forest instead of realizing, as Tom and Treebeard do, that all living organisms have value. As Treebeard points out, Saruman "does not care for growing things, except as far as they serve him for the moment."

> "Middle-earth, by the way, is not a name of a never-never land without relation to the world we live in. . . . It is just a use of Middle English *middel-erde*, altered from Old English *Middangeard*: the name for the inhabited lands of Men 'between the seas.'"
>
> **J.R.R. TOLKIEN**, LETTER TO HOUGHTON MIFFLIN CO., JUNE 29, 1955

The Debate Between the Sexes: One of the most popular genres of medieval literature is the debate, in which two or more characters, often allegorical, discuss subjects such as love, politics, or morality. Treebeard's account of the disagreements between Ents and Ent-wives is a satire on a debate between the sexes. The males enjoy living as free spirits, roaming from wood to wood and taking their pleasure where they find it. Entwives, on the other hand, desire order, peace, and a specific place called "home." The males like nature in the wild, while the Ent-wives prefer structured gardens. Tolkien exploits gender stereotypes to poke fun at human gender relations and to point out that if the sexes disagree too strenuously, as the Ents and Ent-wives did, procreation will cease.

Nature Joins the Fray: The introduction of the Ents broadens the scope of the battle brewing between the Fellowship's forces and the Enemy. The conflict has become more than warfare among the various races and peoples of Middle-earth. It has now begun to involve nature itself. Because Saruman's Orc armies have begun an assault on nature, destroying the forest without reason, nature fights back. The dramatic scene of the Ents marching into battle is a powerful moment and a subtle nod to Shakespeare's *Macbeth,* in which one of the prophecies related to Macbeth's demise says that "Birnam Wood," a forest, will physically move toward a castle. The episode of the Ents reminds us that evil in *The Lord of the Rings* touches the lives of everyone and everything, including trees and entire landscapes. Tolkien wrote *The Lord of the Rings* in the 1940s, before the blossoming of the modern environmental conservation movement, but he foreshadows this era of ecological concerns in his criticism of thoughtless destruction of trees.

Noble Hosts: Here, as in *The Fellowship of the Ring*, nature is rarely an indifferent backdrop but a force for good or evil. From the first moment he meets Merry and Pippin, Treebeard offers them help, treating them nobly and hospitably. Treebeard offers food and shelter to the hobbits out of sheer benevolence, expecting nothing in return. As always in *The Lord of the Rings*, good brings creatures together and evil drives them apart. Hospitality such as the Ents offer is one of the ways Middle-earth resembles ancient Greece as Homer depicted it. In Homer's world, the true measure of a person's nobility is the generosity with which he receives guests.

BOOK III, CHAPTER 5
The White Rider

Aragorn and Legolas agree that their horses did not sound frightened when they ran away. Legolas says the animals spoke "as horses will when they meet a friend." Gimli still believes that the stranger he saw was Saruman. Using his Ranger skills and powers of deduction, Aragorn examines tracks and decides that Merry and Pippin are both alive and that they managed to escape from the Orcs. Aragorn and his companions follow hobbit tracks into Fangorn Forest.

The searchers climb a small hill and look around. With his keen sight, Legolas spots an old man in dirty gray rags passing from tree to tree behind them. No longer trying to hide, the mysterious stranger quickly approaches the three and asks what they are doing in Fangorn. Taking the old man for Saruman, Aragorn pulls out his sword, Gimli raises his axe, and Legolas draws his bow. Before any of them can attack, the old man jumps atop a rock and waves his staff, disarming all three. He tears off his rags and reveals beautiful white robes. Aragorn at last recognizes the old fellow: it is Gandalf the Grey, reborn as Gandalf the White.

Gandalf says, mysteriously, that he "passed through fire and deep water" during his battle with the **Balrog**. After the Balrog lashed Gandalf with his whip, the two plunged a great distance into deep water. The Balrog's fire severely burned Gandalf, but the water extinguished the flames. The Balrog was "a thing of slime, stronger than a strangling snake."

Gandalf began to win the fight. Eventually, the Balrog fled up "the Endless Stair," a secret passageway leading to a high mountain peak. Gandalf followed him. They found "a lonely window in the snow" and emerged above the mists of Middle-earth. Balrog burst into flame anew, but Gandalf managed to hurl him off the mountainside and crush him. Even so, Gandalf could not have survived if **Gwaihir the Windlord** had not rescued him and carried him to Lothlórien, where Lady Galadriel healed him.

Gandalf explains that neither Saruman nor Sauron knows where the hobbits are. Saruman betrayed Sauron by dividing the Isengarders against Rohan, thereby aiding Gandalf's forces. Gandalf notes that Sauron has blundered by concentrating his forces on the search for Frodo rather than guarding the entrance to Mordor in order to block Frodo's entry. Apparently, it has not occurred to Sauron that Frodo might want to destroy the Ring. Gandalf also predicts that the Ents, now fully roused to action, will be powerful in a way no one can foresee. Aragorn, confident that Gandalf will make a superb leader of their forces, hails him as the White Rider. With a long whistle, Gandalf summons Shadowfax, who brings the missing horses to the other three. Apparently, Gandalf has borrowed his favorite steed once more. As the four riders depart for Isengard, Legolas sees great smoke and asks what is going on. "Battle and war!" answers Gandalf. "Ride on!"

> "Though Tolkien lived in the twentieth century, he can scarcely be called a modern writer. His roots were buried deep in early literature, and the major names in twentieth-century writing meant little or nothing to him."
>
> **HUMPHREY CARPENTER**, *THE INKLINGS*

Book III, Chapter 5

From Death, New Life: Tolkien highlights Gandalf's preternatural power and wisdom. The wizard has great insight into the psychology of both good and evil characters, as we see in his subtle understanding of Sauron's psychology. Gandalf knows that Sauron would never imagine that the present possessor of the Ring might want to destroy it rather than use it for his own benefit. Gandalf's wisdom appears related to his near death, as he has returned to life with greater insight. Like many figures in myth who gain superhuman understanding by passing through the underworld, Gandalf's demise or near demise at the end of the preceding volume of the novel marks not failure, but power. Gandalf reappears stronger than ever. Like the ancient Roman hero Aeneas in Virgil's *Aeneid*, who gains wisdom from a passage through the realm of the dead, Gandalf looks death in the face and emerges revitalized. Furthermore, in the Christian tradition of rebirth, Gandalf returns as a purified being, no longer Gandalf the Grey but Gandalf the White. He has been cleansed, as if in death his earlier weaknesses were eradicated. His newly white robes also indicate his increased leadership responsibilities. Saruman has worn white robes for centuries to indicate his position as Head Wizard. He no longer deserves to lead his brethren, however, and Gandalf's white robes show that he is now ready to take up leadership.

BOOK III, CHAPTER 6
The King of the Golden Hall

On the approach to King Théoden's great hall in Rohan, the company notices that the hall appears "thatched with gold." The guards, under orders not to admit strangers, disarm the company and reluctantly let them in. After the travelers return their horses, they meet with Théoden, and his wily counselor **Gríma Wormtongue**. Disconcertingly, the king looks like a beaten man. His head hangs low over his knees. Immediately, he scolds Gandalf for "ruining" his finest steed, Shadowfax, and for always bearing bad news. Wormtongue accuses Gandalf of seeking favors.

Enraged, Gandalf tells the king that Wormtongue is a traitor in the service of Saruman. Wormtongue has destroyed the king's self-confidence as well as his faith in his other chief advisers. King Théoden banishes Wormtongue and appoints his royal nephew, **Éomer**, long an opponent of Wormtongue, top aide and official heir. With Wormtongue gone, the king stands tall and looks years younger. He insists on leading the Riders of Rohan into battle against Saruman's forces. If they can succeed quickly, he argues, they will have only one front left to defend against Sauron. Gandalf and the other Fellowship members present join Théoden.

To protect civilians during his absence, the king appoints Éomer's sister, **Éowyn**, Marshal of Rohan. The king leaves a small military force with her. Unnoticed, Éowyn looks adoringly at Aragorn. As a token of gratitude for the wizard's advice, the king offers Gandalf any gift he wants. Gandalf chooses Shadowfax. That afternoon, the warriors ride off to find Saruman's warriors.

UNDERSTANDING AND INTERPRETING
Book III, Chapter 6

King Arthur and King Théoden: In his description of King Théoden and the court of Edoras, Tolkien draws upon the mythical tales of King Arthur and his court of Camelot. Théoden's Riders evoke Arthur's Knights of the Round Table, and Queen Éowyn has some of the ethereal goodness and beauty of Queen Guinevere in the Arthurian legends. In nodding to ancient British myth in this manner, Tolkien signals his intention to make *The Lord of the Rings* not just a fantasy novel, but a tale with the feel of ancient myth. Like the old stories about King Arthur, Tolkien's novel aims to reveal something important about human nature and fate.

"For all its antiquarian knowledge and antiquarian charm, no one could mistake *The Lord of the Rings* for anything but a work of the twentieth century. It shows above all the difficulties which that century has created for traditional views of good and evil, though it also tries to re-assert them."

T.A. SHIPPEY, *J. R. R. TOLKIEN: AUTHOR OF THE CENTURY*

Trust and Suspicion: Issues of trust underpin the episode at Edoras. In the major crisis of the chapter, Théoden cannot recognize that his long-trusted counselor is a spy and traitor who has undermined the welfare of the kingdom he purports to serve. Wormtongue's smooth talk demonstrates the power of language to deceive and misguide. Trust is also an issue for Gandalf's party, whose members must prove they can be trusted. The guards' reluctance to allow Gandalf into the castle emphasizes that Sauron's evil has cast a pall of suspicion and mistrust over all of Middle-earth. Every stranger automatically comes under suspicion.

Strong Éowyn: As one of the few strong women in Tolkien's epic, Éowyn is an interesting character. Advisers at court recommend that she be allowed to lead the people of Rohan in the absence of the king and his top warriors. They call her "fearless and high-hearted" and point out that everyone loves her. Éowyn gladly accepts the responsibility given her.

BOOK III, CHAPTER 7
Helm's Deep

As they ride to the west across Rohan, Legolas tells Gandalf that he can see a great number of Saruman's soldiers—Orcs and wild mountain men—approaching in the distance. Gandalf advises the king to take his men to Helm's Deep, a natural fortress in a nearby mountain gorge. Gandalf suddenly announces that he must leave on an errand but will return soon.

Saruman's warriors badly outnumber Théoden's force. Nevertheless, the king's men defend themselves through the night at Helm's Deep. Gimli and Legolas are especially effective. The Dwarf beheads two Orcs with one swing of his axe, and the Elf challenges his new friend to a contest to see who can kill more of the enemy. By dawn, each has slain at least forty. Still, wave after wave of Orcs continues the attack. After many hours, the forces of Rohan grow tired. Aragorn is worried to see that the Orcs have crept beneath the Wall and have lit a flaming trail of Orc-liquor below the Riders. Aragorn goes into the Horn burg, the nearby citadel, to find that Éomer has not arrived. Aragorn learns that the Orcs have used their flaming liquid to blast through the Wall and seize it. The Orcs jeer at the Riders in the citadel, telling them to come out and meet their fate at the hands of the Uruk-hai. Suddenly, the roar of trumpets is heard, and King Théoden appears in martial splendor. The Orcs, gripped with fear, retreat. A horseman clad in white appears in the distance. The Riders of Rohan hail Gandalf, the White Rider, on the back of Shadowfax.

UNDERSTANDING AND INTERPRETING
Book III, Chapter 7

Mythic Battle: The appearance of Théoden at just the right moment marks the most dramatic battle scene in the novel thus far. In his masterful depiction of the battle, Tolkien uses all the classic devices of narrative suspense. The scene begins with Aragorn's sinking feeling that the Orc forces are too numerous to withstand. Then, with a clap of thunder and a roar of trumpets, Théoden appears, guided by Gandalf. The thunder and trumpets are not realistic details, but rather mythic additions that enhance the legendary feel of the tale. Real battles may not take place in this somewhat melodramatic fashion, as the grim war scenes in great literature from Homer's *Iliad* to Tolstoy's *War and Peace* remind us. But in *The Lord of the Rings*, Tolkien aims for the more abstract level of myth, in which events do not necessarily unfold as they would in real life.

BOOK III, CHAPTER 8
The Road to Isengard

Saruman's forces flee from Helm's Deep, but few survive. A small forest has suddenly appeared around the exit. Orcs who escape from King Théoden and Gandalf are engulfed and killed by the warrior trees. Several Ents direct the massacre. Théoden, Éomer, and twenty of their horsemen join Gandalf, Aragorn, Gimli, and Legolas on the road to Isengard, Saruman's fortress. Unneeded, most of the Riders of Rohan rest.

Isengard is one of the strongest fortifications in Middle-earth, comprising a huge rock wall, roughly circular in shape, which encloses a shallow valley. A fortified city sits inside the wall. Beneath the floor of the fortress runs a complicated system of tunnels used for storage and housing. Thousands of servants, slaves, and warriors can live there. Saruman also stables and trains wolves underground.

Gandalf and his comrades arrive only to discover that the Ents have already overthrown Saruman and captured Isengard. Saruman has taken refuge in an impregnable, 500-foot tower, which he calls Orthanc (meaning "Cunning Mind"). Near a great rubble heap, Gandalf finds two small figures resting, surrounded by empty wine bottles and bowls. One of the figures sleeps, and the other leans against a broken rock and exhales smoke. The figures are Merry and Pippin, enjoying the spoils of a victory for which they are willing to take credit. Gimli recognizes them and laughs, calling out, "You rascals, you woolly-footed and wool-pated truants! A fine hunt you have led us!" Gandalf orders food and drink for his weary comrades and asks where he can find Treebeard.

UNDERSTANDING AND INTERPRETING
Book III, Chapter 8

Nonchalant Hobbits: The surprising appearance of Merry and Pippin at Saruman's stronghold of Orthanc shows us the humor of which Tolkien is capable. Though *The Lord of the Rings* is famous for its grand epic tone and serious treatment of the nature of good and evil, it also includes its share of humorous, human moments. The humor in the scene at Orthanc arises from the juxtaposition of the solemn and dramatic setting—the immense stone tower standing amid a gorge of rock—and the leisurely, nonchalant attitude of the hobbits who sit there. Merry and Pippin appear oblivious to the battle. Instead of worrying, they are lounging, smoking, chatting, and generally enjoying themselves as if in their natural element. They express more interest in the different varieties of tobacco than in the events that shake the world around them. Once again, Tolkien's portrayal of the hobbits challenges traditional notions of what epic heroes should be like. Tolkien suggests that history lies in the hands of the little people, those who go unnoticed in their own time.

BOOK III, CHAPTER 9
Flotsam and Jetsam

The two hobbits offer Gimli some tobacco, and Pippin gives a beloved pipe of his to Gimli. Aragorn returns the hobbits' knives and the Elf-brooch. Merry, Pippin, and Treebeard explain how Isengard fell. In the company of a horde of treelike creatures called *Huorns*, a small army of Ents traveled from Fangorn Forest to the gates of the fortress. Most of Saruman's troops were attacking Helm's Deep when the Ents arrived. In a matter of minutes, the powerful Ents broke into Isengard, leaving Saruman scurrying to the safety of Orthanc. Treebeard knew he had to kill any of Saruman's forces left hiding underground, so the Ents redirected nearby streams, flooding the complex of caves and passageways so thoroughly that the contents of storage rooms floated across the floor of Isengard.

This morning, a defeated man riding a tired old horse approached Isengard. He was the Traitor of Rohan, Wormtongue. Instead of killing Saruman's spy, Treebeard ordered him to join his master in the tower, saying, "[p]ut all the rats in one trap."

UNDERSTANDING AND INTERPRETING
Book III, Chapter 9

A Merry Perspective: Tolkien tells the story of the overthrow of Isengard primarily through the voices of Merry and Pippin. After food, wine, and a little pipe-weed, the hobbits present their version of the story in the manner of old yarns spun by a fireside. The hobbits point out that they are beginning "in the middle" of the story (or "*in medias res,*" as was the custom in traditional epics),

PIPE-WEED

In his later years, Merry wrote a noteworthy treatise titled *Herblore of the Shire*, in which he discussed the botany of the region, specifically the history of pipe-weed. Tolkien tells us only a portion of the book survives—but that portion is illuminating. Hobbits developed the art of smoking pipe-weed (or "leaf") over several centuries. They preferred to inhale the aromatic smoke through clay or wooden pipes. A hobbit named Toby Hornblower developed the best pipe-weed, probably from plants originating in Gondor and growing wild near Bree. Hobbits enjoyed the relaxing, sometimes euphoric effects of the weed. Tolkien scholars have long debated whether the hobbits' pipe-weed was tobacco or hemp. Merry's treatise is not specific on that point.

and they take their time telling it. They even work in a long song about the Ents. Through Merry and Pippin, Tolkien presents this part of the tale just as warriors would have reported a battle victory in Anglo-Saxon times. The narrative is exciting and interesting, although we might be a little suspicious of Merry and Pippin's biased interpretations.

An Important Gift: Chapter 9 consists of the exchange of information and various trivial items. It is a rather static interlude between episodes of action, but it reveals a great deal. When Pippin gives Gimli his tobacco pipe, we glimpse the everyday world of small pleasures and minor details that he treasures as much as the drama of catastrophic conflict and heroic action. Pippin's pipe is a far cry from the Ring, unrelated to the outcome of history, ignored by kings and wizards, and overlooked by prophets. Nevertheless, the pipe is a significant object, a symbol of the values of caring and friendship that make the Fellowship possible in the first place. Pippin gives Gimli a pipe, a tool of brief respite from the burden of the quest, as a gesture of good will, because Pippin cares for Gimli and wants him to be comfortable. Though a humble gesture, the gift of the pipe embodies the selflessness central to the novel.

BOOK III, CHAPTER 10
The Voice of Saruman

Merry and Pippin marvel at the strength and courage of the Ents, amazed that such docile, friendly beings are mighty warriors. Treebeard has told the hobbits that the forces of evil envied Ents in the First Age. They bred Trolls in imitation of Ents, just as they bred Orcs in imitation of Elves. Gandalf decides that he must speak with Saruman before leaving Isengard. Théoden, Aragorn, and Éomer join him, and Gimli and Legolas insist on tagging along to represent their races. The six climb up twenty-seven steps to the main entrance of Orthanc and summon Saruman. Gandalf warns that Saruman is full of treachery, and his voice can be dangerously seductive.

Wormtongue appears at a high window. Gandalf orders the traitor to fetch his master. Saruman silently appears, looking grave and benevolent. In a hypnotic voice, he speaks first to King Théoden, calling him the mightiest sovereign in the western lands and saying in a sincere voice that he regrets the conflict between their armies. Saruman argues that he alone can help the king fight against Sauron. Saruman focuses only on Théoden, ignoring Gimli and Éomer when they attempt to speak. At last, the old king responds by saying, "We will have peace when you and all your works have perished—and the works of your dark master to whom you would deliver us." Théoden has resisted Saruman.

Saruman turns to Gandalf and reminds him that wizards should support each other. He asks how Gandalf can tolerate such common company. Gandalf laughs out loud and tells Saruman he should have been a court jester. Gandalf offers to release Saruman if he will surrender Orthanc and his powerful magic staff. Saruman refuses and leaves the window. Gandalf demonstrates his superior powers by summoning Saruman back, against his will, and breaking his staff with a verbal command. When Gandalf releases Saruman, the evil wizard can only whimper and crawl away. Suddenly, Wormtongue hurls a heavy, shining ball from the window. To Saruman's dismay, Wormtongue has thrown a valuable palantír at Gandalf and missed. As the group leaves, Gandalf asks Treebeard to surround Orthanc with water, trapping Saruman forever.

UNDERSTANDING AND INTERPRETING
Book III, Chapter 10

Wormtongue, Court Jester: The portrayal of Wormtongue speaking from the window broadens Tolkien's picture of evil. Wormtongue is not an impressive, powerful villain like Saruman, but a lesser figure who embodies corruption and evil on a small scale. Tolkien, as he often does in his fiction, links facility with words, which Wormtongue possesses, to corruption and deceit. When Gandalf reveals Wormtongue's role as a spy against Théoden, Wormtongue responds with a fine speech calculated to turn Théoden against Gandalf. Gandalf neatly sums up Wormtongue by calling him a "jester." A jester deals with language rather than actions, using words playfully for entertainment. Tolkien also portrays Wormtongue as completely unable to control his emotions. Wormtongue's rash toss of the palantír, a great loss to Saruman, suggests the danger of acting on emotion alone. Wormtongue's hysterics emphasize, by contrast, the moderation and self-control that Tolkien values as heroic.

Out With the Old: Saruman has always possessed a powerful ability to control the minds of others. For centuries, he could persuade the wise and intimidate lesser beings. When he confronts the invaders who stand beneath his tower window, Saruman believes he still has the ability to manipulate anyone. In his appeal to Théoden, he sounds serious, kind, and, above all, sincere. He appeals to the king's sense of fair play and his neighborly feelings. Since Wormtongue recently persuaded the king to follow his advice, Saruman must think Théoden an easy target. Two factors have changed, however: the king has benefited from Gandalf's counsel and Saruman's power has deteriorated. After Théoden has resisted evil's appeal, Saruman tries to appeal to Gandalf's sense of class superiority and wizardly bonds, but Gandalf finds his former leader laughable. He emphasizes Saruman's loss of power by making him come and go. Finally, Gandalf breaks Saruman's staff, shattering his symbol of power.

BOOK III, CHAPTER 11
The Palantír

Gandalf warns his comrades that their victory over Saruman might arouse Sauron's ire and put them all in greater danger. The group travels away from Isengard. Pippin asks Merry whether Gandalf seems different now that he has come back from the dead, and Merry replies that the wizard seems both happier and more serious. That night, as Gandalf sleeps, curious Pippin steals—from Gandalf's bag—the dark globe (palantír) that Wormtongue hurled from the window. When he looks inside the transparent ball, it begins to spin. Sauron appears in the globe and questions Pippin without speaking. It is as if he is inside Pippin's mind. The hobbit gasps and loses consciousness.

Gandalf is angry at Pippin. The palantír, literally "that which looks far away," is one of seven ancient seeing-stones that Sauron has turned to evil, using them as devices to communicate with his minions from his tower in Mordor. The palantír works both ways, and Sauron could read Pippin's mind as Pippin was reading Sauron's. Gandalf says Sauron probably thinks that Saruman still possesses the palantír and that Pippin is a captive whom Saruman was showing to the Evil One. In a way, Gandalf says, this helps their cause. He explains that the winged creatures Pippin saw in the palantír are the Nazgûl, the Ringwraiths who pursued the hobbits earlier in the novel.

At that moment, the sky darkens as a vast winged shape passes overhead. Gandalf says it is one of the Ringwraiths. The warriors must disperse immediately. The Ents will stay at Isengard and hold Saruman captive. Pippin will ride on Shadowfax with Gandalf to Minas Tirith, the capital city of Gondor. The others will rally the Riders of Rohan at Helm's Deep.

UNDERSTANDING AND INTERPRETING
Book III, Chapter 11

Curious Pippin: When Pippin succumbs to his urge to gaze into the palantír, he endears us with his understandable flaws. Pippin does not precisely steal the palantír, but he knows he should not be doing what he is doing. Yet Tolkien structures the scene to elicit sympathy for Pippin, narrating from Pippin's point of view to make us understand the hobbit's motivations. Pippin is mostly motivated by boredom, sleeplessness, and fascination with the mysterious object. His moral failing here is nothing more than curiosity, augmented by the pull of the palantír.

Menacing Mordor: Pippin's glimpse of the frightening Nazgûl in the seeing-stone etches the reality of Mordor more clearly in our minds. Prior to this moment, the only character to have actually seen Mordor is Frodo, who glimpsed it from the top of Amon Hen at the end of *The Fellowship of the Ring*. For the other characters, and for us, Mordor has existed only as a vague idea of evil far in the distance. As the novel progresses, Mordor's presence is felt more strongly. Gandalf's words remind us that, though at times the evil of Sauron may slip from the characters' minds, Sauron is constantly watching and searching for the characters, focused obsessively on the Ring.

A Change in Gandalf: The first character to demonstrate dramatic growth in this epic is the wizard Gandalf. Since his battle with the Balrog, Gandalf has changed noticeably. He has returned from the dead, and his friends see that Gandalf is now an even wiser figure. Merry points out that Gandalf seems both kinder and more frightening than before, happier but more solemn. He is also more powerful. While Saruman has grown weaker through corruption and hubris, Gandalf has become stronger through virtue. Gandalf seems more open and caring toward his friends, but he has actually become even more reluctant to share information with them.

Life without Parole: We may wonder why Gandalf does not kill Saruman at the end of Book III. Surely that would eliminate any possibility of Saruman regaining power or doing further harm. However, to mercilessly kill an already defeated enemy would be to mimic the behavior of Sauron or Saruman. Gandalf cannot hope to defeat evil if, in defeating it, he takes on its characteristics. He even offers Saruman total freedom if Saruman will surrender his staff. When Saruman refuses, Gandalf destroys the staff but allows the wizard to live. Gandalf makes Saruman's impregnable tower his prison.

BOOK IV, CHAPTER 1
The Taming of Sméagol

The narrative returns to Frodo and Sam, who are slowly making their way through rugged terrain toward Mordor. Mountains protect the Evil Empire on three sides, forming a natural barrier to invasion from the north, south, and west. Frodo and Sam approach from the northwest with great difficulty. They have reached a cliff from which they can see Mordor straight ahead, but there appears to be no way to descend the steep cliff. Frodo decides to attempt the descent. He slips, falls, slides, and lands bruised but miraculously uninjured eighteen fathoms (108 feet) below. At this point, Sam remembers he has an Elven rope from Galadriel in his pack. He uses it to join Frodo.

Gollum has been following them, intent on regaining possession of the One Ring. Now Gollum descends the mountain on all fours, headfirst, like a hound following the scent. As the creature draws near, he leaps on Sam. They wrestle. Frodo draws his knife, Sting, from its sheath and thrusts it against Gollum's neck, demanding obedience from the creature. Suddenly subservient, Gollum vows total servitude. He suddenly bounds away, attempting escape. The hobbits get him back and harness him with the Elven rope. "It hurts us, it hurts us," hisses Gollum. "It freezes, it bites! Elves twisted it, curse them! Nasty cruel hobbits!"

Sam suggests killing Gollum immediately, for safety and for peace and quiet. Frodo refuses. He tries to convince Gollum that Sauron is their mutual enemy and desperately wants the Ring. If Gollum will help the two on their quest, Frodo will spare his life. Gollum appears to agree and swears by the power of the Ring that he will "be very, very good" and "serve the master" of the Ring, by which he means Frodo. Sam is another matter.

UNDERSTANDING AND INTERPRETING
Book IV, Chapter 1

The Ever-Present Elves: Galadriel's distant influence over the Fellowship continues as Sam finds the Elven rope essential for surviving the plummet from the cliff and for subduing Gollum. We get the idea that Galadriel has always known more than she was willing to reveal. She can assist in the quest, but only to a limited extent. Frodo and Sam must pursue this mission on their own as much as possible.

Mysterious Gollum: This chapter returns us to the fascinating character of Gollum, whom we have not seen up close since Bilbo's encounter with him in *The Hobbit*. Gollum proves to be one of the most complex and indefinable characters in Tolkien's novel. He is literally a slave to the Ring, as his mind focuses on his "Precious" at the exclusion of all else. Gollum's moral nature is split quite drastically, an inward reflection of the division between Sméagol, his identity before he encountered the Ring, and Gollum, the creature he has since become. Gollum's long-standing habit of talking aloud to himself, debating with himself in a neurotic manner, indicates his inner conflict and his lack of a strong identity. After Frodo tames Gollum, Gollum is convincing in his proclamation that he wishes to guide his new master. With the character of Gollum, Tolkien injects a significant element of uncertainty into the plot. Gollum himself appears unsure of what he will do or what his goal is. This sense of utter unpredictability and potential danger pushes the narrative forward, keeping us in suspense throughout Book IV. Tolkien's technique effectively places us in Frodo's and Sam's shoes. Much like the hobbits, we know that the wretched Gollum has selfish intentions, but we have no idea when or how he might act on them.

Compassion and a Hard Head: Frodo combines compassion with practicality. He refuses to kill Gollum partly because killing would pain him. He says Gollum is a pathetic creature who has not really hurt Sam or him. However, Frodo also spares Gollum's life because, he reasons, Gollum might make a very effective guide on the treacherous road to Mordor. Frodo has outgrown some of his naïveté. He realizes that Gollum can be dangerous, but he believes he can control him by appealing to his lust for the Ring. He does not hesitate to threaten Gollum with a knife, knowing that this violent gesture will make the creature fear him. Frodo displays a surprising and forceful mix of suspicion and compassion in his interactions with Gollum, fully aware of the creature's motivation to retrieve the Ring, but sensing that Gollum would not do anything to harm the hobbits overtly.

BOOK IV, CHAPTER 2
The Passage of the Marshes

Gollum has been to Mordor before, and the three quickly move out of the mountains and into the marshes that serve as another northern barrier to Mordor. Even Sam realizes that they would be lost without their "disgusting" guide, whose long neck continually turns this way and that as he sniffs his way along. Gollum, accustomed to life underground, detests sunlight, which he calls the "nassty Yellow Face." He even dislikes the light of the moon.

Food has become a problem. Gollum hunts for "nice fisshes," as he puts it, but settles for any slimy supper (worms, toads, beetles) he can get. The hobbits survive on *lembas*, Elven "waybread" that Galadriel gave them. Because Gollum hates Elves, he will not consider eating *lembas*. As they progress deeper into Mordor, daytime is no brighter than twilight. Lights that look like ghostly campfires from some forgotten era sometimes encircle the three. Looking down into the marshy bog, Frodo sees "dead faces." Gollum advises ignoring these terrifying visions. He explains that they are crossing the Dead Marshes, an area that was once the site of a great battle between Elves and humans and their perennial enemies, Orcs. This is a cemetery that has turned to marsh, and the warriors buried here are restless and unhappy. The travelers should ignore the lights, which could lead to the realm of the dead.

A Ringwraith soars by. Gollum warns that the Ringwraiths see and report everything. As Frodo comes nearer to Sauron's stronghold, the Ring, which he wears around his neck, becomes heavier and heavier. It drags him down, reminding Frodo of the powerful pull of the Eye he saw in Galadriel's mirror. One night, Sam hears the dozing Gollum in conversation with himself, torn between his need to get his "Precious" and his vow to obey the hobbits. The next morning, Frodo, Sam, and Gollum have nearly arrived at the gates of Mordor. The hobbits thank Gollum for fulfilling his promise of guiding them to the gates. A Nazgûl flies overhead for the third time, a sign Gollum identifies as a very bad omen. Gollum refuses to proceed, and Frodo must threaten him with a knife to make him go forward.

UNDERSTANDING AND INTERPRETING
Book IV, Chapter 2

Untrustworthy Guide: In this chapter, Gollum becomes more mysterious and complicated just as his trustworthiness becomes more crucial. When Frodo tamed Gollum in the previous chapter, he had Gollum under his control, and the creature's reliability did not matter much. As the group nears Mordor, however, Gollum assumes more control. No longer a passive slave under Frodo's knife, he is now their guide, on whom they must rely—a slave with power over his masters. Gollum's hatred of the sun reminds us that he is a creature of darkness, a corrupted opposite of Frodo who succumbed fully to the Ring where Frodo resisted fully.

Travelers in the Underworld: The image of Gollum guiding Frodo and Sam through a barren landscape on their way to fulfill their mission echoes images from ancient Greek and Roman epics. In epic tales like the *Odyssey* and the

Aeneid, protagonists must suffer through distressing journeys to the underworld, often guided by shady or unsavory characters. On these ancient journeys, the heroes are often forced to confront the dead and the possibility that they themselves might die. In *The Two Towers*, Gollum leads the hobbits through the Dead Marshes, a realm of the dead with waters that contain ghostly images of the faces of slain warriors and lights that can lure travelers to death. Like the realms of the dead in the classical epics, the landscape of the Dead Marshes is unpleasant, devoid of life and growth. Yet the travelers must complete passage through this barren landscape to complete the quest. As Gollum points out, there is no way to reach Mordor but through the Dead Marshes, just as in the classical epics there was no way for the heroes to complete their quests without a sojourn in the underworld.

Increasing Dread: Mordor becomes an ever stronger, darker reality. As the hobbits approach the dark land, it becomes a clearly felt presence. The landscape bordering Mordor is nasty, full of poison pits and barren stone outcrops, with an overwhelming stench saturating the air. The frightening Nazgûl flying overhead are a constant reminder of the proximity and threat of Sauron. Even the normally confident Gollum is deeply troubled when the Nazgûl flies overhead for the third time, taking it as a very bad omen. This growing atmosphere of evil, along with the uncertainty surrounding Gollum's trustworthiness, heightens the suspense that propels Book IV forward.

BOOK IV, CHAPTER 3
The Black Gate Is Closed

To enter Mordor from this direction, the three must go through the Haunted Pass and the huge Black Gate. Frodo realizes he cannot enter the gate unnoticed. Guards watch over the gate, and soldiers of all kinds go through it. Gollum has mixed feelings. He would like to flee, but he longs for the Ring. Gollum reveals an alternate, secret route into Mordor. The three could swing around the fortress to the west, head south through a path in the western mountains, and find a staircase that leads to a dark tunnel into the Evil Empire. This approach is difficult, and there are dangers that Gollum does not specify. However, Sauron's guards would not expect an enemy to approach from that direction.

Four Nazgûl appear in the sky overhead, and the hobbits know Sauron is observing them. Frodo and Sam grab their knives, but they know that escape is impossible. Gollum senses that Men are heading toward Mordor—Men with long dark hair, gold rings, and red flags. He has never seen anything like them before, but knows they are very fierce. There are always Men entering Mordor now. Sam asks whether the Men have "oliphaunts" with them, as he has heard the creatures described in old poetry. Gollum has never seen an oliphaunt. He urges the hobbits to sleep through the daylight hours and proceed again at night.

UNDERSTANDING AND INTERPRETING
Book IV, Chapter 3

A Journey Like Dante's: Tolkien uses a trope from ancient epics in this chapter: he makes it impossible for the three to enter the final destination directly. In Dante's *Divine Comedy*, Dante, like Frodo, is a traveler motivated by good but forced to go into the mouth of hell to reach heaven. Dante cannot take the shortest path to heaven, but must travel through realms of evil he would otherwise never visit. Similarly, Frodo and Sam must travel to the heart of evil in Mordor to ensure the ultimate triumph of good. The hobbits, as usual, attain their goals not by direct confrontation, but by cunning. They plan to take the back road to a hidden entrance to Mordor rather than fight the guards at Mordor's gates.

Evil Men of Mordor: The danger of Mordor becomes increasingly palpable. In this chapter, we glimpse for the first time the humans associated with the evil kingdom. Prior to this moment, Mordor was merely an idea of evil, and then a place associated with the fantastical, especially the dark shapes of the flying Nazgûl. Now Mordor is connected to the more familiar, yet equally terrifying, world of human evil. The Men of Mordor, with their long dark hair, gold rings, and red flags, remind us that evil is not always inherent in people but is sometimes an outside force that can corrupt good to an almost unrecognizable degree.

BOOK IV, CHAPTER 4
Of Herbs and Stewed Rabbit

Gollum leads Frodo and Sam around the western rim of the valley. They stay off the road, but keep it close on their left and follow its direction. Gollum prefers to travel at night to avoid the sun, and Frodo likes the cover that the darkness gives them. Gradually, the land becomes greener and more fragrant. After several days, they arrive in a country full of woods and streams once known as Ithilien. Gollum coughs and sputters in the verdant setting, but the hobbits rejoice in it. They stop at a stream to drink and bathe. As Gollum sets off to hunt for food, Sam, who has tired of *lembas*, jokingly asks Gollum to bring back something tasty. Frodo sleeps, and Sam watches him, observing the fine lines visible on Frodo's aging face. Sam acknowledges that he feels deep love for Frodo. To Sam's surprise, Gollum returns with two small rabbits.

Sam wants a fire so he can stew the rabbits, but Gollum dislikes fire, which he calls "the nassty red tongues." Frodo says a fire might attract enemies, but what is a hobbit to do when there are rabbits to stew? Sam builds the fire and searches for herbs to flavor the meat. He longs for potatoes, carrots, turnips, onions, bay leaves, sage, thyme, and fresh-baked bread. Gollum can hardly believe that Sam is ruining this tasty bunny meat by cooking it. He leaves again to hunt for something raw to eat.

After a refreshing meal, Sam and Frodo clean their cooking gear in a nearby stream. They look back and see that the fire has spread and become quite visible. Within minutes, four human soldiers from Gondor approach the hobbits. One is named **Faramir**. Some of Sauron's forces are in the area, and Faramir expects a skirmish. Soon, some of Sauron's Orcs and human soldiers attack. Other Gondor soldiers appear out of the brush to help, but Faramir's men rout the enemy. Frodo and Sam watch and worry. An "oliphaunt" appears, thrilling Sam. Faramir plans to take Frodo and Sam with him to a secret location where they can eat and rest safely. Gollum has not returned from his hunt, and Frodo fears for his safety.

UNDERSTANDING AND INTERPRETING
Book IV, Chapter 4

Sam, Selfless Hero: The relationship between Frodo and Sam, already central to the novel, deepens when Sam silently expresses affection for Frodo. Sam is surprised by his feelings of solicitude toward Frodo when he notes the wrinkles appearing on Frodo's aging face. Sam's concern for Frodo, his observation of Frodo's increasingly haggard and weak appearance, foreshadows the greater responsibility Sam will bear during the remainder of the quest. Sam does not benefit from his attachment to Frodo—in fact, his dedication is a great hardship. Sam's loyalty is selfless, which Tolkien finds heroic.

Heroes Must Eat: The narrator's careful attention to the business of finding food brings us down to earth somewhat, reminding us that mundane concerns always exist within the grander scope of the quest. The title of Chapter 4 refers to the stewed rabbit and wild herbs that Frodo and Sam prepare for dinner, emphasizing that gnawing hunger can overshadow even pressing concerns. Such material details ground the epic quest in reality and remind us that however spiritual or lofty the heroes' final goals, the heroes themselves are beings with physical concerns.

The Plight of the Enemy: Tolkien served in the bloody trenches of World War I (1914–1918) and lost most of his best friends there. He knew all about the brutality of human combat (see following page). As Sam watches the skirmish between the Men of Gondor and Sauron's men, he considers the plight of his enemies, perhaps as Tolkien did when he fought. When an enemy soldier falls down dead close to Sam, Sam feels relieved he cannot see the man's face. He wonders what his name is and where he came from. Did he really have an evil heart? What lies or threats had brought the man here to die, so far from home? Wouldn't he rather be with his family, playing with his children, living in peace? The truth, Sam thinks, is that he probably was not so different from the Men of Gondor. He was just a soldier caught in the wrong place at the wrong time.

BOOK IV, CHAPTER 5
The Window on the West

After the skirmish, Faramir and his men briefly rest. Sam falls asleep and wakes to find Faramir interrogating Frodo. Faramir heard a prophecy that a Halfling will arrive bearing something of great value. He asks Frodo what this object is, but Frodo answers only that he is on an errand to deliver the object elsewhere. Frodo makes a great effort not to speak ill of Boromir, even though Boromir tried to seize the Ring for himself. Faramir hints that he suspects Frodo of betraying Boromir.

Faramir reveals to Frodo that Boromir is his brother. Faramir says that once, as he stared at the sea, he either dreamed or actually saw Boromir floating by on a boat, his horn broken. Faramir says he knew Boromir was sailing to the land of the dead. Frodo, who knows nothing of Boromir's death, says it must have been only a vision. Faramir addresses his brother in deep grief, asking what happened to him before his death.

On the way to the hideout, Faramir commends Frodo's truthfulness. Faramir tries again to extract information about the valuable object, familiar to him only as Isildur's Bane, that he knows Frodo carries. He suggests that Isildur's Bane indirectly killed Boromir by causing dissension in the ranks, but Frodo explains that the Fellowship did not quarrel. They reach the secret hideout, a large cave that lies behind a beautiful waterfall. Because the waterfall faces west, it is known as "The Window of the Sunset" (sometimes "Window on the West"). In the cave, they relax and enjoy wine, salted meats, dried fruit, cheese, and fresh bread.

THE BLOODY GREAT WAR

The war of devastating atrocities known as the Great War was supposed to be the war that ended all wars. It began on June 28, 1914, when Austria-Hungary declared war on Russia after Archduke Franz Ferdinand (1863–1914), heir to the throne of the Austro-Hungarian Empire, was assassinated by hostile rebels in the Bosnian capital of Sarajevo. The war escalated into a conflict between the Central Powers (Germany and Austria-Hungary, among others) and the Allies (Great Britain, France, the United States, Russia, Japan, and others). The trench warfare that ensued was ghastly and bloody. Many young British soldiers went to battle thinking the war would be an easy path to glory and wound up dead, dismembered, or tragically disillusioned. Tolkien returned from the front suffering severe psychological wounds.

Sam has a little too much wine and inadvertently reveals that Frodo is carrying the One Ring and that Boromir tried to take it. Faramir knows about the Ring, but unlike his brother, he has no interest in possessing it. He is shocked that Boromir tried to take it. Faramir admires Frodo for bearing the Ring so responsibly.

UNDERSTANDING AND INTERPRETING
Book IV, Chapter 5

Isildur's Bane: On several occasions in Chapter 5, Faramir refers to "Isildur's Bane," his name for the unknown object Frodo carries. **Isildur** was the ancient King of Gondor, who cut the One Ring from Sauron's hand, and a bane is a curse, a cause of ruin. The Ring is rightly called Isildur's Bane, for if Isildur had destroyed it, Sauron could never have returned to power, and Aragorn, Isildur's last surviving direct descendant, would now rule Gondor.

Taking the Blame: Frodo has suffered all manner of hardships, but he has never had to face an interrogation of the sort Faramir conducts when he suspects Frodo of playing a part in Boromir's death. Frodo could easily escape Faramir's suspicions by stating the truth: Boromir was a traitor who sought possession of the Ring himself and betrayed the Fellowship. But Frodo refuses to admit the truth out of regard for Faramir's memory of his late brother. Frodo sacrifices his own comfort and honor to preserve the good memory of someone who betrayed him. The nobility of Frodo's act is impressive. Watching how well he holds up under pressure from the accusatory Faramir, we develop a deeper respect for the hobbit's empathy and strength of character.

BOOK IV, CHAPTER 6
The Forbidden Pool

Shortly before dawn, Faramir awakens Frodo and Sam and asks for their help. He leads the hobbits to a lookout post above a large pool into which the waterfall descends. Faramir points to a strange little creature beside the pool, which occasionally dives in and captures a fish. Faramir asks if Frodo or Sam can identify the trespasser. Frodo realizes that the it is Gollum, who is mumbling, "Dirty hobbits. Nasty hobbits. Gone and left us. . . . No Precious. Nasty Men, they'll take it, steal my Precious." Faramir's men want to kill Gollum, but Frodo begs them not to.

Frodo explains to Faramir that Gollum's passions for the Ring and "tasty fisshes" brought him here. Frodo goes to speak to Gollum alone, and eventually Gollum agrees to leave the pool. Frodo leads him right into the arms of

Faramir's men, who capture Gollum. Gollum, feeling betrayed, spits on Frodo. Faramir privately warns Frodo against trusting Gollum, in whom he sees evil growing, but he does not advise against using him as a guide. With fresh supplies, Frodo, Sam, and Gollum set out once more. Faramir prepares to defend Gondor from an imminent attack by Sauron's forces.

UNDERSTANDING AND INTERPRETING
Book IV, Chapter 6

Pitiable Creature: In this chapter, Tolkien explores the idea of treachery from a surprising new angle, as Frodo betrays Gollum, tricking him into leaving the water and walking right up to Faramir's men, who are waiting for him. Though Frodo does save Gollum's life by convincing Faramir's men not to kill him, in doing so he betrays him. The fact that Gollum still elicits our pity despite all his whining and seeming deceitfulness highlights the creature's complex character. Tolkien's portrayal of Gollum as a childish creature who resorts to flattery of the hobbits makes him pitiable and pathetic. We pity him for his helpless enslavement to the Ring. Furthermore, this episode marks the first time we have seen Frodo do anything willfully deceitful to another individual. When Gollum spits in Frodo's face after his capture, it is hard to sympathize with Frodo.

BOOK IV, CHAPTER 7
Journey to the Cross-roads

For the time being, an eerie peace seems to have fallen across the land. Perhaps Sauron has focused his attention on Gondor so completely that his already sparse western border guards are not at their stations. Frodo and his fellow travelers have no trouble with Orcs or other enemies during this leg of their journey, but something strange is happening. The atmosphere over Mordor is even gloomier than usual. At high noon, the sky is brown.

Gollum says they must head for the Cross-roads, where they will decide how to cross the Mountains of Shadow and enter the heart of Mordor. The route across the mountains is called Cirith Ungol, "The Spider's Pass." Gollum recommends taking a secret route through Cirith Ungol, which is safer than the main road because Orcs will not find them, but difficult and treacherous in another way that he does not specify. On the way to the Cross-roads, they come across a headless statue of an ancient king of Gondor desecrated with graffiti. The stone head lies nearby.

UNDERSTANDING AND INTERPRETING
Book IV, Chapter 7

A Vision of Death: The headless, graffiti-covered statue the hobbits discover is one of many poetic moments in *The Lord of the Rings*. The statue has no importance to the plot, and Frodo and Sam learn nothing crucial from it. They simply see the statue and continue on their journey. Nevertheless, the statue has an aura of meaning, not only for the hobbits, who pay it such rapt attention that Gollum must drag them away, but for us. The broken statue of an ancient king of Gondor is a reference to the 1818 poem "Ozymandias" by Percy Bysshe Shelley, one of the most prominent figures in the Romantic movement in English poetry in the early nineteenth century. Tolkien, a professor of Anglo-Saxon literature at Oxford, was certainly familiar with the poem, which tells of a wanderer in the desert who comes upon the beheaded statue of a once great Egyptian king now a "colossal wreck, boundless and bare." Shelley's poem is a meditation on how worldly power vanishes with time and how the mighty fall. The headless statue is a fitting symbol of the kingdom of Gondor, where wicked usurpers have replaced once powerful noble lords.

BOOK IV, CHAPTER 8
The Stairs of Cirith Ungol

Gollum guides Frodo and Sam to the valley of Minas Morgul. All three are momentarily transfixed by the chilling sight of the Tower of the Moon rising in the distance, but Gollum finally urges them onward. The way is hard, and a horrid stench in the air makes it difficult for the hobbits to breathe. Frodo begs for a moment's rest, but Gollum and Sam insist on continuing. As they start moving again, Minas Morgul erupts in a deafening thunder, and troops appear. Frodo sees a great mass of cavalrymen all dressed in sable, guided by a dark horseman whom Frodo identifies as the Lord of the Nazgûl. Frodo knows that this is only a tiny part of Sauron's vast army, and his heart goes out to the people of Gondor.

Suddenly, the horseman stops, and Frodo fears he has spotted them. Frodo stands still, but almost against his will his hand moves toward the Ring hanging on his neck, which would give him the strength to confront the Lord of the Nazgûl. But Frodo exercises his will, and his hand grasps the phial (or starglass) of Galadriel, which helps him forget the Ring. The Ringwraith continues on his way.

J.R.R. Tolkien

FRODO'S WYRD ✺ Tolkien sometimes refers to Frodo's destiny, by which he means the Anglo-Saxon *wyrd*, not the Latin *fate*. Fate determines people's actions as well as the outcome of those actions. For believers in fate, every gesture and moment is scripted. The Anglo-Saxon concept of wyrd is more complex. For believers in wyrd, people have free choice. Wyrd presents a problem or responsibility, but how you play the hand you have been dealt is up to you. Frodo's wyrd is to bear the One Ring.

Frodo remains distressed, however, by the convergence of dark forces. He fears that he has taken too long to reach Mordor and it is too late to fulfill his mission of destroying the Ring. Gollum urges the hobbits steadily onward, up an interminable set of stairs. Frodo becomes dizzy and feels that he cannot go on, but Gollum forces them to continue. Frodo looks down and sees that they are above Minas Morgul. After what seems like miles uphill on the stairs of Cirith Ungol, as the twisting mountain is called, Gollum leads Frodo and Sam into a dark crevice to rest. The two hobbits fall into a discussion of the old songs and prophecies, wondering whether they themselves will become characters in future songs, perhaps sung by their own children.

Frodo and Sam privately talk about how far they can trust Gollum. Frodo asserts that no matter how selfish Gollum may be, he is no friend of the Orcs, and therefore may be considered a reliable guide. One night, Sam awakens to find Gollum caressing the sleeping Frodo. Sam accuses Gollum of sneaking around in the dark. Gollum is offended, saying he was not sneaking. Frodo wakes and settles the argument, telling Gollum he is free to go off by himself if he wishes, but Gollum says he must guide the hobbits to the end.

UNDERSTANDING AND INTERPRETING
Book IV, Chapter 8

Predicting Literary Stardom: The importance of songs and singing resurfaces in Chapter 8 in an interesting new way, as Sam and Frodo explicitly speculate that their own quest might someday be the subject of songs. Songs have been sung in the novel frequently, never as mere entertainment but always as a record of historical or prophetic knowledge. Before the invention of writing, cultures maintained their traditions and myths through the oral performance of sacred stories. Collective cultural memory was passed on through songs and poems rather than through manuscripts. Gandalf reminds us of this role of oral story-telling when he gives Legolas and Aragorn important messages about their fates by reciting bits of poetry to them in Chapter 5. Here, Sam and Frodo discuss the cultural importance of songs, but they do so with the awareness that they themselves might feature in songs sung by their own offspring. This speculation is a moment that makes us realize that *The Lord of the Rings* is itself a chronicle, just like the songs of Middle-earth, and that the characters have predicted their own place in the narrative we are reading, although they predicted songs, not novels.

A Moment of Tenderness: We see an intriguing aspect of Gollum when Sam awakens to find him caressing Frodo with the appearance of love and affection. It is no surprise that Sam views Gollum's action with suspicion and accuses Gollum of sneaking around his master. What is surprising is that Gollum seems innocent. We have been so used to viewing the creature with uncertainty, doubting his loyalty to the hobbits he serves, that it is a shock to realize he may genuinely care for Frodo.

BOOK IV, CHAPTER 9
Shelob's Lair

At the foot of a great gray wall is an opening to a cave. Gollum suggests that they all enter the cave, which leads to the heart of Mordor. He does not mention that the cave is known as "Shelob's Lair." Sam notices an unspeakable stench that oozes from the cave opening. As the group carefully progresses in the darkness, Gollum, who has lived most of his life underground and prefers the dark to daylight, walks faster and faster. Hours go by. As he falls behind, Frodo staggers from the difficult ground and the increasing stench.

The hobbits see a dim fork in the pathway. Gollum has long since disappeared and cannot tell them which way to go. Suddenly, Frodo feels intense hostility and danger emanating from the darkness. They hear a bubbling hiss but can see nothing. Sam shouts to Frodo to raise the phial of Galadriel. The phial shines a strong light and illuminates hundreds of tiny eyes, all of them staring at the hobbits. The eyes belong to Shelob, a giant spider-monster ever hungry for creatures to devour and used by the evil Sauron to guard his passages.

Although terrified, Frodo takes out Sting, his sword, and with it and the phial, he walks boldly toward the eyes, which retreat as he advances. The creature quickly backs away. One by one, its eyes waver and close. They have never seen such brightness. The creature turns and escapes into the shadows. The hobbits head for the end of the tunnel, but cobwebs stretched across the passageway block them. Handing the phial to Sam, Frodo cuts their way through with Sting, and they can finally see the exit from the tunnel. They dash outside.

Outside the cave, Sam finds reason for alarm. Frodo's unsheathed sword glows blue, and a red light in a distant lookout tower suggests that Orcs are in the area. Sam quickly hides the phial, which he still holds.

Looking toward Frodo, Sam sees something huge moving from his left, coming out of a shadow under a cliff. It is the most loathsome shape he has ever observed, and it flashes toward Frodo with deadly purpose. Sam tries to call out, but something grabs him from behind, covering his mouth. It is Gollum, who has attacked Sam. He gloats, saying he will strangle Sam while Shelob kills Frodo. But Sam manages to break Gollum's hold. They land on their backs, Sam on top. As soon as Gollum can squirm free, he flees. Spinning around, Sam rushes wildly toward Frodo. Frodo lies motionless as Shelob stares down at him. She has bound Frodo in thick webbing and begins to drag him away.

UNDERSTANDING AND INTERPRETING
Book IV, Chapter 9

The Deadliest Enemy: Frodo and Sam's encounter with the revolting spider Shelob is the culminating danger of their journey, and in fact, it is horrifying not because Shelob is so monstrously disgusting, but because Gollum turns out to be so dangerous. For the first time in the entire novel, Frodo and Sam get tricked into a bad situation. Before this point, Sam and Frodo have faced only obvious, undisguised dangers, such as the hovering Nazgûl, the kidnapping Uruk-hai, and the mistrustful guards of Gondor. Those tests of endurance have been difficult, but easy to see and combat. With Gollum's treachery comes a new kind of trial, one that stems from deception and wrongful trust. Gollum does not attack the hobbits or threaten them, as their previous enemies have. Instead, he wins their confidence over an extended period of time and then betrays them. As an enemy, the pathetic Gollum now appears more dangerous than all the others. He has played upon the natural goodness of the hobbits and exploited it to his own advantage. We can see exactly why the hobbits fell for his game because we have felt pity and affection for Gollum throughout the narrative, just as they sometimes have.

A Female Villain: As Frodo's nemesis, Shelob differs from previous villains in the novel in several ways. Unlike Saruman or Wormtongue, the giant spider-monster is incapable of speech and perhaps incapable of rational thought. A creature of instinct, she follows only her hungry stomach. She knows nothing of world domination, unlike Sauron. Shelob makes a surprising figure of evil because she is an animal, and it is hard for us to imagine animals being so thoroughly and inherently evil. Moreover, Shelob is the first and only appearance of an evil female force in *The Lord of the Rings*. The narrator stresses Shelob's gender, repeatedly calling the spider "she." Furthermore, the narrator explicitly tells us how Shelob devours her babies, rendering her a perverse mother figure.

BOOK IV, CHAPTER 10
The Choices of Master Samwise

Frodo's Elven sword, Sting, lies a few feet away. Without thinking, Sam grabs it and attacks Shelob. One swipe of the sword cuts a claw off her foot. Another destroys one of her eyes, and a third slices her vast belly. Shelob charges with the intent of dropping her awesome body weight on Sam and smothering him. As Shelob lurches toward him, Sam points the Elven sword straight at her belly. Shelob's own force impales her on Sting. She has never known such pain. Her body lurches back, but she yearns for one more try at Sam.

A voice from far away speaks to Sam, and he grabs the star-glass and points it at Shelob, shouting Elven words he does not understand. The brilliance of the star-glass shocks and confuses Shelob. She quickly crawls back to her lair, leaving a trail of putrid yellow slime from her belly wound. Sam tries to revive Frodo, but it seems his friend is dead. Sam must make a choice. He can stay with Frodo and die fighting Sauron's Orcs, who must be nearby, he can pursue Gollum and seek revenge, or he can try to fulfill Frodo's mission and carry the One Ring to the Mountain of Fire. With a broken heart, Sam concludes that he must pursue the quest. He takes the Ring from around Frodo's neck and slowly begins the lonely trek toward the volcano.

Frodo is almost out of sight when Sam notices Orcs creeping toward his friend. Rage engulfs Sam. He thinks the Orcs will eat Frodo if he leaves. Quickly placing the Ring on his finger, Sam returns to the battle site. The Ring works wonders. Sam is now invisible and can understand everything the Orcs are saying in their own language. The Orcs take up Frodo's paralyzed body and carry it away.

Sam follows behind, listening to the guards' conversation. One Orc, named Shagrat, tells the other, Gorbag, that Shelob has been wounded. Gorbag is impressed that any creature could hurt Shelob and cut through her cobwebs. He imagines the creature must be very powerful. Shagrat says he has orders from above to retrieve Frodo safe and sound, with a careful examination of all his possessions. Gorbag wonders whether Frodo is even alive, but Shagrat says

Frodo is just stunned. Sam is amazed to hear that Frodo is alive. The Orc guards carry Frodo away, slamming doors behind them and preventing Sam from following.

UNDERSTANDING AND INTERPRETING
Book IV, Chapter 10

Thank Galadriel: In these chapters, we see several examples of Galadriel's continuing influence. When Frodo sees the Ringwraiths, he reaches for the Ring, and only the phial that Galadriel gave him when he left Lothlórien prevents him from grabbing it. Galadriel's influence on Sam is repeated and profound. As Shelob approaches the hobbits in the tunnel, Sam has a vision in which Galadriel urges them to use the star-glass in darkness. When Frodo wields it, the star-glass chases off Shelob. During his battle with Shelob, Sam suddenly speaks an Elven language he does not know, and this time *he* uses the star-glass to dispense with Shelob. As he bends over Frodo's apparent corpse, Sam realizes that this is the very scene he witnessed in Galadriel's mirror: Frodo lying pale-faced and unconscious under a dark cliff. Galadriel can help the hobbits only in limited ways, but her assistance is clear and important.

Heroes in Low Places: As the title of Chapter 10 indicates, the novel ends with a surprising focus not on Frodo, who has been the protagonist and Ring-bearer for all of the novel thus far, but rather on Sam. It is Sam who assumes possession of the Ring and takes on the great responsibility of bearing it. The decisions Sam makes in this chapter arguably demonstrate more quick thinking and courage than we have seen throughout the novel from Frodo. For all of the inferiority and servility that Sam feels, he may be made of stronger stuff than the hobbit he considers his master. The larger moral lesson of this revelation is clear: those of low social rank can be heroes just as easily as their masters. In a moment of hardship and challenge, even the lowliest person may emerge as the savior of the world.

Conclusions

The last pages of *The Two Towers* leave us in great suspense. In part, the suspense is simply plot-related. We want to find out whether Sam can successfully complete the mission and destroy the Ring. The personal and emotional aspect of the novel's conclusion is equally suspenseful. Sam and Frodo have been such a close team throughout Book IV that it is hard to imagine what might happen now that they are separated. When the Orc guards slam the gates in Sam's face, denying him access to Frodo, we wonder whether Sam's extraordinary devotion to Frodo will be an impediment in the crucial role he has assumed for himself. Now that Sam has the Ring, he could go his own way. Yet his attachment to Frodo may keep him from doing so. The choice between commitment to one's friends and the need to follow one's own destiny will no doubt be difficult for Sam.

V

THE RETURN
OF THE KING

The Return of the King

An Overview

Key Facts

Genre: English fantasy; quest novel; third volume of epic trilogy

Date of First Publication: 1955

Setting: Closing years of the Third Age on Middle-earth

Narrator: Anonymous, omniscient, third-person

Plot Overview: Sauron's troops lay siege to Minas Tirith, the capital city of Gondor. King Théoden and the Riders of Rohan, on route to Minas Tirith, hope to intervene before the city falls. Aragorn and a small force of supporters also hurry to defend the city. Meanwhile, Frodo struggles to destroy the One Ring in the Mountain of Fire. He receives exceptional assistance from Sam and a surprise from Gollum. Trouble brews in the Shire.

Style, Technique, and Language

Style—Christ Figure: Both Frodo and Gandalf serve as sacrificial victims at various times, but the clearest Christ figure is Aragorn, who fulfills the prophecies about the return, or second coming, of the King to Gondor. Aragorn's journey through the Paths of the Dead parallels the apocryphal account of the "harrowing

"The need to be, if only for brief moments, in a world of coherence, where all is relevant and has meaning, is a profoundly human need and one that was for most of our culture's history satisfied by religious myths. . . . That world, for many, no longer exists. . . . Tolkien, for our time, has created such a world."

RANDEL HELMS, *TOLKIEN'S WORLD*

of hell"—Christ's descent into hell after his death on the cross. This story was especially popular among medieval audiences. When Aragorn heals the wounded in Minas Tirith with only the touch of his hand and a kiss, it recalls Christ's work with the sick as recorded in the Gospels. Interpreting Aragorn as a Christ figure does not mean the third volume of *The Lord of the Rings* cannot be understood except as a systematic allegory of the Christian narrative. The biblical overtones in Aragorn's rise to the throne are simply a motif that underlines the images of sacrifice, redemption, and rejuvenation in the Zion-like city of Minas Tirith.

Technique—Appearance Equals Character: In *The Lord of the Rings*, members of the same race share the same characteristics, and these characteristics are reflected in outward appearances. Like all Elves, Legolas is soft-spoken and ethereal, as his attractive visage suggests; like all Dwarves, Gimli is brutish and proud, as his stocky size suggests; like all Ents, Treebeard is slow-moving, strong, and wise, as his tree-like appearance suggests. Men are complex. They have great physical strength proportionate to their size, yet their personalities are confused and ill-defined, as though their history lies mostly ahead of them. Hobbits are popularly interpreted as Tolkien's depiction of the common man, modern yet pre-industrial. They are humble, jovial, and social, as their small size suggests.

Language—Brutal Simile: In this volume more than in others, Tolkien uses a direct, sometimes blunt style characterized by simple similes, short sentences, action verbs, and concrete nouns. His similes are often brutal and are never merely decorous. Enemy tents sprout "like a foul fungus-growth" around beleaguered Minas Tirith. The face of Sauron's messenger twists "like some wild beast that, as it crouches on its prey, is smitten on the muzzle with a stinging rod." Sauron's troops pour through the Black Gate as swiftly as swirling waters flow when a sluice opens. Confusion reigns "as when death smites the swollen brooding thing" that lies at the center of an ant colony. These vivid images emphasize the urgency of this volume's events.

Characters in *The Return of the King*

THE FELLOWSHIP

Aragorn (Strider): The heir of Isildur and the throne of Gondor, the king to whom the title *The Return of the King* refers. Aragorn, also known as Elessar and Elfstone, claims his right to the throne near the end of the novel.

Frodo Baggins: The brave but unassuming hobbit who bears the Ring to Mordor. Increasingly burdened by the Ring's power, Frodo assumes a more passive role in this volume than in the two previous volumes.

Gandalf the White (Mithrandir): The great wizard who leads the forces of the West. Gandalf, resurrected from apparent death in *The Fellowship of the Ring*, is sometimes a soldier and a mystic, but most of the time an advisor to human political rulers. Gandalf possesses supernatural abilities, but his powers of speech are his greatest tool.

Gimli: The one Dwarf member of the Fellowship. Headstrong Gimli traverses the Paths of the Dead with Aragorn, despite his crippling fear.

Legolas: A courageous Elf. Legolas, like Gimli, plays a smaller role in *The Return of the King* than he does in *The Fellowship of the Ring* or *The Two Towers*. He bravely fights in the march against Mordor.

Meriadoc (Merry) Brandybuck: The fourth hobbit in the Fellowship. Merry, separated from his friends, desperately seeks the approval of King Théoden. Merry is the primary focus of the chapters about the Riders of Rohan.

Peregrin (Pippin) Took: A young hobbit. Pippin, separated from his friends in Book V, abandons his troublesome ways and acts as the intermediary between Gandalf and Denethor. Pippin is the primary focus of the narrative in the scenes in Minas Tirith in Book V.

Samwise (Sam) Gamgee: Frodo's loving friend and fierce supporter. Sam changes from an insecure sidekick to a determined and shrewd guardian. He emerges as the true hero of *The Return of the King*, performing the physical and sacrificial deeds expected of a great hero while maintaining his humble, light-hearted nature.

HOBBITS

Bilbo Baggins: The central character of *The Hobbit*, Bilbo has adopted his younger cousin, Frodo, as an heir. Bilbo spends much of the last part of this epic in Rivendell, writing his memoirs—which supposedly become the source material on which Tolkien bases his epic.

Elanor: Sam and Rose's first child. Elanor is named after a flower in Lothlórien. Her name means "Sun-star."

Rose Cotton: Sam's sweetheart. Rose and Sam marry during the spring, after Sam's return from the War of the Ring. They live with Frodo and their daughter, Elanor, at Bag-End.

ELVES

Arwen Evenstar: The beautiful daughter of Elrond. As an Elf, Arwen could live forever, but because she wants to marry Aragorn, a human, she becomes mortal.

Celeborn and Galadriel: The Lord and Lady of Lothlórien. They arrive in Minas Tirith after Sauron's defeat.

Cirdan the Shipwright: The boatman and Keeper of the Havens. Cirdan sails Frodo, Bilbo, Gandalf, and several Elves to the West and the Blessed Realm.

Elrond Halfelven: The wise master of Rivendell. At the end of the novel, Elrond travels with the other Elves and Frodo to the West, beyond the Great Sea.

Gildor: A leading Elf and a friend of Gandalf. Gildor gave Frodo and his friends shelter when they were first hiding from the Black Riders. He crosses over to the Blessed Realm near the end of this volume.

HUMANS

Beregond: A Gondorian Tower Guard. He shows Pippin around Minas Tirith during the hobbit's first day there. Beregond breaks the law of the Guard by leaving his post, but he successfully stops Denethor from killing Faramir.

Barliman Butterbur: The innkeeper of the Prancing Pony in Bree. He welcomes Gandalf and Frodo back to the inn on their return journey to the Shire.

Denethor: Father of Boromir and Faramir. Denethor serves as the Steward of Gondor in the absence of a rightful heir to the crown. Denethor descends into madness. Proud and wise, he succumbs not to any evil tendency, but to the belief that he cannot save Minas Tirith. Denethor attempts to kill his son Faramir.

Éomer: Nephew of King Théoden of Rohan and brother of Éowyn. Éomer opposed court adviser Gríma Wormtongue and then won the king's trust with Gandalf's help. Éomer is Théoden's declared heir and will one day rule Rohan. He initially urges his father not to go to battle, but bravely goes to battle himself after his father dies.

Éowyn: Éomer's sister. A strong leader, she serves as Marshal of Rohan in the king's absence. Driven by a desire for combat and for Aragorn's affection, she disguises herself, takes the name **Dernhelm**, and rides to battle in Gondor. Éowyn eventually marries Faramir.

Faramir: Boromir's brother, Denethor's son, and eventually Éowyn's husband. In contrast to his father, Denethor, who tries to kill him, Faramir is noble and brave, and immediately recognizes Aragorn's claim to the throne.

Rangers of the North: Thirty of Aragorn's friends and kindred who ride from the Shire borders to join him in the fight against Sauron.

Théoden: King of the Mark and the leader of the Riders of Rohan. Théoden acts as a foil to Denethor. Whereas Denethor neglects Minas Tirith by committing suicide, Théoden bravely sacrifices his life on the battlefield for the sake of the West.

OTHER ALLIES AND BENEVOLENT BEINGS

Gwaihir the Windlord: Swiftest of the great eagles. Near the end of this volume, Gwaihir and the great eagles again serve the free people of Middle-earth.

Riders of Rohan: The cavalry of the nation of Rohan, also known as *Rohirrim*, which means, literally, "Masters of Horses." The Riders are the finest warriors on horseback in Middle-earth. Extremely skillful and fierce in battle, they can defeat even opponents who greatly outnumber them.

Treebeard: The oldest surviving Ent. Initially, he appears little more than a gentle and benevolent tree, but he proves to be a fierce warrior when roused to anger. In this volume, he releases Saruman and Wormtongue from imprisonment in the tower of Orthanc because he cannot stand to cage anything for long.

Woses: Wild Men of the Woods. They hate Orcs and Sauron, so they volunteer to serve as scouts for King Théoden and help him reach Minas Tirith swiftly.

J.R.R. Tolkien

ENEMIES AND MALEVOLENT BEINGS

Black Riders (the Nazgûl, Ringwraiths): Led by the **King of the Ringwraiths**, these mysterious figures represent Sauron and the forces of evil. Some are used as spies and fly on giant winged creatures, terrifying their foes. The Black Riders can survive only as long as the One Ring survives.

Gollum (Sméagol): A bestial creature who once owned the Ring. Gollum pursues Frodo throughout the epic, hoping to regain his "Precious." Gollum becomes Frodo's perverse double, representing what Frodo could become under the influence of the Ring.

Gríma Wormtongue: Once King Théoden's top adviser, now Wormtongue works as Saruman's servant and agent. Eventually, Wormtongue turns on Saruman.

Haradrim: Human warriors from the South. Traditional enemies of Gondor, they support Sauron in the War of the Ring. In battle, they rally around giant pachyderms called "oliphaunts."

Lieutenant of the Dark Tower: A deputy to Sauron who has subjected himself so thoroughly to the Evil One that he cannot remember his own name. Although the Lieutenant is a living creature, his face is a skull, and fire burns in his eye sockets and nostrils.

Lotho Sackville-Baggins: A hobbit living in the Shire. Known as "Pimple" in his early years and "the Chief" during the year of corruption in the Shire, Lotho is weak and greedy. He works for Saruman and helps the corrupt wizard gain control of hobbit property. Under Saruman's orders, Wormtongue murders Lotho when Lotho is no longer of use.

Saruman the White: The deposed wizard and enforcer of the Shire's brief police state. Out of pride, Saruman refuses the forgiveness of Gandalf and Galadriel. Near the end of this volume, Saruman's diminished powers are reflected in his nickname, **Sharkey**.

Sauron: The Dark Lord of Mordor and creator of the One Ring. We never encounter Sauron himself in the novel, but Sauron's Great Eye scans the land. The destruction of the Ring would rob Sauron of his power.

Troll-Chief: Pippin kills the giant Troll just before it can chomp off Beregond's head. The Troll lands on Pippin when it falls, severely injuring the hobbit.

Reading

The Return of the King

BOOK V, CHAPTER 1
Minas Tirith

After riding for several nights on the great steed Shadowfax, **Gandalf** and **Pippin** arrive at Minas Tirith, the capital city of the nation of Gondor. Minas Tirith, which was originally built as a fortress, consists of seven ascending levels. A stone wall with a reinforced gate encircles each level. The gates face different directions, so that an invader would have to zigzag back and forth from one gate to the next, effectively overcoming seven different fortresses before reaching the peak of Minas Tirith. Once formidable, the city is slowly falling into decay.

Gandalf warns Pippin to avoid the subject of Aragorn, who plans to press his legitimate claim to the kingship of Gondor. The two go to visit **Denethor**, who serves as Gondor's Steward in the absence of a legitimate king. In the Hall of Kings, the high throne remains empty. Denethor sits on a black stone chair at the foot of the throne's steps. He stares blankly at his lap and holds the broken horn of his dead son, **Boromir**, who died at the hands of the Orcs in *The Two Towers*.

From the outset, a palpable yet unspoken tension emerges between Gandalf and Denethor. Denethor asks Pippin questions about the company, deliberately ignoring Gandalf. Specifically, Denethor asks Pippin about Boromir's last stand in defense of the hobbits. Pippin realizes he owes Gondor and its Steward a debt, and driven by a strange impulse, he offers his sword to Gondor in service and payment. Denethor, flattered and amused, accepts Pippin into his Guard. Pippin senses Gandalf growing angry beside him. Denethor and Gandalf stare at each other with intensity.

Finally, Denethor bitterly accuses Gandalf of being a power-hungry manipulator. Denethor says he will rule alone until the day the King returns to Gondor. Gandalf responds that his only goal is to care for the good in Middle-earth during the current period of evil.

After the interview, Gandalf explains to Pippin that Denethor can read minds. Gandalf wishes that **Faramir**, Denethor's remaining son, would return to Gondor. Pippin spends most of the rest of the day looking for something to eat. A friendly warrior named **Beregond** looks after Pippin. The two hear the far-off cries of a flying Nazgûl (**Black Rider**), riding a terrible steed with enormous wings that darken the sun.

Warriors arrive at Minas Tirith to help in the fight against Sauron. Unfortunately, they number only 3,000 by the end of the day. Denethor had hoped for ten times that number. Gandalf explains to Pippin that for some time there will be no dawn, for the Darkness has begun.

UNDERSTANDING AND INTERPRETING
Book V, Chapter 1

Physical Evil: The idea of darkness and obscurity is important in this chapter. Gandalf and Pippin ride to Gondor in darkness, and the chapter ends with the descent of permanent night. Darkness will be an important element throughout the rest of the novel. The darkness is metaphorical, suggesting the protagonists' growing sense of uncertainty and dread. The darkness is also literal, however, a physical indication that evil forces are drawing near. Darkness literally descends when the wings of the Nazgûl's steed darken the sun, creating terrifying shadows on the earth below. Gandalf claims that evil has the next move in a grand metaphysical game of chess. Evil acts as if it is a physical substance, spreading out over Gondor and finally enveloping Minas Tirith in darkness at the end of Chapter 1.

City of Weakened Strength: The city of Minas Tirith stands on the brink of Gondor and Mordor as a symbol of good and hope, particularly for the race of Men. The cities of Elves and hobbits we have seen thus far in *The Lord of the Rings* are hidden within forest glens or the countryside, offering peaceful reprieve for visitors. Minas Tirith, in contrast, boldly rises above ground, seven circles rising from the side of a mountain, symbolizing the bravery, resilience, and ambition of the race of Men. In ancient religions—as well as in the mystical variants of all the major monotheistic religions—the number seven was often considered the number of perfection, and the city's rise from the ground suggests that it is straining up toward heaven. Moreover, the city is white, in contrast to the darkness of Mordor, reminding us of the Christian association of the color white with purity of spirit. Despite these signs of strength, however, the city is weakening, becoming decayed and vacant. Minas Tirith, like Celeborn and Galadriel's realm of Lórien, is pure and noble but cannot summon an inward vitality to match its outward elegance. In this portrayal of Minas Tirith, Tolkien draws on the idea, frequently explored in ancient mythologies, of a kingdom suffering because its king is deteriorating. The popular story of the Fisher King, depicted variously in the Arthurian romances, tells of a wounded king so closely tied to the land that his kingdom is barren and unfruitful until the day the king's health improves. In similar fashion, Minas Tirith's empty houses and sad trees mirror the downtrodden Denethor and the empty throne.

Ambiguous Steward: Denethor, much like the city under his command, possesses a regal bearing and appearance that belie his inner decay, paranoia, and trepidation. Denethor is an unusually ambiguous character in this epic, which usually sets up simpler tensions between light and dark, good and evil, West and East, Gondor and Mordor, and so on. Denethor is neither wholly admirable nor wholly detestable. His demeanor remains dignified enough to speak elegantly to Pippin, yet he also appears curt and distracted, as though something churns beneath his outward calm. Furthermore, the mere fact that Denethor dislikes Gandalf, whom we trust unequivocally, warns us that all is not right with the Steward.

J.R.R. Tolkien

BOOK V, CHAPTER 2
The Passing of the Grey Company

The story returns to Aragorn, King **Théoden**, **Éomer**, and their small group of comrades. On the night that Gandalf and Pippin ride off on Shadowfax, Théoden prepares to rejoin his troops at Helm's Deep. Before they can depart, thirty horsemen, **Rangers of the North**, arrive. The Rangers are Aragorn's friends and kin. He welcomes the company enthusiastically but points out that he has not sent for assistance. The riders tell him that **Galadriel**, the Lady of Lothlórien, made the request.

The Rangers are bearing messages to Aragorn from Rivendell. **Lord Elrond's** brief note seems cryptic: "The days are short. If thou art in haste, remember the Paths of the Dead." Elrond's daughter, **Arwen**, wrote a note saying, "The days now are short. Either our hope cometh, or all hopes end." She also sent a tall, wrapped staff, apparently a standard for a banner.

King Théoden takes **Merry** as his squire. The king plans to gather all the help he can in Rohan and move on Minas Tirith. Aragorn follows Elrond's advice and decides to leave Théoden and ride with the Rangers through the terrifying Paths of the Dead. **Legolas** and **Gimli** volunteer to join him. Aragorn informs Legolas and Gimli that he used the *palantír*, the Seeing Stone that Saruman used to communicate with Sauron, to confront Sauron. Aragorn claims that he successfully bent the stone's power to his own will. In so doing, Aragorn has alerted Sauron that he is the heir to the throne of Gondor. Gimli guesses that Sauron will now release his forces sooner because he knows that Isildur's long-awaited heir exists. Aragorn believes a hasty attack will prevent Sauron from searching for Frodo or thoroughly preparing his troops for the invasion.

By riding the Paths of the Dead, Aragorn believes, he will fulfill a prophecy. In ancient days, mountain warriors betrayed Aragorn's ancestor, Isildur, by promising to help him fight Sauron and then failing to fight. Isildur cursed the men, making it impossible for them to enjoy peaceful deaths until they fight against Sauron and fulfill their oath. According to the verse, the Sleepless Dead, or Oathbreakers, must fulfill their oath by obeying Isildur's heir when he returns to call them from the Stone of Erech.

On their way to the Paths of the Dead, Aragorn's company stops to rest and eat with **Éowyn** and the people of Rohan whom she protects. Éowyn all but professes her love for Aragorn and begs to ride with him, but Aragorn will not allow her to leave her post. At the Dark Door leading to the cave under Haunted Mountain, Legolas calms the horses and convinces them to enter. Gimli says the Paths of the Dead frighten him, but he must pass through the cave if Legolas and the others do. After a long and terrifying time underground, the company emerges unscathed. Aragorn calls to the Dead and orders them to follow him. Legolas sees shapes of warriors, horses, and pale banners following in procession. All across the countryside, lights go out in homes and hamlets. Doors slam shut as folk hide or run from the ghostly caravan.

UNDERSTANDING AND INTERPRETING
Book V, Chapter 2

Aragorn's Christ-like Journey: Tolkien often insisted that *The Lord of the Rings* was not an allegory (a symbolic rendering of established tales and archetypes). Nevertheless, the mystical trip through the Paths of the Dead casts Aragorn as a Christ figure, and the events of Chapter 2 as a whole reflect the Passion of Jesus Christ as portrayed in the Gospels and popular medieval literature. Drawing from the Gospel of Nicodemus, an apocryphal writing, the medieval church said that after Christ's death on the cross, he descended into hell to redeem those believers who had already died and to preach to the lost souls held captive there. Then, Christ rose again on earth and eventually ascended to heaven. All this happened just as holy writings foretold it would. Following Christ's trajectory, Aragorn descends into the underground Paths of the Dead, where he speaks to the spirits of the Dead. Then he leads the Dead out into the waking world, where they affirm their devotion to him. All this happens just as messages and songs foretold it would. Like Christ, Aragorn knows of the prophecies and acts in part because he knows he must fulfill them. Aragorn repeatedly affirms that divine right and his own will make his feats possible, not his heroic skill.

The presence of these biblical parallels does not mean that Tolkien misrepresented his intentions for *The Lord of the Rings*. The comparisons to Christ are far from a systematic allegory, and more than one character fits the role of a Christ figure in the trilogy. As mythology for England, *The Lord of the Rings* promotes a specific moral and religious understanding, implying that the Christian principles of sacrifice, redemption, and forgiveness are central to the way the world worked even before the formal appearance of Christianity as a religion.

Éowyn as Feminist: Tolkien rarely deals with women in his fiction, but in this chapter, Éowyn gives an impressive speech espousing the cause of feminism. She protests, to Aragorn, the limitations she suffers because she is a woman. Éowyn accuses Aragorn of believing that a woman's place is in the home. She is tired of watching others achieve when she knows she could be as effective as any man. Éowyn feels like she is locked in a cage, where she must stay until old age has left her useless. Aragorn responds tersely that a battlefield is no place for a woman.

HOBBITS AND SQUIRES

Both Pippin and Merry become squires to the chief knights of Gondor and Rohan. King Théoden refers to Merry as his esquire, a title that marks the first step on the path to knighthood. To become a knight, a seven-year-old boy would move into the home of a knight and serve as his page for about five years. When he reached puberty, the boy could become an esquire (squire), serving the knight in the field and in the home while training in the mastery of weapons. Over the centuries, the term "esquire" has come to mean a member of the gentry or a person of standing just below a knight.

BOOK V, CHAPTER 3
The Muster of Rohan

King Théoden gathers his supporters so they can make the long trip to Minas Tirith and help defend Gondor against Sauron's warriors. His son and top officer, Éomer, suggests that he stay at home and rest, but Théoden refuses. He will not cower or retire like an old man. With his troops, the king proceeds toward Gondor. Warriors from across the land join him as he rides. Although they need to get to Gondor quickly, Théoden doubts that his 6,000 horsemen can reach Minas Tirith in less than a week.

The king visits Éowyn so her brother, Éomer, can say goodbye to her and the soldiers can pick up supplies. Éowyn speaks sadly of Aragorn's mission to the Paths of the Dead. Hope seems to have left her heart. The sun has stopped rising; a great Darkness has settled over the land. Théoden tells Merry that he must stay behind. He is too small to handle the kind of horse that the Riders of Rohan will use for the trip. Merry insists that he must join the battle, but Théoden says no. Later, in private, a soldier whom Merry does not know, **Dernhelm**, offers to share a steed with the hobbit, secretly carrying him into battle. Dernhelm is smaller than most of the Riders but is determined.

UNDERSTANDING AND INTERPRETING
Book V, Chapter 3

Judgment Day: The terrible gloom emanating from Mordor reminds us that the war brewing in Middle-earth is more than mere political wrangling. It is not just a dispute over stolen property (the Ring) or a battle over territorial claims (the realm of Gondor). Rather, the war is a vast, cosmic battle with universal implications. The darkening of the sky is strikingly reminiscent of the way the heavens transform in the Book of Revelation in the Bible. Along with the dark sky, other signs point to what Christian doctrine calls the Day of Judgment, among them the Dead returning to life from the Paths of the Dead. Christianity says that before Judgment Day, when the dead will be resurrected, a fierce battle and a darkened sky will foreshadow a cataclysmic change in the nature of existence. Tolkien makes overt references to the Book of Revelation to heighten the cosmic importance of the War of the Ring.

A LORD AND HIS THANES

Tolkien alludes to the Germanic code of *comitatus* when King Théoden assembles his warriors from around the Land of Rohan. Comitatus, which figures in the Anglo-Saxon epic *Beowulf*, was a Germanic honor system, established in the fifth and sixth centuries, that defined the relationship between a king or lord and his warriors (often called "thanes," a word that Théoden uses). Thanes swore allegiance to their lords and swore to fight for them, to the death if necessary, whenever called on to do so. The thanes also promised to avenge their lord in the event of his murder. For  their loyalty, the lord rewarded his thanes with protection, land, and, often, the spoils of war.

BOOK V, CHAPTER 4
The Siege of Gondor

For the time being, Denethor assigns Pippin the position of "esquire of the chamber." He will run errands for the Steward and might be required to sing occasionally. Near noon, Pippin hears a cry outside the walls of the city. Five **Black Riders**, Ringwraiths, are attacking a small group of horsemen racing toward the protection of the outer walls. It is Faramir and his border patrol. With Gandalf's assistance, they escape harm.

Faramir reports his meeting with Frodo and Sam, and Pippin notices Gandalf's hands trembling with fear when he learns where **Gollum** was leading the hobbits. Still, Gandalf points out the happy fact that Sauron did not know where the Ring was when Faramir last saw Frodo. Now, perhaps Sauron is too preoccupied with attacking Gondor to notice Frodo.

Denethor believes that the power of the Ring would serve him well, and he is angry that Faramir let the Ring slip through his hands. Denethor bitterly remarks that Boromir, his other son, would have brought him a "mighty gift"— the Ring. Gandalf points out that Boromir would have kept the "gift" for himself. The two argue.

The next morning, Denethor sends Faramir to protect the outlying ruins of Osgiliath, where Mordor's armies are likely to strike first. Faramir dutifully accepts the perilous—in fact, nearly suicidal—assignment from his father. Scouts report that Sauron has mustered an awesome force of Trolls, Orcs, humans, and a few "oliphaunts" (elephants) under the command of the **King of the Ringwraiths**. However, Sauron does have one military flaw. Most of his warriors are foot soldiers, and his cavalry is weak. If the Riders of Rohan can arrive in time, they have a good chance.

Faramir's men fight well at Osgiliath, but they are forced to flee for their lives in the face of overwhelming odds. Faramir, a superb commander, manages an orderly retreat and loses only a third of his men. As he nears the gates of Minas Tirith, he sustains a severe wound from one of the Ringwraith's poisoned arrows. Gandalf and the few horse soldiers from the city ride to his rescue. That night, Sauron's forces surround Minas Tirith and lob fireballs into the outermost circle of the city's walled defense. They also light on fire the heads of those soldiers of Gondor who died at Osgiliath and toss them over the wall.

Stricken with sudden bitterness and grief, Denethor locks himself in the Tower with Faramir, who is now delirious with fever from the arrow wound. Pippin looks on as Denethor weeps, cursing Gandalf. Meanwhile, Gandalf takes over the defense of Minas Tirith. The army of Mordor launches an attack on the outer wall of the city. Denethor tells the desperate messengers who arrive in his court that everyone in the city should give up and burn in the fires.

Denethor calls for his servants and orders them to carry Faramir to the Hall of Kings, where Gondor's leaders are laid to rest. Denethor places Faramir on a marble table and tells his servants to surround him and his son with wood and oil, and then, when he says so, to throw a lighted torch on the pyre. Pippin warns the servants not to obey Denethor's orders, as he has obviously gone mad. Pippin quickly seeks help and finds Beregond, who dares to break orders and leave his military post to try to help. Pippin goes in frantic search of Gandalf.

The armies of Mordor, led by the Lord of the Nazgûl, approach the gate of Minas Tirith with a great battering ram. On their third strike at the great iron door, the door shatters. The Black Captain enters the first ring of the city, and all flee in terror before him. Pippin watches as Gandalf stands alone before the Black Captain. Gandalf orders the Lord of the Nazgûl to return to Mordor, to nothingness, but the Ringwraith only laughs and says, "Old fool! This is my hour. Do you not know Death when you see it?" He throws back his hood to reveal a crown set on an invisible head. His sword bursts into flames, ready to strike. Suddenly, a cock crows, and a great clamor of horns sounds from the north. The Riders of Rohan have arrived.

UNDERSTANDING AND INTERPRETING
Book V, Chapter 4

A Father's Cruelty: For reasons that are not quite clear, Denethor openly prefers his son Boromir to his son Faramir. Boromir is strong and bold, and perhaps his father admires his assertiveness. Faramir, although more reflective than his brother, is a courageous and intelligent military leader. After Denethor learns of Boromir's death, Faramir asks if his father wishes he had died in Boromir's stead. Denethor's response is candid to the point of cruelty: "I wish that indeed," he says. Despite this bad treatment, Faramir remains loyal to his father and volunteers for the extraordinarily dangerous task of ambushing the enemy forces as they cross the Anduin River.

A Battle from Pippin's Perspective: As commentators have observed, one of Tolkien's great strengths is his ability to write convincingly about war. Tolkien not only fought and sustained injury in World War I, he wrote his novel in the years surrounding World War II—a war in which Germany bombed the heart of the English homeland. Tolkien writes about battle generally, without graphic detail, and only briefly from the viewpoint of those actually fighting, a technique that allows him to maintain perspective. "The Siege of Gondor" is narrated in the third person, as is the entire epic, but it is told from the perspective of the chapter's only hobbit, Pippin. Tolkien does not explain Pippin's thoughts and emotions, just what he sees and hears. We know only as much as what he overhears in Denethor's court, discusses with Gandalf, or observes as might a citizen of Minas Tirith. This restricted knowledge of events increases our sense of suspense and fear. We watch with Pippin as retreating men stumble frantically for the city gates and learn in horror that the enemy's firebombs are actually human heads set on fire.

Denethor's Madness: Recalling the legendary image of the Roman Emperor Nero fiddling as Rome burned, Denethor's actions in the midst of impending doom reveal much about his character. While a great war for the very freedom of Middle-earth rages outside Gondor's walls, Denethor turns his attention inward, locking himself in the Citadel and mourning his own demise. Denethor desires complete power or none at all. With the destruction of Minas Tirith at hand, he tries to exert control by taking the lives of himself and his son. Denethor coveted the Ring and wanted it to return glory to Gondor, and this lust for the Ring leads Denethor to madness, paranoia, and insecurity. As critic Rose Zimbardo notes, the Ring's wicked effect is to rob people of personal identity. Just as those who wear the Ring become invisible, those who focus their energies on obtaining the Ring lose their sense of self in the overwhelming desire to harness a great power and control others.

BOOK V, CHAPTER 5
The Ride of the Rohirrim

In this short chapter, the narration returns to the previous night and explains the arrival of the "Rohirrim" (another name for the Riders of Rohan) from Merry's point of view. Merry wonders if King Théoden has discovered that he disobeyed orders and hitched a ride with the king's cavalry. They are less than a day's ride from Minas Tirith. Merry hears a rumbling noise in the distance and wonders if it is the sound of the city under siege.

Woses, Wild Men of the Woods, have volunteered to serve as scouts for Théoden. They know of an old shortcut that the Riders of Rohan can take to the city. The cavalry mounts immediately and charges toward the capital. As dawn breaks, the city is within sight. Théoden looks sadly on the destruction of Minas Tirith. Suddenly, a great flash of light and a booming sound comes from the city.

Reinvigorated, Théoden commands his Riders into battle with a great cry "more clear than any there had ever heard a mortal man achieve." The band of skillful warriors drives into the heart of the enemy. They sing as they fight, for the "joy of battle" is upon them.

The shouting Rohirrim rout the Orcs and armies of Mordor. The Darkness dissipates with a fresh wind from the sea. At the arrival of the Rohirrim, the Black Captain senses the Darkness fading and the tide of battle turning. He vanishes from the city gate to enter the fray. The chieftain of the Southrons, allies of Mordor, leads his men against Théoden. Though outnumbered, Théoden and Éomer charge through the enemy scimitars handily, striking down the Southrons' chieftain.

UNDERSTANDING AND INTERPRETING
Book V, Chapter 5

Dumpy, Brutish, But Helpful: The Woses are reminiscent of the Ents, who appeared in *The Two Towers*. Both tribes are closely associated with nature, have little contact with the civilized world, but come to the aid of the Fellowship as a way of countering the Orcs. As with the Ents, the Woses cannot remain neutral in the war. Taking refuge in the forest offers no escape, as even the forest-dwellers have been forced into the fray, compelled to offer their support to one side or the other. There is nothing heroic about the Woses, who are dumpy and brutish in appearance and show none of the grace or nobility of other races the Fellowship has encountered thus far. The Woses make no gracious offer to aid the Fellowship further when their job is done; they vanish after the group has found its way. The commonness of the Woses stresses the value of the aid they provide. They are not typical heroes in the knightly style, but ordinary folk whose participation shows how great the scope of the War of the Ring has become.

A Sudden Leap to Immortality: The rejuvenation of Théoden in the midst of battle provides the morale boost the warriors have needed. Théoden's resurgence illustrates the importance of character in a leadership position and suggests the tremendous potential of the mind when jolted by the right motives. The king gazes gloomily at the destruction of Minas Tirith until the blast from the city jolts him, prompting him to utter a cry of more clarity than seems mortally possible. It is as if Théoden himself is becoming immortal, at least in the sense that the moment of his battle cry will endure in the memory of the Rohirrim. No doubt, he is stirred to this superhuman intensity by his sentimental attachment to Minas Tirith. Tolkien was fascinated by the hidden psychological impulses that prompt humans to superhuman deeds and that bring heroism within the grasp of everyone who can experience intense emotions.

BOOK V, CHAPTER 6

The Battle of the Pelennor Fields

A fierce battle takes place on the Pelennor fields that surround Minas Tirith. A massive black beast swoops down on Théoden, hitting his horse with a poisoned dart. The steed rears up and the king falls beneath his horse and is crushed. The Lord of the Nazgûl looms above on the back of his flying beast. Terrified, Théoden's guards flee in panic—all but Dernhelm and Merry. Merry repeats to himself that he must serve his knight, but his body shakes from fear, and he cannot open his eyes. Thrown from his horse but unharmed, Dernhelm challenges the Black Captain, laughing in his face when he boasts of his power. Merry hears Dernhelm speak and recognizes the warrior's voice. Dernhelm is really Éowyn, the Lady of Rohan, in disguise, her face "the face of one that goes seeking death, having nothing to hope."

Éowyn attacks the mounted Ringwraith and slices open the throat of his giant beast. The Ringwraith strikes Éowyn with his mace, shattering her shield, breaking her arm, and knocking her to her knees. As the Ringwraith moves in for the kill, Merry, recovering his senses, stabs him, shearing his mantle and passing the blade into the sinew behind his knee. Éowyn quickly takes advantage of the Ringwraith's surprise and thrusts her sword between the Ringwraith's crown and mantle, destroying him. A shrill wail is heard, and his armor is suddenly empty. King Ringwraith is never again seen in Middle-earth. Despite their triumph, both Éowyn and Théoden appear to be dying, and Merry is seriously wounded.

Noristhebattlewon.The **Haradrim** warriors alone outnumber the Riders of Rohan, and they rally around their oliphaunts, which carry huge battle towers. The dying King Théoden appoints Éomer his heir. Éomer, seeing Éowyn's fallen body, leads the Rohirrim in a furious attack. The Men of Minas Tirith, led by Imrahil, Prince of Dol Amroth,

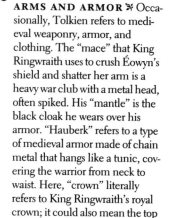

ARMS AND ARMOR ❧ Occasionally, Tolkien refers to medieval weaponry, armor, and clothing. The "mace" that King Ringwraith uses to crush Éowyn's shield and shatter her arm is a heavy war club with a metal head, often spiked. His "mantle" is the black cloak he wears over his armor. "Hauberk" refers to a type of medieval armor made of chain metal that hangs like a tunic, covering the warrior from neck to waist. Here, "crown" literally refers to King Ringwraith's royal crown; it could also mean the top of his head or any armor covering the head.

emerge from the city and drive the enemy from the gate. Théoden's body is taken to the city, along with Éowyn. Imrahil alerts the rescuers that Éowyn is not dead.

The allies of Mordor reassemble as new soldiers of Sauron arrive from Osgiliath. The Men of Rohan and Gondor dwindle. As the tide turns against Gondor, a fleet of black enemy ships appears on the Anduin River. Éomer fears he is defeated but continues to fight bravely, laughing in hope and despair. All at once, the foremost ship raises a banner emblazoned with the White Tree of Gondor and the crown and stars that stand for Gondor. Arwen of Rivendell created this flag of jewels and *mithril* and sent it to her champion, Aragorn, who has arrived with a stunning force. At the lead are Legolas and Gimli.

Sauron's forces are caught between Aragorn's hammer and the anvil of Éomer. They do not stand a chance. Those who are not slaughtered drown as they try to escape across the Anduin River, which runs red.

UNDERSTANDING AND INTERPRETING
Book V, Chapter 6

Boasting and Bragging: Throughout *The Lord of the Rings*, Tolkien shows his heroes engaging in the Anglo-Saxon epic tradition of boasting before battle. We see examples of such boasting throughout *Beowulf*: Unferth at the mead hall, Beowulf with Breca, Beowulf and Grendel. The boasts resemble what today we might expect to hear before a professional wrestling exhibition, a heavyweight boxing match, or during an intercoastal rap feud. Typically, each side threatens the other with great harm while exaggerating its own strengths. In this chapter, Éowyn and the King of the Ringwraiths exchange such boasts. King Ringwraith coldly bellows that Éowyn must get out of the way, because his monstrous beast wants to devour King Théoden. If she persists in defying him, says the Ringwraith, Éowyn will find herself in "the houses of lamentation, beyond all darkness, where thy flesh shall be devoured, and thy shriveled mind be left naked to the Lidless Eye." No "living man" can stand up to the mighty Ringwraith. Éowyn laughs, pointing out that she is not a man, and she plans to kill the Ringwraith. With her golden hair cascading down and her intent fixed, Éowyn renders King Ringwraith speechless.

A Turning Point: This chapter marks a turning point in *The Lord of the Rings*. The conflict established in *The Fellowship of the Ring* remains unresolved, since the Ring still exists, but a great accumulated tension now finds some resolution. Gondor's ultimate salvation arrives in a manner that upsets the black-against-white, east-against-west conflict. Aragorn's arrival suggests that he has the ability to transcend such categories. Aragorn emerges from the south, and he comes riding in Mordor's own dark ships, complicating the distinction between the forces of good and evil. Aragorn's unusual entrance via the Paths of the Dead suggests that his claim to the throne extends over both east and west, the living and the dead. Furthermore, Aragorn's sword, Andúril—reforged after centuries of remaining broken—symbolizes the reunification of the lands and peoples Sauron has divided.

Unconventional but True Heroes: Tolkien was suspicious of the archetype of courage displayed by the heroes of the Norse sagas and mythologies he studied. Tolkien commented that heroic courage was a "potent but terrifying solution." A classic hero acts with blind or impulsive courage, which may be effective but is not necessarily admirable. Tolkien prefers to emphasize the heroism of those whose courageous deeds arise from their ideals and sense of moral obligation, not from their natural fighting instincts. To this end, he casts two unlikely candidates, Éowyn and Merry, as heroes. Both characters represent somewhat marginalized segments of the population of Middle-earth—hobbits and women. The conspicuous scarcity of women in *The Lord of the Rings* highlights the irony of Éowyn's sacrifice for Théoden. It is Éowyn who manages to slay the terrifying Lord of the Nazgûl, whom no man has been able to defeat. To win the opportunity to act, Éowyn has had to show cunning, care, and dedication to the cause of Rohan. Merry's heroism emerges from a sense of moral obligation and duty, not stealth or cunning. When thrown from his horse before the Nazgûl, Merry cries and whimpers, longing to be courageous but unable to open his eyes. When Merry sees the Nazgûl strike Éowyn, he responds out of pity, wonder, and the "slow-kindled courage of his race." Merry's courage represents Tolkien's ideal of heroism—undemonstrative, reflective, and unexpected. As T.A. Shippey notes, Tolkien's ideal—as represented in the novel's main protagonists, Sam and Frodo—is hobbit heroism, not human heroism.

BOOK V, CHAPTER 7
The Pyre of Denethor

The narration shifts back to the beginning of the Battle of the Pelennor Fields and to Pippin's perspective. Gandalf sits atop Shadowfax after the King of the Ringwraiths has withdrawn. The horns of the Riders of Rohan have just sounded in the distance. Pippin runs up to Gandalf and begs him to help save

Faramir, who will be burned alive by his father if someone does not intervene. Gandalf wants to pursue the Dark Rider, but he feels he must go with Pippin.

At the mausoleum, Beregond is fighting to stave off Denethor's guardsmen, who have been ordered to kill him. Beregond has already killed two of them. Denethor throws open the door, drawing his sword, but Gandalf lifts his hand and the sword flies from Denethor's grip. The wizard decries Denethor's madness, and Denethor replies that Faramir has already burned. Rushing past, Gandalf finds Faramir still alive on the funeral pyre. Amid Denethor's protests and tears, Gandalf lifts Faramir and carries him away with a strength that surprises Pippin. Denethor, the wizard says, does not have the authority to order Faramir's death or his own.

Denethor laughs. Standing proudly, he produces from his cloak a *palantír* similar to the Stone of Orthanc. He warns that the west is doomed. He has foreseen the black ships of the Enemy approaching. The Steward condemns Gandalf for bringing a young upstart Ranger to replace him as ruler. Denethor wants things to remain as are in Minas Tirith. He springs for Faramir, but Beregond stops him. Grabbing a torch from a servant, Denethor lights the funeral pyre and throws himself into the raging fire, clutching the *palantír*.

Gandalf and Beregond carry Faramir to the Houses of Healing. As they exit, the House of Stewards collapses in flames, and Denethor's servants run out.

Soon after, they hear a great cry from the battlefield. It is the sound of Éowyn and Merry defeating the Lord of the Nazgûl. A sense of hope returns as the sun breaks through the Darkness. Gandalf discusses Denethor's *palantír* with Pippin and Beregond. Gandalf says he had always guessed the Steward possessed one of the seven seeing-stones. The wizard surmises that Denethor, in his growing distress, began to use the stone, and through it he fell prey to the lies of Sauron.

UNDERSTANDING AND INTERPRETING
Book V, Chapter 7

Leaders and Foils: The pall of Lord Denethor's suicide looms over these chapters, despite the arrival of Aragorn and the victory over the Black Captain. Tolkien places Denethor in sharp contrast to each of the west's other three prominent leaders—Théoden, Gandalf, and Aragorn. Chapters 6 and 7 take place at the same time, though from different perspectives. Gandalf and Beregond hear the cries of the Black Captain just as the House of Stewards crumbles in flames; Pippin watches Denethor place himself on the burning pyre just as Théoden prepares to speak his final words to Merry. The parallels between the two rulers show them to be foils, counterpoints to each other. Théoden dies sprinting ahead of his men into battle, drawing the attention of the Lord of the Nazgûl and allowing Éowyn to strike down the Black Captain. Denethor, in contrast, removes himself from his people, withdrawing into isolation and madness. Théoden displays the sort of bravery necessary to lead and to improve the welfare of his kingdom, whereas Denethor shows only passivity and self-involvement.

Wizard and King: Just before Denethor's suicide, he and Gandalf engage in a confrontation that highlights the contrast between them. Pippin has been unable to understand the tension between Gandalf and Denethor, even questioning Gandalf's role, wondering what purpose or good Gandalf's wizardry serves in the broader scheme of Middle-earth. The wizard's role is clarified in his final standoff with Denethor. Gandalf's virtue lies not so much in his mystical powers or even his wisdom, but in his ability to see possibilities for change in each individual and to extend charity. Gandalf offered Théoden forgiveness and redemption for his former misdeeds, and now he offers counsel and a second chance to Denethor. Before Denethor commits suicide, Gandalf tells him, "Come! We are needed. There is much that you can yet do." While Denethor remains strong enough to resist Sauron's will, however, he has fallen victim to Sauron's lies. Denethor gains only knowledge, not wisdom, from the *palantír*. The sphere shows the Steward images such as the black ships approaching, but it provides no explanation for these images. Denethor misinterprets the knowledge the *palantír* gives him, darkly assuming that the ships of the Enemy foretell the doom of Minas Tirith, when in reality they herald its salvation. Denethor cannot distinguish between knowledge and real wisdom, a distinction that Gandalf can make.

BOOK V, CHAPTER 8
The Houses of Healing

King Théoden's men gently cover the body of their king with a cloth of gold. Faramir, Éowyn, and Merry have been carried to the Houses of Healing. Faramir and Éowyn appear to be near death. Merry received some sort of evil poison when he struck King Ringwraith. Faramir suffers from a fever that will not abate. Although the healers of Gondor are wise and skilled, certain illnesses from Mordor baffle them. A recent flu-like malady has confounded even the wisest healer. They call this sickness "the Black Shadow."

The eldest of the old wives serving the wounded recalls a maxim of ancient lore: "The hands of the king are the hands of a healer, and so shall the rightful king be known." Gandalf says that the maxim is literally true, and they must call for Aragorn. When the old wives request Aragorn's aid, he gladly goes to the Houses of Healing, dressed in Ranger garb. Aragorn quickly assesses the situation and begins to chant Faramir's name, making each repetition fainter until those watching can only see his lips move slightly. When he finishes, Aragorn looks up and asks for *athelas*, a rare healing herb. The old wives know the plant as "kingsfoil," and they collect this rare herb from a nearby forest.

Aragorn takes two leaves, breathes on them, and crushes them in his palms. Immediately, the air in the room tingles with a sparkling joy. Aragorn then casts the crushed leaves into bowls of steaming water. The fragrance reminds observers of "dewy mornings of unshadowed sun" in a land that exists only in fleeting memories. Faramir stirs and opens his eyes. He pledges his allegiance to Aragorn, calling him his king.

Aragorn examines Éowyn and says that the chief threat to her health comes from the arm that held the sword that stabbed the Ringwraith. His evil was so strong that it infected Éowyn. Furthermore, Wormtongue's poisonous words have affected Éowyn, and she suffers from a longing of the heart that cannot be requited. Aragorn knows that *he* is the object of Éowyn's love. He applies two more leaves of kingsfoil and assures everyone that he can revive Éowyn, but she must wake to hope, not despair, or she is lost. He asks her brother, Éomer, to call her to consciousness, which he does successfully. She must rest for ten days, and she must be encouraged to desire life.

Merry's case is the least severe. He, too, has suffered an evil infliction from stabbing the Ringwraith, but his spirit is strong. Aragorn calls Merry back to life and uses the last two leaves of kingsfoil to revive him. Merry immediately announces that he is hungry and wants some pipe-weed. All through the night, Aragorn heals the wounded of the city. News spreads quickly that the king has returned. Aragorn has shown himself to be a king and a healer. He receives the royal name Elessar, which means Elfstone. As prophecies foretold, "Elfstone" refers to the precious emerald brooch that Aragorn wears, commemorating his love for Arwen. Aragorn also receives the name Envinyatar, which means the Renewer. As a healer, Aragorn has renewed the strength and hope of the people.

UNDERSTANDING AND INTERPRETING
Book V, Chapter 8

A King Unmasked: Finally, in Chapter 8, Aragorn emerges as the redeemer of Minas Tirith. Under Denethor, the city suffered decay analogous to the debilitated condition of its ruler. Aragorn, in contrast, brings life to the city. Not only does he defeat the armies of Mordor, he heals the wounded and the dying with his touch and presence. Once again, Aragorn fulfills the role of a Christ figure. Aragorn's selflessness stands out even more clearly against the selfishness of Denethor, who, rather than give life to others, takes his own life and attempts to take the life of his son. Aragorn's claim to the throne is finally recognized when Faramir wakes from his fever and immediately pronounces Aragorn king.

Lovesickness Strikes: In the matter of Éowyn's malady, Tolkien reverses standard literary stereotypes. Aragorn correctly diagnoses Éowyn's condition: in addition to the broken arm and poison that she received from the Ringwraith, she is lovesick. Lovesickness was an important element of the concept of courtly love developed in the late Middle Ages. It was also a factor in the chivalric code discussed in many works of literature, including *Sir Gawain and the Green Knight* (anonymous, c. 1375), one of Tolkien's favorite works. In traditional depictions of courtly love, a male knight falls hopelessly in love with a lady of the court who is married or betrothed, and his love usually goes unrequited. The knight devotes himself to serving his lady, and as she continually refuses him, he becomes lovesick, a condition that resembles a severe case of the flu. He gets a fever, feels queasy, loses his appetite, has difficulty sleeping or concentrating, and generally acts as if he wants to die. Here, Tolkien reverses the literary trope by making a lady sick with love. Éowyn loves Aragorn so deeply that she cannot see the point of life without him, despite the fact that Aragorn has offered her no encouragement and usually acts as if he is unaware of her existence. Healing Éowyn's broken arm is easy, and curing her from the Ringwraith's poison is within Aragorn's ability. But curing her lovesickness is another matter.

CHIVALRY As a medieval scholar, Tolkien was expert in chivalry and courtly behavior, such as the kind seen in the chivalric romance *Sir Gawain and the Green Knight* (anonymous, c. 1375). Tolkien refers to chivalry throughout *The Lord of the Rings*. Chivalry came about, indirectly, as a result of Muslims and Vikings who invaded Europe between the years 700 and 1000. It became necessary to train cavalry to fight these invaders, and training for cavalry led to development of rules of deportment for knights and the squires who served them. These rules became known as the chivalric code.

CHESS IS WAR

The game of chess evolved from *chaturanga*, which originated in India during the sixth century A.D. *Chaturanga* is a Sanskrit word that refers to the four divisions of an Indian army: cavalry, infantry, chariots, and elephants. From its inception, chess was considered a game of war in which the winner was the player who directed his forces most skillfully. Throughout the Middle Ages, rulers from Persia to China and Western Europe worked out military strategies with chess in mind. Tolkien alludes to that practice in *The Return of the King*, in which military leaders pit foot soldiers against cavalry, catapults against archers, and elephant forces against a highly mobile navy in an attempt to destroy or capture the opponent's king.

BOOK V, CHAPTER 9
The Last Debate

The morning after the great battle, Legolas and Gimli leave their encampment and walk into the city of Minas Tirith to speak with Merry and Pippin. Along the way, the residents stand in awe at the sight of Legolas, who is "fair of face beyond the measure of Men." Gimli is proud of his Elf friend. The hobbits are eager to hear of their friends' adventures. Legolas says he will tell the tale and make it short. He speaks of the haunted road under the mountains and how the Dead followed them out, obeying Aragorn's every command. They rode ninety-three leagues to a point on the Anduin River, where they captured Sauron's fleet of fifty ships. The dead swarmed over the ships, causing Sauron's terrified men to leap overboard. Along the way, Sauron's forces tried to intercept Aragorn but soon fled before the fearsome might of the Dead.

After the victory at the river, Aragorn dismissed the Dead and assured them that their debt was paid. He had no further need of them, because warriors, townsmen, ranchers, and farmers from across the area had been following Aragorn's progress and wanted to join this great leader who could master even the Dead. Thousands of fresh troops embarked with Aragorn and sailed or rowed to Minas Tirith, where they contributed to the victory.

As Legolas tells his story, with only a few interruptions from Gimli, Aragorn meets with the military captains of Gondor and Rohan near the spot where Théoden fell. The question is what to do next. Gandalf points out that the Free People of Middle-earth have only defeated Sauron's first wave. More waves will follow. Gondor and Rohan cannot win a military victory. Their only hope is to distract Sauron until Frodo can destroy the Ring. To this end, the captains agree to attack and to march toward Mordor in two days' time. Their attacking army may number no more than 6,000, but this bold move will force Sauron to believe that Aragorn has the Ring and plans to use it against Mordor. Meanwhile, the hopes of all good folk in Middle-earth lie with Frodo and Sam.

UNDERSTANDING AND INTERPRETING
Book V, Chapter 9

A Dark Tale Told: Legolas's tale is an interesting departure from Tolkien's typical habit of depicting events firsthand, as they unfold. Hearing a story second-hand reminds us of the importance of oral tradition in the ancient cultures Tolkien studied and of the author's attempt to recreate this tradition in Middle-earth. We sense that one day, many generations later, Legolas's tale will become

LEECHING AND SWEATING

The old wives of Gondor are known for their *leechcraft*, a medieval medical treatment used by healers, physicians, and barbers. Leeches (bloodsucking annelids or worms) supposedly drew bad blood or evil "humours" out of the body. Bloodletting was generally ineffective and often did more harm than good, resulting in dehydration and weakness. Other medieval medical treatments were not much better. Sweating caused excessive perspiration but did sometimes help break a fever. Purging through vomiting was only helpful in certain cases of poisoning. Treatment for the plague consisted of burning incense, because the horrid smell of the dead or dying was thought to carry the disease. Sterilization of instruments was unknown, so surgery usually resulted in infection.

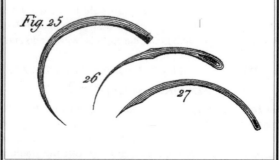

Fig. 25

26

27

a folktale or a myth, part of the cultural legacy of Elves or Men. In an interesting twist, Gimli refuses to talk about what happened on the Paths of the Dead. Gimli says he wishes to keep the memories of his journey on the Paths of the Dead in darkness forever and never bring them to the light of day. Hearing Legolas narrate the tale that Gimli refuses to speak reminds us of the fragility of the oral tradition—a story may be lost forever if it is not retold.

The Weakness of Evil: In these chapters, we discover that the forces of the Enemy, just like the forces of Gondor, experience fear. The Dead overwhelmed the Enemy not with military maneuvers or well-aimed arrows, but with psychological manipulation. The mere appearance of the Dead caused the Enemy to flee. Legolas expresses amazement that the troops of the Dark Lord were overcome by terror. The fact that even the soldiers of Mordor are scared reminds us that the battle between good and evil in *The Lord of the Rings,* however cosmic in scope, is still a clash between imperfect creatures with their own limitations. Similarly, Gandalf highlights Sauron's limitations by pointing out that Sauron probably mistakenly believes that Aragorn has control of the Ring and will use it to attack Mordor for his own glory. Sauron's blindness to the possibility of selflessness is the only failing that the forces of good can exploit to overthrow him.

BOOK V, CHAPTER 10
The Black Gate Opens

Two days later, Aragorn and Gandalf assemble an army and begin a march of several days toward the Black Gate where Sauron reigns in his Dark Tower of Barad-dûr. Merry has not recovered sufficiently to join them, but Pippin proudly represents the Shire. Gandalf and Aragorn ride toward the Black Gate with a small envoy, including Gimli, Legolas, Pippin, Éomer, Imrahil, and Elrond's sons—representatives of each of the races of Middle-earth that oppose Sauron. The envoy calls for Sauron to emerge and submit to the justice of Gondor. After a long period of silence, the Lieutenant of the Dark Tower emerges with an embassy of black-clad soldiers. The Lieutenant has served the Evil One so faithfully that he cannot remember his own name. He calls himself the **Mouth of Sauron**.

The Lieutenant mockingly presents Aragorn and Gandalf with "trophies": Sam's sword and Frodo's *mithril* breastplate. Seeing the sword and breastplate, Pippin cries out in grief. Tactically, this is unwise because the Lieutenant can confirm that these "trophies" do in fact belong to one of Sauron's enemies—

THE BLACK SHADOW

The first local occurrence of the Black
Shadow, a disease that even Gondor's
wisest healers cannot cure, is an allusion to
the medieval "Black Death," a pandemic
of plagues (bubonic, pneumonic, and
septicemic) that killed a third of Europe's
population over the course of just two years
(A.D. 1348–1350). Symptoms included
vomiting, fever, infection of the lungs or
blood, and coma. The plague spread from
the Crimea to Mediterranean ports and
then across Europe, carried by flea-infested
rats. England was hit especially hard, losing
more than half its citizenry. Outbreaks
continued, less severely, for more than
400 years.

someone Pippin recognizes. Gandalf warns Pippin to be silent. Sauron has a deal to offer. Aragorn and Gandalf can choose to proceed with their hostility, in which case Sauron will torture Frodo and Sam "as long and slow as our arts in the Great Tower can contrive," perhaps for years. He will release the hobbits only when they are broken and destroyed, so that Aragorn and Gandalf can see what their choice has wrought. Alternately, they can choose to withdraw beyond the Anduin River and disarm forever. They must rebuild Isengard to its former condition. The Lieutenant will reside there and rule the entire west.

Gandalf realizes that if Sauron had the Ring, there would be no need for negotiation. He would control everything immediately. Since Sauron is trying to make a deal, Frodo and Sam must be free and might yet destroy the Ring. Gandalf and Aragorn keep the sword and *mithril* breastplate but reject the Lieutenant's terms.

The Lieutenant feels sudden terror at Gandalf's rebuke. He turns and retreats to the Black Gate. As he does, the army of Mordor—ten times larger than that of Gondor—pours out of the Gate. Drums roll, fires blaze, and the sun turns red. A great company of brutal hill-Trolls charges into Pippin's company. One of the Trolls pounces on Beregond, but Pippin stabs the Troll with his sword. The Troll topples forward and crushes the startled Pippin, who begins to lose consciousness. He bids farewell to the world. Just as everything turns dark, Pippin hears a great clamor of voices shouting, "The Eagles are coming!" Pippin thinks he must be confusing his story with Bilbo's.

UNDERSTANDING AND INTERPRETING
Book V, Chapter 10

A Mood of Irony: Irony pervades the closing chapters of Book V. Legolas and Gimli note the irony that Aragorn defeated Mordor's forces with spirits of the Dead who themselves once worshipped Sauron. In a strategic sense, the march to Mordor is ironic because Sauron thinks he is cunningly luring Aragorn's forces in, when actually Aragorn's forces approach Mordor of their own accord to distract Sauron. The deepest irony lies in the confrontation with the Lieutenant before the Black Gate. We know that the Lieutenant's bold words are only a show. In the final moments of *The Two Towers,* Sam cast aside his sword in favor of Frodo's, and the Orcs did not kill Frodo, but did take off his *mithril* coat. Armed with his lies, the Lieutenant does not expect to be so coldly dismissed by a military force only one-tenth the size of his own.

The Strength of Words: As usual, Gandalf uses words to vanquish the Lieutenant, not force. In answer to the Balrog in the Mines of Moria and the Lord of the Nazgûl at the gates of Minas Tirith, Gandalf abandoned his formidable magic powers in favor of the power of words, confronting his enemies with speech and commanding them to turn from their violent intentions, and here, he commands the Lieutenant with words, yelling, "Begone!"

BOOK VI, CHAPTER 1
The Tower of Cirith Ungol

The story returns to Frodo and Sam. Orcs have captured Frodo and taken him to their stronghold, the Tower of Cirith Ungol, which stands near **Shelob**'s Lair. Sam, on the ground below, searches desperately for an open entrance. He feels he must rescue Frodo or die in the attempt. Sam is tempted to use the Ring. He puts it on for a moment and begins to imagine himself as Samwise the Strong. Remembering his love for Frodo, he shakes off such thoughts and removes the Ring.

Pressing on with a shrug, Sam halts helplessly before the gate, as if held by a web. He is under the influence of the Two Watchers who forbid all entrance to Cirith Ungol. Sam unconsciously draws the phial of Galadriel from his breast and extends it forward. Its great light pierces the gloom, and Sam passes quickly through the gate. The Watchers let out a shrill cry.

Inside, Sam notices the bodies of dead Orcs as he reaches a narrow staircase. The dark figure of an Orc moves down the stairs, sees Sam, and halts, perceiving Sam as a great shadow brandishing an Elven blade that shines brightly in the darkness. The terrified Orc turns and runs up into the tower. Sam follows stealthily, jovially terming himself the "Elf-warrior." Upstairs, Sam can hear the Orc, Snaga, speak to another Orc, Shagrat. They are the only two Orcs left in the tower. Shagrat orders Snaga to descend, but Snaga will not go back downstairs. Snaga runs into an unknown chamber of the tower, leaving the furious Shagrat alone. Sam reveals himself to Shagrat and moves to attack, but the Orc, overwhelmed by the power of the Ring, runs around Sam and out the door.

Sam looks desperately for Frodo but cannot find him. He begins to sing to himself. His song draws a snarl from Snaga, who mistakes Sam's voice for Frodo's. Sam follows the sound of the snarl and finds the Orc climbing a ladder through a hidden door in the ceiling. Sam climbs after Snaga and attacks him in the secret chamber. In a panic, Snaga charges Sam, trips over him, and falls through the hidden door to the hard floor below.

Frodo lies naked on a heap of rags in the middle of the room. He is surprised to see Sam and utterly elated to find that Sam has saved the Ring. Suddenly, Frodo demands that Sam hand over the Ring, calling Sam a thief. He grabs the Ring. Then, as if emerging from a trance, Frodo apologizes to Sam, whom he saw for a moment as a greedy Orc. Frodo and Sam outfit themselves in Orc gear and climb down the ladder. With the phial of Galadriel, the two hobbits move past the Watchers and out into Mordor. Suddenly, the terrifying cry of a Black Rider rends the sky above them.

UNDERSTANDING AND INTERPRETING
Book VI, Chapter 1

Poisoning an Old Friendship: The physical presence of the Ring dominates the opening of Book VI. The Ring inflicts trouble upon the only relationship that has remained pure throughout the novel thus far: the devoted friendship of Frodo and Sam. We have never seen discord mar the camaraderie of these two hobbits on their long journey through Middle-earth. But with Sam's sudden and unexpected possession of the Ring, the relationship falls victim to jealousy and wrongful accusations. When Frodo sees Sam with the Ring and demands it back, calling his loving friend a thief, we witness the power of the Ring to distort reality and make people feel an illusory sense of power. Sam toys with some mild delusions of grandeur when he wears the Ring, but these are more comic and endearing than evil, leading us to feel more strongly the unfairness of Frodo's accusations. The injury is even greater because it comes at a moment of reunion after extreme bravery on Sam's part. Though Frodo apologizes soon afterward and Sam accepts the apology, the memory of Frodo's unkind words lingers in our minds as further proof of the Ring's destructive power.

The True Hero: Sam's reaction to the Ring's seductive power reminds us why he emerges at the end of *The Lord of the Rings* as the unexpected hero of the novel. Sam wears the Ring and, to some degree, experiences the same delusions of grandeur and fame that all its wearers feel. He fantasizes about achieving fame as "Samwise the Strong," a fantasy that shows his susceptibility to the vanity that the Ring inspires. But what allows Sam to remove the Ring is his ability to think of Frodo, whom he loves. Love for others is precisely what the Ring tries to destroy, setting all its wearers on courses of greed in which bonds of loyalty and love no longer matter. Sam does not succumb to the Ring's malevolence. His intense devotion to his friends is unmatched even by Frodo, who earlier took off the Ring through the strength of his own will, not through the strength of his love for another. The irony of Sam's thoughts—that he, an ordinary gardener hobbit, is too common to wear the Ring—is that he is actually the Ring's safest keeper and perhaps the single most noble character in the epic.

BOOK VI, CHAPTER 2
The Land of Shadow

Frodo and Sam scurry to cover and elude the Ringwraith. Although they can see the Mountain of Fire (sometimes called "Mount Doom" or "Orodruin") in the distance, it is still more than fifty miles away. Sam thinks of Galadriel and half-jokingly tells Frodo that he would like to ask the Lady of Lothlórien for two more gifts: clean water and plain daylight. To his amazement, the gloom disappears with the next day's dawn. Before long, the two discover cool water trickling nearby. That night, Sam notices a white star twinkling high over the mountains. Its beauty nearly breaks his heart. For a moment, he sees the evil of Mordor as only a small and transient blot on the history of Middle-earth.

Frodo and Sam continue moving northward. They overhear two Orcs quarreling and talking about a rumor that a great Elf in bright armor is on the loose. They also mention a creature they call "that gobbler," which Frodo concludes must be Gollum. Sam soon catches a glimpse of Gollum flitting among some rocks, stalking them. A company of Orcs suddenly appears. Apparently, Sauron has ordered his southern guard to join him at the Black Gate. Since the hobbits are still wearing Orc clothing, the company captain assumes they are small Orcs and orders them to fall into line. Frodo and Sam march along with the Orcs until another company of Orcs meets them at a crossroads. Orcs being Orcs, the two companies dispute the right of way. A fight breaks out, and in the melee, the hobbits crawl off without notice.

UNDERSTANDING AND INTERPRETING
Book VI, Chapter 2

Strength in Weakness: Sam and Frodo mingle with the Orcs and survive, a development that reminds us of the utility of the hobbits' nondescript appearance and general modesty and ordinariness. A more noble and knightly presence, like that of Aragorn or Théoden, would have stood out from the Orc contingent and immediately been attacked. But because Frodo and Sam are not much to look at, they pass unnoticed even when swept along in the midst of the marching Orc army. Moreover, their proximity to the Orcs allows them to over-hear the rumor that a great Elf in bright armor is on the loose. The hobbits are thus allowed to see what knights like Aragorn cannot: the nervous and anxious side of the enemy. Elrond's words from the earliest parts of the novel, in Book II, ring true. The nature of the Ring-quest is such that the weak and the small are just as likely to succeed as the strong.

BOOK VI, CHAPTER 3
Mount Doom

The next morning, Sam gains new strength and a grim sense of responsibility. He wakes Frodo and pushes him on toward Orodruin. The land before them is cold and dead, dotted by countless craters and hollows. The hobbits crawl east-ward from hiding place to hiding place. After a few miles, Frodo is nearly spent, his mind and body tormented by the terrible weight of the Ring. He refuses to give the Ring to Sam. Frodo says he is losing all memory, all sensation except for conflicting obsessions to destroy or serve the Ring.

At last, Frodo and Sam reach the base of Mount Doom. The Ring so burdens Frodo that Sam must carry him. When they are more than halfway up the mountain, the hobbits fall to the ground exhausted. Then they both hear a voice inside their heads calling, "Now, now, or it will be too late!" Sam staggers on, carrying Frodo on his back. Suddenly, someone strikes them from behind. It is Gollum, more intent than ever on stealing the Ring. He struggles viciously with the hobbits until Frodo commands him to leave and Gollum falls to his knees. Sam considers killing the creature, but Gollum looks so pathetic that he cannot. He turns his back on Gollum and follows Frodo.

At the edge of the volcano, Frodo yells that he will not go through with this deed—the Ring is his! He slips it on his finger and disappears. Just then, Gollum attacks again, crashing into Sam from behind and driving Sam's head against a stone. Gollum scurries to where he last saw Frodo and begins wrestling with his unseen foe. In seconds, the world turns to chaos. Sauron finally realizes that Frodo has the Ring and sends his remaining Ringwraiths to attack by air. As Sam struggles to his feet, he sees Ringwraiths rapidly approaching and Gollum standing on the edge of the volcano's abyss, madly struggling with the invisible Frodo. Gollum pulls his hands up to his mouth and his white fangs gleam as he chomps on what appears to be pure air. Frodo screams and at once becomes visible, falling to his knees at the chasm's edge.

Gollum is ecstatic. He holds up Frodo's bloody, severed finger. On the finger, the One Ring flames with living fire. Gollum whirls, dancing like a madman. Then he steps too far, wavers on the brink for just a moment, and falls into the depths of the volcano, still holding the Ring. A horrible noise rings out as if Middle-earth is about to explode. Sam quickly leads Frodo away from the teeming volcano. The sky bursts with lightning and black rain, and the Ringwraiths crackle, shrivel, and dissolve.

Frodo's eyes become peaceful as he stands with Sam. His burden has lifted. Frodo says he is glad to be with Sam "at the end of all things."

UNDERSTANDING AND INTERPRETING
Book VI, Chapter 3

A Quest Completed: The completion of the quest marks the central climax of *The Lord of the Rings*. While the novel has included several separate, progressively larger climaxes, such as the overthrow of Saruman and the battle for Gondor at the Pelennor Fields, the deposit of the Ring into the Cracks of Doom resolves the major conflict presented at the outset of *The Fellowship of the Ring*. All of the markings we might expect from the climax of such a voluminous quest narrative are in place: Mount Doom erupts, towers fall, and Sauron's dark shadow vanishes in the wind. The effects of Frodo's success are endless. Middle-earth is freed from Mordor's evil influence, ensuring renewed hope and progress for its inhabitants. And although Frodo does not emerge from the fray with the typical hero's booty of treasure or a maiden, he has gained self-understanding and the knowledge that the most important person in world to him is Sam.

Passive Hero: Frodo continues to add to the picture of hobbit heroism that Tolkien has developed throughout the novel. Frodo's heroism has become subtle; he is a hero simply because he has carried the Ring this far for this long. The Ring now burdens him so greatly that he is forced to become passive, carried up Mount Doom as he weeps. Even when, at the last minute, Frodo says he refuses to destroy the Ring, he does not undermine his heroism. That Frodo willed himself to move forward as far as the Cracks of Doom is evidence enough of his heroism.

Active Hero: Sam's self-sacrificing heroism on the journey up Mount Doom complements Frodo's passivity in its gentleness and love. As Sam carries Frodo up the mountain, he is struck by the fact that his master is lighter than he expected. When Frodo struggles with an uncontrollable urge to grasp the Ring, Sam gently removes his master's hand from his chest and holds his palms together. The image suggests two men praying, implying that Sam redeems Frodo spiritually.

The Weight of Evil: The last leg of Frodo's journey reveals much about the ambiguous nature of evil. At first glance, the Ring seems to embody physical evil, literally dragging Frodo into the earth. The Ring is immensely heavy, and it sucks away Frodo's bodily strength. Interestingly, however, when Sam picks up Frodo (and the Ring on Frodo's finger), he finds his friend quite light. He can remove Frodo's groping hand from the Ring with a gentle tug. The different reactions of the hobbits to the Ring suggests that only the Ring's wearer perceives its heaviness. Its physical force is not "real," but a manifestation of the great weight on the Ring-bearer's heart and spirit. This fits with Tolkien's idea that physical symbols of evil have real power only over those who are tempted by them.

BOOK VI, CHAPTER 4
The Field of Cormallen

The narrative returns to the moment before Pippin loses consciousness near Sauron's Black Gate. As Sauron's forces surround Aragorn's army, a slaughter seems certain. Suddenly, Gandalf looks north and, with a voice rising above the din of battle, cries, "The Eagles are coming!" Gwaihir the Windlord and a host of great eagles are speeding to Gandalf's assistance once more. Suddenly, a horrible shriek comes from the Dark Tower. The earth groans and quakes beneath the feet of the warriors. Sauron's tower collapses, and the Black Gate crumbles. Orcs and Trolls flee in terror.

Meanwhile, Sam is trying to lead Frodo away from the volcano. They have no chance of outrunning the river of fire descending the slope toward them. They have resigned themselves to death, but the Windlord miraculously carries Gandalf to the Mountain of Fire just in time to rescue Frodo and Sam.

When Sam wakes, he finds himself on a soft bed in Ithilien, the eastern lands of Gondor, next to a sleeping Frodo. He first comments on the extraordinary dream he has just had and then cries out in astonishment that his dream actually happened. Gandalf tells him that from now on, the year in Gondor will always begin on March 25, the day that Frodo and Sam destroyed the One Ring—and Sauron with it. Gandalf says that a great Shadow has departed. He asks the hobbits to dress in their worn and ragged attire and escorts them out of the wood. They are to attend a reception hosted by the King of Gondor.

A great throng of people awaits the hobbits. At their emergence, the crowd bursts into thunderous applause, singing songs in praise of the hobbits. Frodo and Sam approach a great throne, where Aragorn welcomes them. He lifts them and sets them on the throne, and the joy of the people flows over them like a warm wind. In a regal ceremony, Frodo bequeaths his knife Sting to Sam, who initially resists but finally accepts the gift. That evening, Frodo and Sam attend a generous feast, where they are reunited with their old companions. Sam is greatly surprised by Pippin, who seems to have grown several inches. The next morning, King Aragorn prepares to enter the great city of Gondor as its rightful ruler.

UNDERSTANDING AND INTERPRETING
Book VI, Chapter 4

The Hand Recedes: This chapter, which marks the public acknowledgment of the end of Sauron's reign, features a number of prominent images of vanishing shadows. The great Darkness, extended outward like a giant hand over the land, suddenly vanishes. Sauron has always been associated with a hand; his finger wore the Ring, and his greedy nature is well represented by the image of a grasping hand. When Sam and Frodo rout Sauron, this hand dissipates like a shadow in the light, or like smoke in the air. The symbolism of this quick fade is clear: Sauron's power was never substantial or real. It was always just an airy illusion, a castle in the air that was fated to dissolve. When Gandalf stands outside the Black Gate, Tolkien explicitly mentions that no shadow falls upon the wizard. As a figure of supreme good, Gandalf can resist Sauron's evil.

Recognition at Last: The festivities at the court of Gondor mark an important step in the hobbits' development. Their reception at the court marks the first time they have been treated with anything close to great respect and admiration. Before now, their presence was met either with wary suspicion, as when the hobbits arrived at Éomer's court and Faramir's stronghold in *The Two Towers*, or with outright hostility, as at the inn at Bree in *The Fellowship of the Ring*. Though the hobbits have been pursuing a goal of value to all civilization since their first step out of the Shire, their significance has not been right fully rewarded or even acknowledged anywhere they have visited. Finally, at the reception in Gondor, the reunited hobbits are treated to rapturous praise and applause, with no shadow of suspicion or darkness falling over the ceremony. The hobbit outsiders, whom others have often viewed as children not to be taken seriously, have now, in a sense, grown up. They finally receive due recognition, having shown the world their worth.

BOOK VI, CHAPTER 5
The Steward and the King

The narrator moves back to the time before the quest ended. After Aragorn's army marches toward Sauron's stronghold, Lady Éowyn rises from her healing bed and requests an audience with Faramir, now Steward of Gondor. In a sad, angry voice, she says she wants to fight the enemy in battle. The Lady touches Faramir's heart. He sees she is not only beautiful, but bold and possessed of a deep spirit. He convinces Éowyn that she is too late to join the march on Mordor. War probably will come to Minas Tirith soon enough, and she should allow herself to grow strong in preparation for that dreaded event. He moves the lady to a room with a window facing east so she can look in Aragorn's direction. However, soon Éowyn and Faramir take strolls together in the gardens almost every day. Soon Faramir realizes he has fallen in love.

For days, they stare to the east, waiting for word of Gondor's success, until eventually they see the Darkness break. As sunlight shines through the sky, the citizens of Minas Tirith break out in song. Messengers soon arrive telling of Aragorn's victory. The conflict resolved, Éowyn's longing for war fades, and she and Faramir agree to wed.

Aragorn's coronation is May 1 in Minas Tirith. Frodo is the crown bearer, and Gandalf places the White Crown on Aragorn's head. Faramir pledges his loyalty. He will keep the title of Steward and live with Éowyn in the beautiful fiefdom of Ithilien. Beregond will serve as captain of Faramir's guard. The city of Minas Tirith begins to revive. Its walls are restored, and the city is filled with trees, fountains, and laughter. Ambassadors from many lands arrive in Gondor, and Aragorn shows mercy by rewarding both the faithful and the enemies of the West. Gandalf explains that the Third Age of Middle-earth has passed. The war against Sauron is over, and Aragorn's reign in the age of Men has begun.

The Riders of Rohan depart on May 8, but Aragorn requests that the members of the Fellowship of the Ring stay in Minas Tirith for a special event that is to take place Midsummer's Day. On Midsummer's Eve, a large party arrives from Rivendell and Lothlórien, including Elrond, Galadriel, **Celeborn**, and the guest of honor, Arwen. The next day, Aragorn and Arwen finally wed. With Gandalf's encouragement, Aragorn plants a sapling "of the Eldest of Trees" in the main courtyard of Minas Tirith to commemorate his marriage and new reign.

UNDERSTANDING AND INTERPRETING

Book VI, Chapter 5

"Nothing Is So Beautiful as Spring": Tolkien was an expert on medieval festivals and customs. When the citizens of Gondor choose to celebrate the New Year on March 25, the date that Frodo and Sam destroyed the Ring, they also recognize the vernal equinox, which occurs just a few days earlier. On the vernal equinox, the sun crosses the equator, making day and night of equal length ("equinox" means "equal night") in the Northern Hemisphere. In agrarian areas especially, the vernal equinox is a time of natural beginning and rebirth. The revised date of the Gondorian New Year thus has traditional as well as historic relevance.

A New Age: The revival of Minas Tirith marks the rise of the Age of Men, as Gandalf announces when the city suddenly flourishes again. This notion of one age giving way to a new one is an ancient idea. The Greeks, for example, envisioned consecutive epochs symbolized by various metals—the Golden Age being the best and earliest age. In Middle-earth, the transition of ages is foretold in *The Fellowship of the Ring*, when Galadriel sadly suggests that the power of the Elves will continue to diminish in the future, whether or not Frodo's mission is successful. The new age is also foreshadowed in *The Two Towers* with the news that there are no young Ents, as the Ent-wives disappeared long ago. The era of the Ent race, like that of the Elves, appears to be passing away. Humans, represented by Aragorn, are to assume primacy in the world during this new age, which presumably continues through our own present day. This transition to human rule allows us to picture our own world as a continuation of Tolkien's Middle-earth. We may imagine that our lives have been made possible because of the heroism of Frodo and his cohorts.

A Fresh Start: Aragorn's marriage to Arwen is a surprise in some ways, as there has been little focus on female characters in the novel thus far. Still, the wedding fulfills several symbolic functions. On a literal level, it warms our hearts to see two such noble characters united. The marriage is especially touching because Arwen, an Elf, had the opportunity to sail west across the Great Sea and live eternally, but gave up her immortality in order to be with the mortal Aragorn. On a broader, mythical level, the wedding symbolizes the ideas of continuity and unity. As in Shakespeare's comedies, which nearly always end with a wedding, the marriage of Aragorn and Arwen suggests that life goes on, and past divisions will be reconciled. The wedding, itself a beginning, represents the regeneration of a fresh, new world after the fall of Sauron.

BOOK VI, CHAPTER 6
Many Partings

Arwen presents Frodo with two gifts. The first is a precious star-shaped gem which Frodo wears around his neck where the Ring used to be. The second is a voyage. Arwen, now mortal, cannot accompany her father when he departs for the "Havens," sailing to the West, but she will send Frodo in her place, if he wishes it.

After the wedding, most of the principal characters ride to Rohan for King Théoden's funeral. His warriors lay him in a golden bier in a house of stone, covered by a great mound that rises on the eastern side of the Barrowfield of Rohan Royalty. They place many of the king's possessions, weapons, and armor in the bier. After the funeral, Éomer hosts a great feast in honor of the wedding of his sister and Faramir.

On a short visit to Isengard, Gandalf learns that **Treebeard** has released Saruman and Wormtongue but kept the keys to Orthanc. Gandalf suspects that Saruman managed to talk his way out of his prison, but Treebeard says he simply hates to cage any living thing. Still, Treebeard looks like he is withholding information.

The Fellowship of the Ring disbands for the last time. Legolas takes Gimli to explore Fangorn Forest. Aragorn and Arwen depart for Gondor. Gandalf and the hobbits, meanwhile, turn toward Rivendell to visit Bilbo before returning to the Shire. On the way north, Gandalf spots a pathetic old beggar and his assistant slouching and whining at the side of the road. These creatures are Saruman and Wormtongue. Saruman curses Gandalf and the hobbits as they pass.

At Rivendell, there is a joyful celebration of Bilbo's 129th birthday. Bilbo is cheerful but has aged noticeably. The hobbits enjoy a good visit but are eager to return home. Bilbo sends his manuscripts, notes, and diaries with Frodo and Sam to prepare them for publishing. Elrond privately tells Frodo that Bilbo will be able to make only one more journey. During this season of the year, when leaves turn gold before they fall, Frodo should look for Bilbo in the woods of the Shire. Elrond will be with him.

UNDERSTANDING AND INTERPRETING
Book VI, Chapter 6

Respect for Trees: Tolkien treats trees with special respect throughout the epic, as we see again when Aragorn plants a tree as a symbol of his reign and marriage. Shortly before he marries Arwen, Aragorn tells Gandalf that he wonders what will happen to Gondor when he dies. Who will rule? Gandalf gently reminds Aragorn that kings usually pass on the crown to offspring. The wizard takes Aragorn out of the city and into the mountains, where they find a sapling that is a descendant of the oldest trees in Middle-earth. As a symbol of celebration and of his intent to continue his royal line, Aragorn carefully plants the tree by a fountain in his courtyard.

A Long Ending: One complaint that readers of *The Lord of the Rings* sometimes make is that the denouement—the portion of the narrative following the climax—is excessively long. Five full chapters follow Frodo and Sam's successful completion of the quest at the Cracks of Doom. This lengthy finale, however, highlights the impossibility of considering *The Return of the King* as an individual work separate from the other two volumes of *The Lord of the Rings*. Together, the three volumes form a single novel and narrative. Given the extraordinary length of the novel as a whole and the dramatic intensity of its climax, an exceptionally long coda is not uncalled for.

BOOK VI, CHAPTER 7
Homeward Bound

On October 6, the four hobbits and Gandalf set out for Bree. Frodo is having physical problems from various wounds that he received during the past year. In addition, darkness has crept over his soul. He says he can return to the Shire, but things will never be the same for him there or anywhere. Gandalf observes that some wounds "cannot be wholly cured."

At Bree, the travelers discover that many things have changed, and not for the best. Gandalf's old friend **Barliman Butterbur** still owns the Prancing Pony Tavern, but business has been poor. Despicable characters have moved into the area, and few of the town's residents go out at night. Visitors from the Shire have also been few, and a disreputable element has gained control of the hobbits' homeland. Gandalf tries to assure Butterbur that better times are on the way. The Rangers have won the war in the South and will soon help keep order in Bree.

Gandalf explains how Sauron was defeated and Aragorn became King of Gondor. Butterbur is astonished, since he knew Aragorn as the Ranger Strider. Butterbur has a delightful surprise for Sam. The hobbit's packhorse, old **Bill**, made it all the way back to Bree on his own. Sam visits Bill in the stable. The next day, business at the inn is brisk, as many visitors, unable to restrain their curiosity, come to gawk at Gandalf's party. Many people ask Frodo whether he has written his memoirs yet. Finally, the company sets off. Gandalf tells the hobbits that he will not accompany them to the Shire, because he has to meet with **Tom Bombadil**. He assures them that this will not be their last meeting. His horse, Shadowfax, makes a leap, and Gandalf is gone. Frodo remarks that it feels as though he is falling asleep again, his adventures now over.

UNDERSTANDING AND INTERPRETING
Book VI, Chapter 7

Retracing Their Steps: The gradual return of the company to the Shire brings the narrative full circle, revisiting many characters and locales we have seen before. The Fellowship almost literally retraces its steps from *The Fellowship of the Ring* and *The Two Towers* in reverse order, giving us a chance to glimpse how people and places have changed now that the burden of Sauron's evil has been lifted from Middle-earth. Whereas Frodo was earlier an object of great suspicion, especially after his accidental wearing of the Ring in the tavern in Book I, now he is the object of great admiration and wonder in Bree, with throngs of people asking if he has written his memoirs yet.

Source Material: Bilbo's and Frodo's memoirs add an interesting twist to the narrative structure of the novel. Tolkien implies that these memoirs form his source material for *The Hobbit* and *The Lord of the Rings*. The author suggests that the mythology he has recorded is not his own creation, but a much older set of lore he has retold. The idea that the story of *The Lord of the Rings* existed before Tolkien's retelling bolsters Tolkien's suggestion that the novel be read as an ancient myth for England, a link to a narrative and a world that precede our own time.

BOOK VI, CHAPTER 8
The Scouring of the Shire

On October 31, Frodo, Sam, Merry, and Pippin attempt to cross the bridge over Brandywine River to enter the Shire. Human and hobbit guards standing behind great spiked gates block the way. The guards report that they work for "the Chief," referring to Frodo's distant cousin **Lotho** ("Pimple") of the disreputable **Sackville-Baggins** family branch. We soon learn that Lotho's boss is an outsider named **Sharkey** who has gained control of most hobbit property, including taverns, homes, woods, and crops. Sharkey has hoarded all the pipe-weed and beer and has wantonly destroyed some of the oldest trees in the Shire. He has taken up residence in Bilbo and Frodo's old home, Bag-End.

J.R.R. Tolkien

The four comrades progress toward Hobbiton. They again find the way blocked. The ruffians back off when they see that these hobbits are willing to fight, but Sam and Pippin expect more trouble. Merry suggests that the four comrades spread out and "raise the Shire," gathering all ablebodied hobbits for a showdown with Sharkey's gangsters. Frodo agrees. Soon the hobbits number 200 strong, armed with axes, hammers, knives, swords, staffs, and a few bows. They overthrow a group of twenty bullying ruffians, killing one.

> "Each age must pass, but in every age, if the inhabitants of the world set right the balance of a time that may seem in their eyes to be 'out of joint,' if they capture the past in poetry—as the Elves do—and if they plant seeds for coming generations, they can insure a new birth and can thereby contribute in their turn of time to the cycle of endless renewal."
>
> **ROSE A. ZOMBARDO**, *TOLKIEN: NEW CRITICAL PERSPECTIVES*

Frodo urges the hobbits to avoid bloodshed if at all possible. He particularly opposes killing other hobbits, even if they work for Sharkey. The next day, however, is one of the bloodiest in the history of the Shire. In the legendary **Battle of Bywater**, the hobbits kill seventy of one hundred Sharkey gangsters and lose nineteen loyal Shire citizens. To close matters, the four Fellowship companions and several other armed hobbits march on Bag-End to find Sharkey. To their surprise, Sharkey is none other than Saruman, now well-fed, his eyes gleaming with amusement and malice. He tells Frodo he has enjoyed corrupting the Shire. Wormtongue serves as Saruman's slave, and under Saruman's order, Wormtongue has murdered Lotho, whose services were no longer needed.

Frodo tells Saruman to leave and never return. Saruman attempts to stab Frodo, but the *mithril* mail-coat, which Gandalf has returned to him, saves the hobbit once more. Frodo orders his supporters, who want to kill Saruman, to hold their peace. Angry, Saruman calls Wormtongue to the road and kicks his groveling slave in the face. Something in Wormtongue snaps. He pulls a hidden knife, grabs Saruman from behind, and slits his throat. Before Frodo can intervene, three hobbit arrows kill Wormtongue.

Book VI, Chapter 8

Bully Saruman: In these closing chapters, we witness Saruman's complete debasement. No longer powerful enough to toy with kings or consort with heads of state, he must content himself to take his revenge on hobbits. Saruman is a bully, and like most bullies, he behaves in a cowardly manner in the face of a fair fight. After Frodo banishes Saruman from the Shire, the fallen wizard tries a sneak attack on the hobbit he purports to scorn. For all Saruman's posturing, in the end he behaves like a petulant schoolboy, taking out his rage on his underling instead of facing his real enemies.

Loving Kindness: Medieval theologians especially valued *caritas*, a Latin term meaning "charity" or "loving kindness." Caritas is the love of God for humanity and, more to the point here, love for one's fellow beings.

Caritas is at the core of the compassion that we see in Gandalf, Frodo, and Sam. Here, when the hobbits rally to rebel against Saruman's ruffians, Frodo quickly urges them to avoid bloodshed if possible. He even grants Saruman his freedom out of pity for the wizard, a shell of a formerly great being. Frodo even offers to grant Wormtongue succor if only he will leave Saruman.

BOOK VI, CHAPTER 9
The Grey Havens

The next two years pass swiftly. Sam leads an effort to renew the countryside. Sam opens the box that Galadriel gave him when he left Lothlórien and spreads its contents—fine Elven dust—on the Shire's ground. By spring, trees are flourishing, and in the span of one year, twenty years' worth of growth occurs. Frodo becomes ill in mid-March of that spring, but recovers enough to attend Sam's wedding to his old sweetheart, **Rose Cotton**. The couple accepts an invitation to live with Frodo at Bag-End.

In the early autumn, Frodo has a relapse. He confides to Sam that some of his old wounds will never heal. Sam and Rose's first child, a daughter named **Elanor** after a beautiful golden flower in Lothlórien, is born March 25 of the next year. When little Elanor is almost six months old, Frodo has a private meeting with Sam. He wants his old friend to join him on a mysterious journey. Sam guesses that Frodo wants to travel to Rivendell for the celebration of Bilbo's 131st birthday.

On the morning of September 21, Sam and Frodo set out. They meet up with a large group heading west. Among the travelers are many fair Elven folk, including **Gildor**, Elrond, and Galadriel. Bilbo rides with them, sleepy but eager to move on. Frodo explains to Sam that they are going west to the Havens and from there to the Blessed Realm. They will have to leave Sam at the Havens, because it is not yet his time to depart from Middle-earth. Frodo has made Sam his heir. He foresees that Sam will become a civic leader and that he and Rose will have several more children, some of them named Frodo-lad, Pippin, Merry, Rosie-lass, and Goldilocks. Sam fights to hold back tears.

> "This pity as charity or love binding one man to another cements together the 'fellowship' of the hobbits and later the differing species; the 'chain' of love it creates contrasts with the chains of enslavement represented by Sauron's One Ring."
>
> **JANE CHANCE NITZSCHE**, *TOLKIEN'S ART: A MYTHOLOGY FOR ENGLAND*

Gandalf waits for them at the Havens. He too will ride the Elven ship to the Blessed Realm. The Third Age is over, and his mission is complete. The Days of the Ring have gone, and the time for Elves and wizards is about to pass. Merry and Pippin meet the group at the Havens so that Sam will not have to return to Hobbiton alone. **Cirdan the Shipwright** helps everyone aboard. He is very tall and old, but his eyes are keen as stars. "All is now ready," he says. Frodo smells a sweet fragrance blowing off the western sea and hears singing coming to him from across the water. He is not afraid. As he looks west, Frodo can see "white shores and beyond them a far green country under a swift sunrise."

To Sam, the evening grows darker as the boat pulls away. He is glad to have Merry and Pippin with him for the long, silent ride home. They never look back. When Sam reaches Bag-End, there is a yellow light in the window and a fire within. Rose and Elanor wait for him. Rose has kept the evening meal warm. Sam draws a deep breath and enters his happy home. "Well, I'm back," he says.

UNDERSTANDING AND INTERPRETING
Book VI, Chapter 9

Trouble at Home: Though the final troubles of the Shire police state may seem out of place in the novel, they reinforce the ideas of corruption and temptation that Tolkien has frequently explored throughout the epic. Ever since Pippin learned to control his curiosity after stealing the *palantír* from Gandalf, or since Frodo was torn between desire and duty when debating whether to put on the Ring or take it off, the ability to control one's urges and to understand oneself have been of paramount importance. In the crisis in the Shire, Tolkien explores the problem of corruption on a social rather than an individual level. The hobbits have likely assumed that while they journeyed to Mordor on their mission, the homeland they left behind remained quiet, peaceful, and safe. However, it turns out that the familiar is just as open to corruption and danger as the exotic. Even the seemingly wholesome hobbit race—all of which is endowed, to varying degrees, with Frodo's heroic qualities—is subject to the same failings as any other race in Middle-earth. Tolkien seems to warn against over-romanticizing one's own homeland and people.

Back, but with a Difference: Sam's brief closing words neatly encapsulate the nature of the hobbits' return to the Shire in the final chapters of *The Lord of the Rings*. The hobbits are not home; they are "back." They have arrived at the place from which they started, although both the Shire and they themselves have changed drastically. The Shire is where they belong, and the new wisdom they have gained on the quest enables them to rebuild and restore order to their realm, just as they have restored order to Minas Tirith. The hobbits show that they have gained a set of skills from living with members of the races of Men, Elves, and Dwarves. The hobbits speak with curt confidence to Saruman's stooges and betray a knowledge of military strategy in the Battle of Bywater. Sam has become more forthright, and Merry and Pippin are literally taller. Later, Frodo, in his encounter with Saruman, displays the grace and forgiveness he has learned from Gandalf and Sam.

Preserving Life: Things gradually return to normal after the police state is disrupted, and Sam proceeds to live his life as if he had never left the Shire. Frodo's sacrifice stands in even clearer relief than before when we suddenly understand that his adventure was less about improving life than about preserving it. Just as Frodo struggles upon the deposit of the Ring into the Cracks of Doom, the hobbits struggle to understand a journey for which the goal has been simply to preserve Middle-earth as the beautiful land it has been for so long. Frodo explains to Sam, "It must often be so, Sam, when things are in danger: some one has to give them up, lose them, so that others may keep them." Frodo, for his part, has given up his normal life and commonness by his experience with the Ring's great power. In the end, he must join those whose lives are not common, but mythic.

Conclusions

The company that boards the ship at the Grey Havens contains representatives of many of the races in Middle-earth. Those who board the ship, though different from each other, are now mythic heroes. According to Gandalf, the next age will be dominated by Men, led by Aragorn and Éomer. Tolkien uses the image of the sea as it is frequently employed in literature to convey the notion of endless possibility, eternity, or obscurity. As the group on the ship sails away into the misty, indefinite horizon, so Tolkien imbues *The Lord of the Rings* with the qualities of long lost, pre-historic lore.

SUGGESTIONS
FOR FURTHER
READING

Auden, W.H. "Good and Evil in *The Lord of the Rings.*" *Tolkien Journal* 3 (1967): 5–8. Reprinted in *Critical Quarterly* 10 (1968), 138–142.

Becker, Alida, ed. *The Tolkien Scrapbook*. New York: Grosset and Dunlap, 1974.

Blackwelder, Richard A. *A Tolkien Thesaurus*. New York: Garland, 1990.

Bloom, Harold, ed. *Modern Critical Interpretations:* The Lord of the Rings. Philadelphia: Chelsea House Publishers, 2000.

Campbell, Joseph. *The Hero with a Thousand Faces.* New York: Pantheon, 1949.

Carpenter, Humphrey. *J.R.R. Tolkien: A Biography*. London: George Allen and Unwin, 1977.

Carpenter, Humphrey. *Letters of J.R.R. Tolkien*. Boston: Houghton Mifflin, 1981.

Chance, Jane. The Lord of the Rings: *The Mythology of Power*. Lexington: University of Kentucky Press, 2001.

Clute, John, and John Grant, eds. *The Encyclopedia of Fantasy*. New York: St. Martin's Press, 1997.

Foster, Robert. *A Guide to Middle-earth*. New York: Ballantine Books, Inc., 1971.

Haber, Karen. *Meditations on Middle-earth*. New York: St. Martin's Press, 2001.

Hammond, Wayne G., and Christina Scull. *J.R.R. Tolkien, Artist & Illustrator*. Boston: Houghton Mifflin, 1995.

Tolkien, J.R.R. *The Silmarillion*. Boston: Houghton Mifflin, 1986.

INDEX

Index